Life on

Australian Locomotives

Map of Victoria

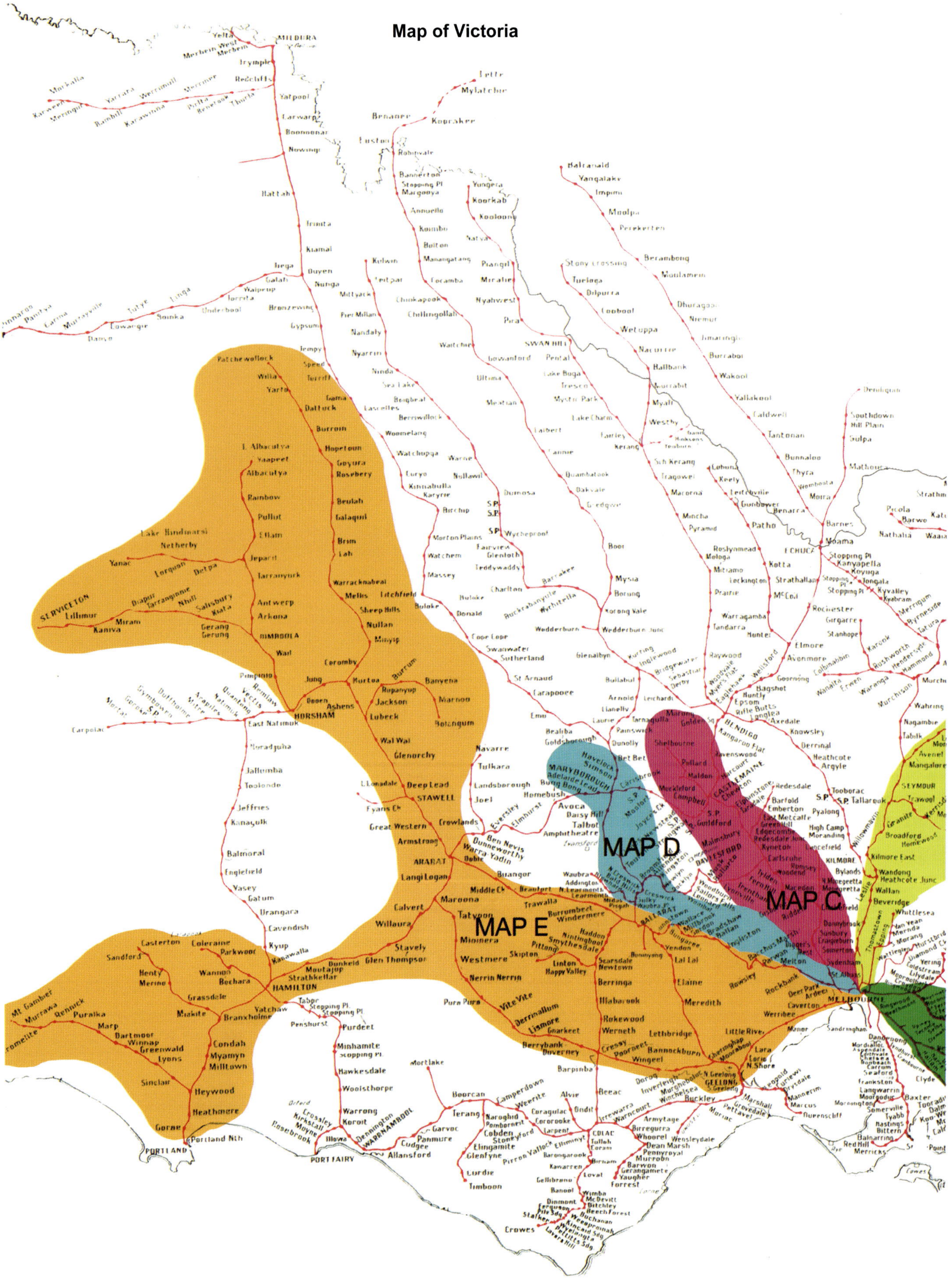

Life on Australian Locomotives

David Barnett

EACH MAP SHOWS A RELEVANT PORTION OF THE VICTORIAN RAILWAYS AND IS ENLARGED AND DETAILED ON THE FOLLOWING PAGES

- **Map A:** Shows locations in Prologue and Chapters 1, 9 and 11
- **Map B:** Shows locations in Chapters 2, 4 and 7
- **Map C:** Shows locations in Chapters 3.
- **Map D:** Shows locations in Chapters 6 and 10.
- **Map E:** Shows locations in Chapters 14 and all remaining Chapters.

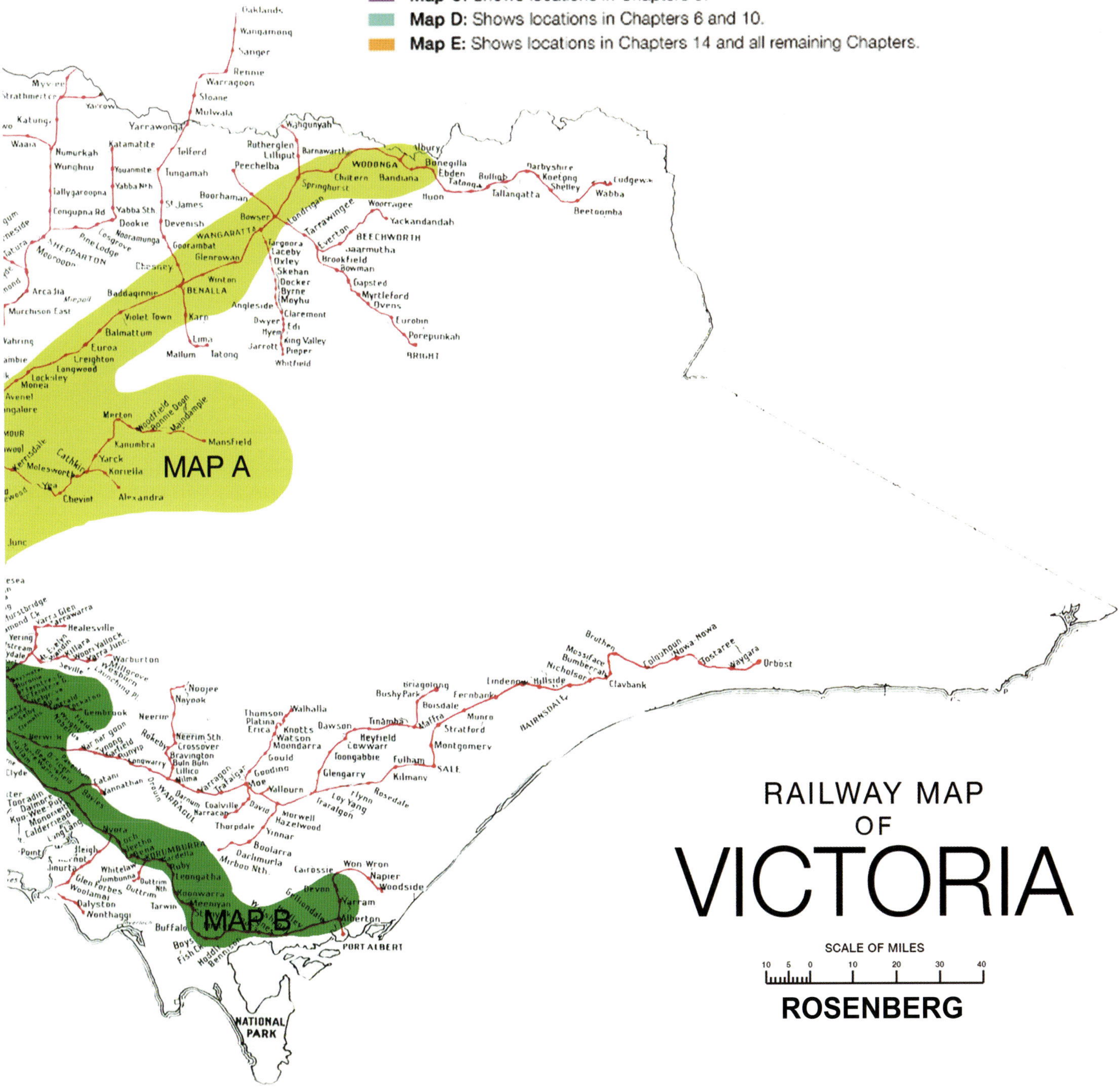

RAILWAY MAP OF VICTORIA

SCALE OF MILES

10 5 0 10 20 30 40

ROSENBERG

For Philip and Christopher

First published in Australia in 2015
by Rosenberg Publishing Pty Ltd
PO Box 6125, Dural Delivery Centre NSW 2158
Phone: 61 2 9654 1502 Fax: 61 2 9654 1338
Email: rosenbergpub@smartchat.net.au
Web: www.rosenbergpub.com.au

National Library of Australia Cataloguing-in-Publication data:

Creator: Barnett, David Maxwell, 1936– author.

Title: Life on Australian locomotives / David M Barnett.

ISBN: 9781925078527 (paperback)
ISBN: 9781925078626 (ebook epub)

Notes: Includes index.

Subjects: Barnett, David Maxwell, 1936-

Fire fighters–Australia–Biography.

Locomotives–Australia.

Dewey Number: 363.37092

Cover and map design by Norman Barnett

Printed in China by Everbest Printing Co Limited

Contents

A spotless R707 makes an impressive sight as it drifts north at speed between Kilmore East and Broadford on a Bi-Centenary Special in 1988. (David Barnett)

Foreword

From time to time a book on railways is published that has a Foreword or Preface written by some noted railway figure such as a Departmental Manager, Senior Engineer, Politician, Ministerial Advisor or high ranking Head Office official. The writer praises the book's author for their lively tale of railway activity, well researched technical detail and for providing an interesting 'behind the scenes' look at day-to-day railway operations.

If this is what introduces the book, you can be pretty sure that it is a bland and disappointing account of its subject matter. Senior figures and Head Office personnel know very little about day-to-day railway operations. If they did, they would most likely try and put a stop to them!

So if an author has this kind of official sanction, interesting, humorous and absorbing material is unlikely to appear in his writing.

Life on Australian Locomotives is not one of those books. It deals with events in steam locomotive cabs that were completely unauthorized by any Head Office department and far removed from official sanction. Later, when the author is officially on the footplate, it describes circumstances, incidents and happenings well away from Head Office scrutiny, which take place in remote locations and at times when even the most keen railway enthusiast would not be awake.

With this kind of adventure in store, you are invited to don your overalls and cap, climb into the cab and enjoy the aromas of oil, steam and steel. The brake test is complete and our starting signal is at 'proceed'. We receive the 'right away'. A brief, distinctive hiss of air confirms the release of the independent engine brake and the regulator is eased open. Steam issues from the cylinder cocks and with a short whistle we are moving into the era when a steam regulator was a sceptre, and a blue starched cap a crown.

David Barnett
March 2015

MAP A:
Shows locations in Prologue and Chapters 1, 9 and 11

MAP B:
Shows locations in Chapters 2, 4 and 7

MAP C:
Shows locations in Chapter 3

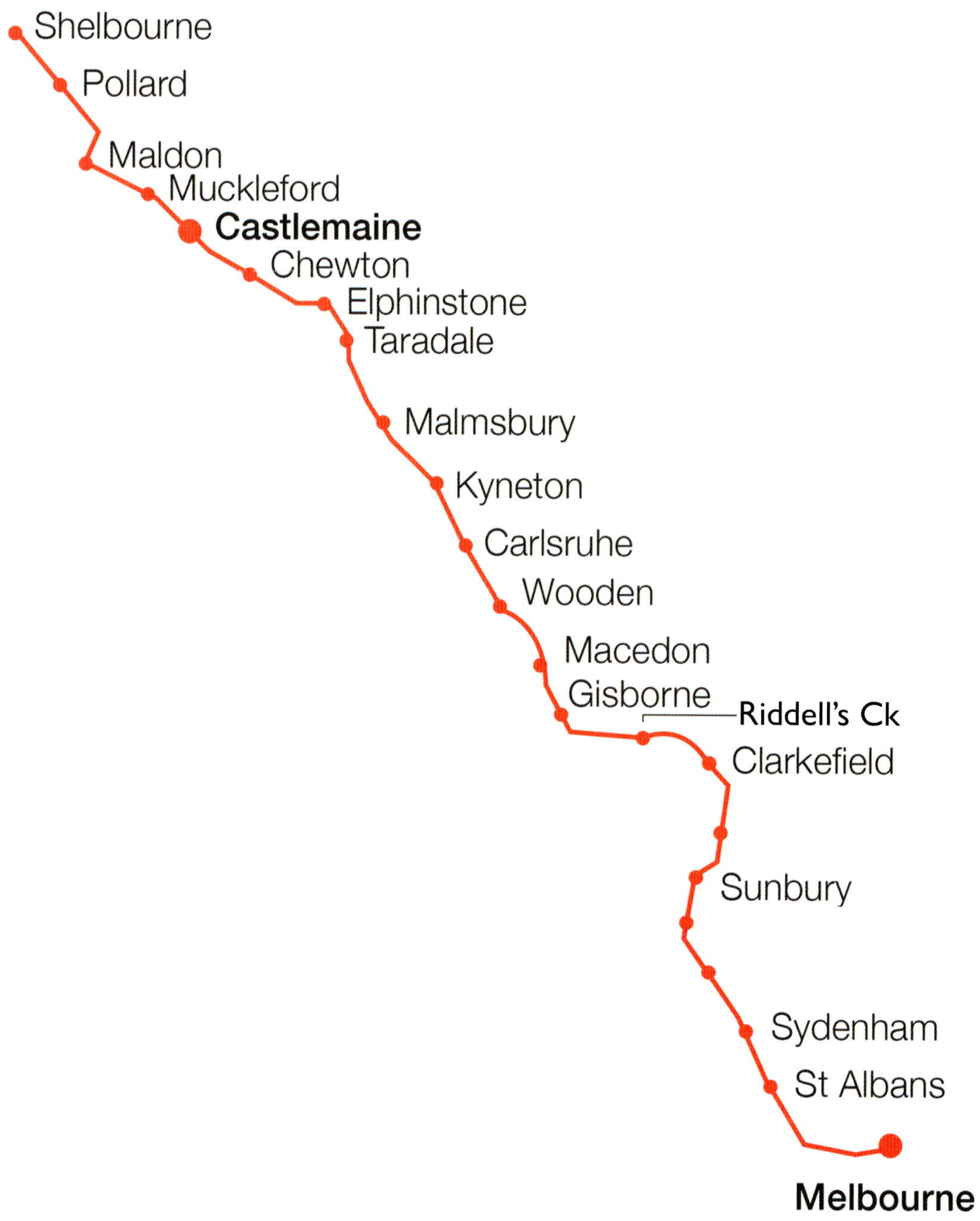

MAP D:
Shows locations in Chapters 6 and 10

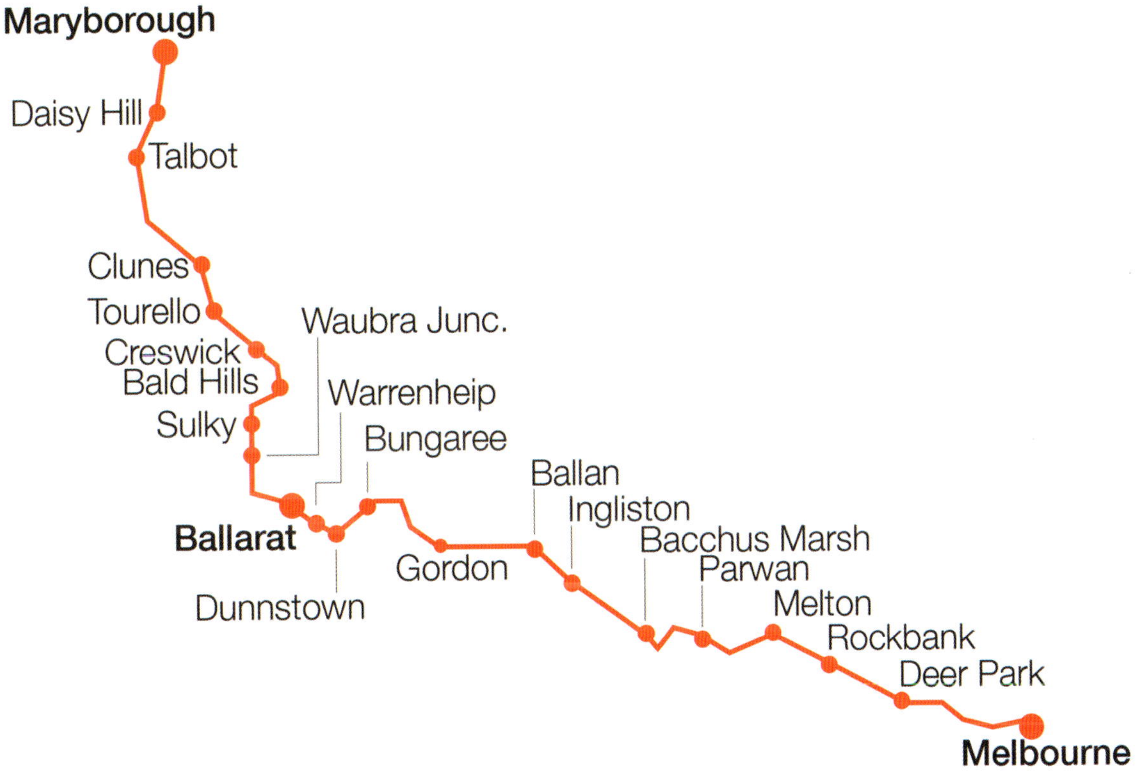

MAP E:
Shows locations in Chapter 14 and all remaining Chapters

Prologue Ahead of Schedule

If ever there was a train required to depart and arrive on time, it was the Spirit of Progress.

In the late 1940s, the Spirit to Albury was hauled by one of four, royal blue, streamlined, three-cylinder S class 4-6-2 steam locomotives. When at North Melbourne, these were stabled outside the depot, adjacent to its south-west wall. Wodonga crews ran the train. Sign-on time was 4.35 pm. The crew would pick up their engine stores and proceed to the locomotive, which was stabled facing funnel-first towards Melbourne.

The S class were too long to fit on a turntable. Turning was accomplished by their traversing a loop at the back of the depot, with a similar arrangement being provided at Wodonga.

On arrival at their engine, the crew would oil and otherwise prepare it for the 190½ mile journey to Albury. To assist in timekeeping, the Spirit engines were bunkered with the best Maitland coal.

On the day with which we are concerned, the fireman tested the gauge glasses (see Glossary), turned on the blower, opened the dampers, and fastened open the firebox doors. They revealed a yawning firebox with a grate area of 50 square feet. He pushed down the banked fire, using the long pricker.

Picking up the shovel, he placed coal around the firebox, gradually building up the fire to raise steam.

On the road, he would be stepping on the treadle that activated the small air cylinder connected to the firebox doors enabling their hands-free operation..

The S class cab was roomy. It surrounded the engineman with the distinctive aroma of oil, steam and steel, boasted two steam gauges, one on each side, two enormous brass injectors to feed the boiler and an air brake with a 'straight air' portion for use on the locomotive, independent of the brakes on the train. Everything was on a big scale.

A little after 5.30 pm, the mellow chime whistle sounded and the S backed away from the depot and around the loop. The huge, streamlined, 12-wheel tender led the way to the sound of a muted and erratic three-cylinder exhaust, characteristic of an S class running in reverse. The engine soon arrived at the TR (train running) point, where, now facing funnel-first to Albury, it stopped. The fireman climbed down and telephoned the signalman to announce the engine's presence.

After a brief delay, it was signalled to proceed. All the while the turbo generator hummed pleasantly, accompanied by the gentle rhythm of the single-stage air compressor and the ever-present aroma of steel, bathed in oil and steam, an atmosphere that was both musical and reassuring.

With a steady hand and a practised eye the driver guided the locomotive through a myriad of signals to Spencer Street's No. 1 platform. He stopped short of the 11-car consist and the fireman swung down to check the coupling alignment on the tender and baggage car. These being satisfactory, he gave the driver an 'ease up' sign and the huge streamlined bulk eased back on to the Southern Hemisphere's premier train. The fireman checked that the couplings were secure, coupled up the brake pipes, opened the brake pipe cocks and returned to the cab.

The platform was alive with people and

charged with the drama and pathos of departure. Travellers and friends pressed along first- and second-class corridors into spacious compartments, admiring the polished wooden panels, carpets, leather upholstery, arm and head rests, ceiling lights, individual reading lights, air-conditioning and the general luxury and comfort of it all. Conversation was normal, yet a kind of silence prevailed. Sounds of the city, present on the platform, were absent on the train, giving the city view from the landscape windows an individual quality.

Over the station's loudspeakers, the 'Man in Grey' announced, in distinctive and never to be forgotten tones: 'Spirit a' Progress, to Albury and Sydney, now standing in Platform Number 1. First-class cars, rear end of train; second-class cars, engine end of train.'

A train examiner soon arrived at the head end, inserted his key into the specially machined slot on the regulator quadrant and the brake test got under way. The guard came up, took the driver's name, advised details of the load, '11 cars, 555 tons', checked watches, exchanged pleasantries and left. At a signal from the train examiner now at the other end of the train, the driver released the brakes and the air compressor thudded out its rhythm as it recharged the main reservoir. The fireman busied himself with the shovel and the orange glow of the firebox gradually became white, while an injector sang its song putting water into the boiler.

The train examiner returned to the cab, reported all was well, retrieved his key and strode off. The fireman turned off the injector, the driver signed the speed recorder chart and all was ready. As the departure time of 6.30 pm approached, the steam gauges nudged the working pressure of 200 psi. The platform was now characterized by final embraces and handshakes, followed by a last minute stepping aboard by those whose place was on the train. Handkerchiefs were held at the ready to signal last goodbyes, and faces pressed close to windows to ensure final words were comprehended.

Train announcements and departure bell were followed, right on 6.30 pm, by the stationmaster signalling 'right away' to the guard, who in turn signalled this with his green hand lamp to the fireman, who acknowledged it with a green lamp from the engine. The whistle sounded its mellow chime, the driver eased the regulator open a fraction, steam hissed from the cylinder cocks, and the Spirit moved.

Bystanders and well-wishers moved back as the train gently commenced its journey, walking the first few paces with it as they waved handkerchiefs and gloves to the now receding faces at windows. The dining car rolled by with its spotless white linen, uniformed stewards and well-dressed diners. Each royal blue liveried vehicle passed with barely a sound until finally the parlour car, with its comfortable armchairs and tastefully curved rear end, announced that the train had passed.

For those on the platform it was time to go home.

For those on the locomotive it was time to get busy. Keeping steam at a maximum and smoke to a minimum, the fireman kept the firebox white hot. The highlight of the run through the suburbs was the sweeping downgrade curve that took the train through Pascoe Vale and on to the Glenroy Bank. Working on a wide open regulator and a gradually lengthening cutoff, the big Pacific began to get into its stride as it stormed over the Pascoe Vale level crossing at 55 mph and went pounding up grade towards Glenroy!

Through Broadmeadows with the grade behind it, speed had stabilized at 16 to 17 mph and the powerful exhaust offered no suggestion that the engine was being pushed beyond its capabilities.

The run to Seymour was uneventful. The engine steamed well, rode well, pulled well and passed through the Seymour platform at the regulation 30 mph, on time.

Once again the regulator was opened wide, the cutoff lengthened and the train went blasting up the rising grade towards Mangalore with the rhythmic three-cylinder exhaust reverberating through the surrounding countryside. Sighting the Mangalore 'Distant' signal, the fireman lowered the automatic staff exchanger to pick up the staff for the Mangalore–Avenel section. The staff arrived with a dull clang. The exchanger was hauled up, the small hoop and pouch removed, and the names engraved on the staff rod called out by the fireman as he delivered the safe working assembly to the driver: 'Mangalore–Avenel'. The driver took the staff, checked the names, and stowed it away within easy reach for the next exchange.

By now the train was on the 1 in 125 down grade away from Mangalore. Here the timetable called for 70 mph. The locomotive crew were familiar with the way the engine rode at various speeds, and soon realized that the usual cab acoustics and vibrations that this section of the track produced were present, but a glance at the speed recorder showed that they were nevertheless falling short of the mark, for the speed shown was 64 mph.

Perhaps a brake was sticking. The fireman looked back along each side of the speeding cars, but no telltale shower of sparks or any other evidence of faulty brake equipment responded to his gaze. Also, the driver's brake gauges showed normal readings. Everything looked in order. The regulator was therefore eased open from its drifting position, the cutoff adjusted to suit, and within a very short time the speed recorder was showing 70.

For the rest of the journey, everything went well. The engine and train rode smoothly. When speed was checked at curves, the speed shown on the speed recorder fell back as expected and advanced again when steaming resumed.

The incident after Mangalore was fading from memory when, on the approach to Wodonga, both men happened to look at their watches. They were eight minutes ahead of time! The train was promptly eased back to below 30 mph in order to absorb as much time as possible before arriving at Albury.

After all, they must avoid attracting the attention of the officials in Melbourne, otherwise there would be correspondence flowing back and forth for weeks.

In this, however, they were already too late. Reports to Train Control from signalman between Violet Town and Wodonga recorded the Spirit as being three minutes ahead at Benalla, six minutes ahead at Wangaratta, and as we have seen, eight minutes up on the timetable at the city on the border.

After turning the 11-car train on the Wodonga loop and stabling their engine, the driver and fireman conferred. Their engine had given a faultless performance and there was obviously nothing wrong with the mechanicals of the locomotive. There was something, however, that wasn't quite right; and that something could only be the speed recorder. Accordingly, before signing off, the driver filled out an Engine Repair card with the instruction, 'Check speed recorder'. This was duly handed to the night-shift fitter. He checked the mechanism and found everything to be in order. There was nothing to even suggest that the device was faulty. He therefore wrote on the card, 'speed recorder checked and ok', entered the date, signed his name, and handed the completed item to the night depot foreman, who read it, acknowledged it and placed it in the box for completed Engine Repair cards.

The same engine was rostered for the south-bound Spirit of Progress the next morning. Unaware of the previous evening's events, the morning crew signed on, prepared their steed, pulled the Spirit cars tender-first from Wodonga to Albury, ran around their train and got ready for the trip to Melbourne. Departing at 7.50 am, they were soon scorching the ballast at over a mile a minute, with the exhaust steam evaporating while the accompanying smoke provided a silent testimony to the train's passing as it slowly dispersed in the crisp morning air. The chime whistle sounded its melodic warning at stations and level crossings, and the distinctive beat from the three cylinders announced that a 2200 plus horsepower S class was indeed in charge. Running under clear signals the crew made good time. With the speed recorder hovering over the 70 mph mark, the train was more than fulfilling its designers' expectations. The bogies on each car provided a carpet slippers ride and superior sound insulation meant conversation in each compartment could be carried out in a whisper, if this was desirable.

Passing through Wangaratta the driver glanced at his watch. Three minutes ahead of time. They'd been keeping within the speed limit so there was nothing wrong there. The automatic staff exchanges had been normal, the fireman was by no means overtaxed and everything was as it should be. On towards Benalla.

The big Pacific was soon pounding up the long climb to Glenrowan, the syncopated rhythm of the exhaust reverberating on either side of the right of way. The automatic staff exchanger performed its duty with a reassuring clang and the words 'Glenrowan, Benalla' were briefly audible in the cab.

Passengers at the second sitting for breakfast were leaving the dining car, and the tables were being prepared for morning tea as Violet Town went past like a newspaper in the wind as the Spirit continued its exhilarating progress south. This was railroading at its best.

With the 1 in 125 up grade from Avenel to Mangalore almost over, the fireman prepared to lower the staff exchanger for the last time as the train approached double track. There was a long whistle, then a brake application, then another whistle, shorter than the first, as the driver acknowledged the Mangalore 'Distant' being lowered from 'caution' to 'clear'. In the distance, the Home and Starting signals also dropped their arms to 'proceed'. A hiss of air under each car announced the release of the brakes and the train passed smoothly through the station with Mangalore's line side instrument picking up the lowered staff exchanger's final delivery.

The incident at the 'Distant' signal caused the driver to examine his watch.

Other people elsewhere were also examining their watches. Among them was Seymour Train Control. A few minutes earlier the Mangalore signalman had advised that the Spirit was 10 minutes ahead; should he let it through? 'Yes, let it through'. And so it was that the Mangalore signals went to 'clear'. Seymour quickly communicated the early running to Melbourne. An investigation team was immediately assembled to meet the train.

The driver was at a loss as to why he was so far ahead of time. Nevertheless he was, and the best course of action was to run the next 60 miles at an easier pace. This was done by keeping the speed to a maximum of 60 mph. This provided the opportunity to check the speed recorder. Mileposts were selected, and with the needle sitting on 60 each man's watch was used to measure the time. Sixty seconds to the mile! That, it seemed, ruled out the speed recorder.

Seven minutes had been dropped by the time Broadmeadows went by, and a couple of fortuitous signal checks before North Melbourne, helped by an agonizingly slow—to bystanders anyway—journey along Spencer Street's No. 1 platform, allowed the train to arrive on time. Coming gently to a stand, it stretched its length comfortably in the station and said goodbye to each traveller.

Meanwhile, knowledgeable men in suits and felt hats from the Rolling Stock branch were waiting. Their understanding of thermodynamics, applied mechanics, mathematics and chemistry knew no bounds. When it came to the finer points of living, however, they had the interpersonal skills of a battering ram. Their course of action was already decided. Using words of one syllable, as was their want, they let it be known that the speed recorder on this S class was going to be replaced on this very day, the engine being needed to run the Spirit that evening. The engine was to be run immediately to its stabling point at North Melbourne, where the changeover would take place. This information was communicated through tight lips and facial expressions that carried as much compassion as your average European wasp. The engine crew were treated either as if they were not present, or addressed in a nondescript third person manner, of the kind used by members of the Spanish Inquisition.

Accordingly, the men on the footplate delivered their locomotive to its required location, handed it over to a hostling crew for servicing (see Glossary), signed off, and promptly left the depot environs lest they be charged with trespassing.

Meanwhile, members of the mechanical staff arrived to remove the offending speed recorder. The depot foreman, briefed that morning by the Chief Mechanical Engineer, saw to it that the guilty item was replaced with one that had been thoroughly overhauled. Thus the engine cab played host to the grunts and sighs and expletives of two fitters and their assistants as they carefully fitted the replacement. It was not easy. Not only were they working in a confined space, but they were also handling a very heavy piece of equipment.

Eventually the task was complete.

The offending speed recorder was put aside for examination and everyone sighed with relief.

In due course, briefed on the events of the last 24 hours, the evening departure crew arrived at the locomotive.

The cab had been swept clean and the new speed recorder was firmly in place.

At the appointed time, with preparation complete, the engine backed around the reversing loop to the TR point. With its presence announced to the signalman, it moved gracefully across the Spencer Street yard, easing through the cross overs and turn outs and onto its train. Both enginemen kept an eye on the speed recorder. There was nothing unusual. However, as their speed so far had barely reached 15 mph this was hardly surprising.

At 6.30 pm they were away. The first major test for the recently replaced item of gleaming brass and impressive dials came as the big 4-6-2 wheeled its load down the grade and around the curve at Pascoe Vale. The needle rose to 55 and the experience of both crew told them that this was exactly what they were doing. They went through Broadmeadows at 17 mph and proceeded on to Seymour. The trip was uneventful. At no time were they in doubt that on a 65 mph curve, with the speed recorder needle showing that reading, that this was exactly how fast they were going. Aware that they were under scrutiny, they passed through the Seymour yard at the regulation 30 mph, right on time. Seymour Control informed Melbourne, 'Spirit of Progress, on time at 7.56 pm.'

On hearing this, the mechanical staff and other senior officials in Melbourne breathed more easily. Their relief was short lived.

As they accelerated up the grade towards Mangalore, the fireman lowered the staff exchanger. Passing the station at about 40 mph, the instrument picked up the outgoing staff, was hauled back into cab, the staff retrieved and 'Mangalore, Avenel' called by the fireman and echoed back by the driver. Speed increased. Avenel flashed by to the sound of the clang of the staff exchanger as the Spirit roared north. Train controllers on the north-eastern line maintained close supervision of the times recorded as it passed each station.

By the time Benalla was reached, it was four minutes ahead of schedule. At Wangaratta, six minutes, and at Wodonga, nine minutes. On passing through Springhurst, the engine crew well and truly realized that for some unknown reason they had been running too fast. Was the new speed recorder as faulty as the one it replaced? From Springhurst to Albury they kept the speed close to 60 mph but this made little difference to their time of arrival.

The train was turned and the big S class rolled into its allotted road at the Wodonga depot.

No one was surprised when the foreman announced that the engine was withdrawn from traffic pending a thorough investigation into the reasons for it consistently running ahead of time.

The investigation commenced the next morning. The speed recorder was removed and with it the compete drive assembly. It was discovered that the heavy vertical drive shaft from the driving wheel gearbox to the recorder in the cab had sustained a long fracture, leaving two large adjacent, but completely separate, abutting portions of the shaft in place. These were maintained in their vertical alignment by their undamaged holding brackets, with the top section resting on the lower one. The two portions of the shaft provided a 'friction drive' to the cab-mounted speed recorder. The heavy mass and high inertia of the upper portion meant that this drive worked quite well until the engine's speed rose above 65 mph. At higher speeds, the vibration from the cab assemblies caused the speed of the top portion to fall behind that of the lower, resulting in the engine having to be run faster for the speed recorder to register, say, 70 mph — a speed that had already been attained, but not recorded. Estimates put the lag between the upper and lower shaft pieces at eight or nine miles an hour. Thus, when the crew observed 70 on the speed recorder, their actual speed was nearer 80. Hence the reduction in running times. A new vertical drive shaft solved the problem and all was well.

For obvious reasons, these incidents were kept very quiet, with only those involved being aware of them. Some leaks did occur, but fortunately for the Victorian Railways these were inconsequential.

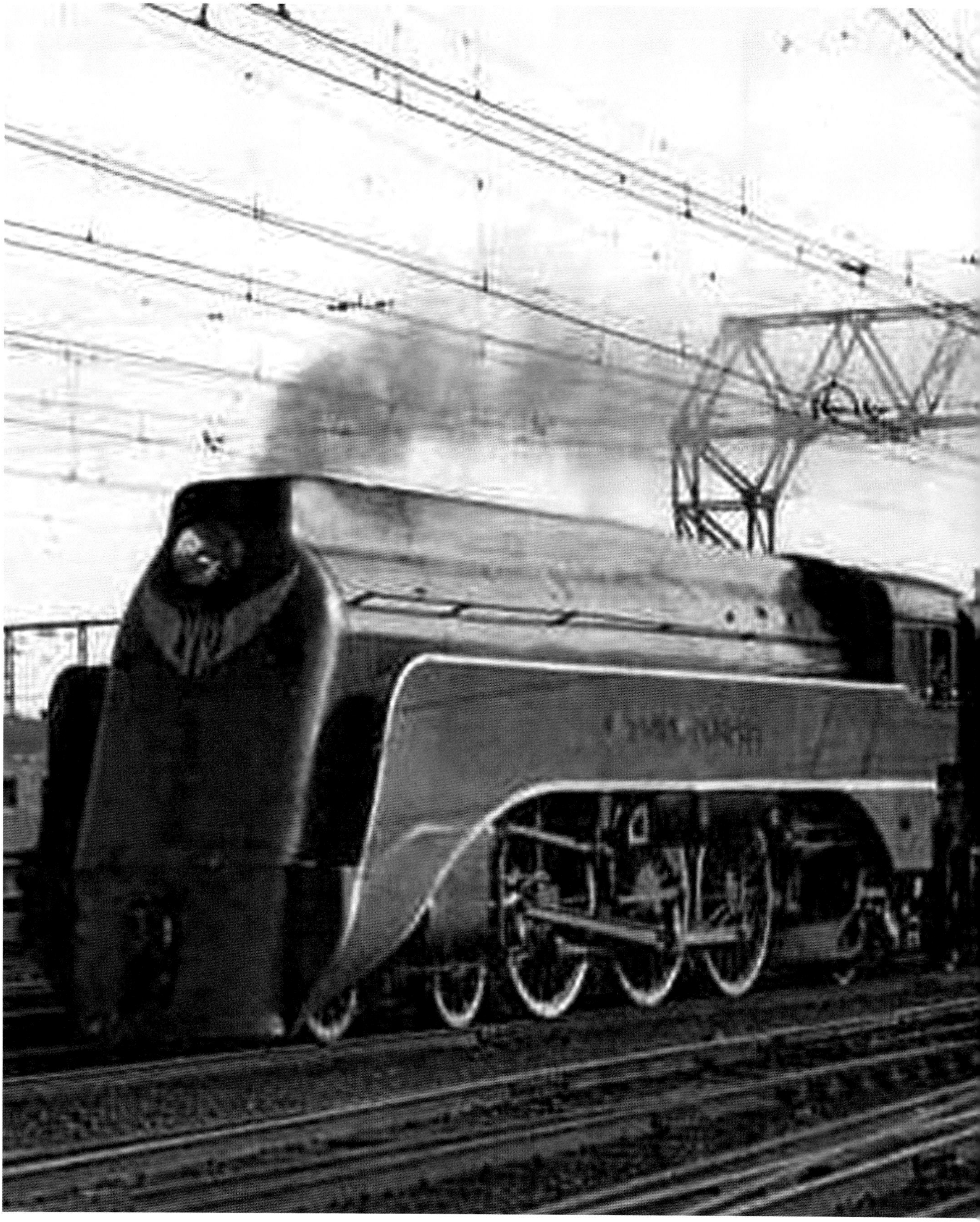

June 11, 1938, saw S300, Matthew Flinders, arriving at Spencer Street in charge of a still new Spirit of Progress. The train consist is rare and unusual. It comprises two baggage cars and eight other Spirit cars, making 10/450 tons. Note the top arm on the signal gantry pulled off at 'clear', admitting the train to the platform road. (W.A.G. Lewis)

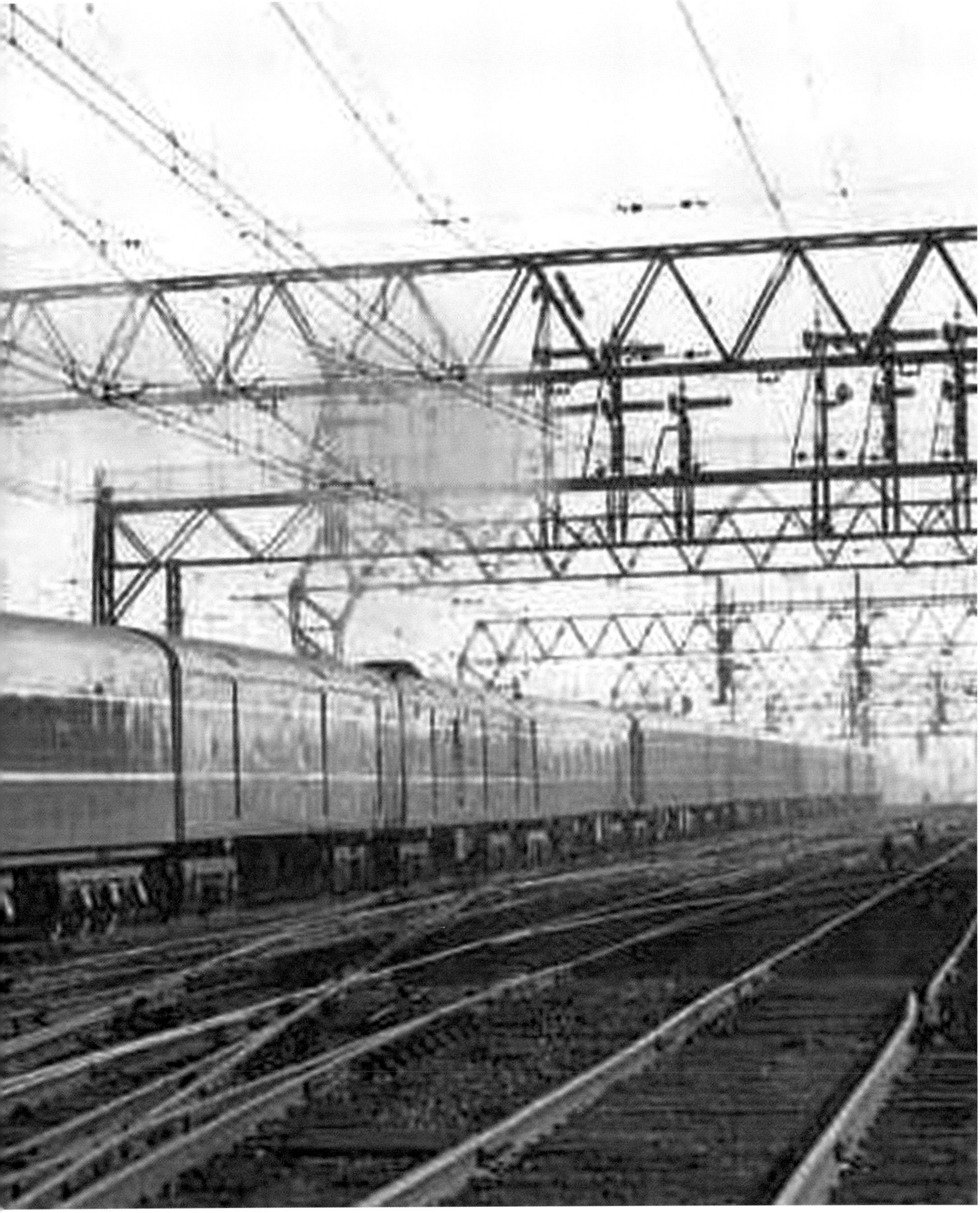

PART 1: WITHOUT OFFICIAL AUTHORITY

1 From a Distance

In my pre-school years I liked steam locomotives from a distance. Up close I was terrified!

So it was that whenever my mother took me into Melbourne by train from our suburban home in Eaglemont, I would peer anxiously along Flinders Street station's platform No. 1. The aim was to make sure we were not about to encounter some steam hissing monster. Most of the time I was disappointed. We usually arrived before the departure of the morning passenger train to Gippsland and my peering revealed an ominous black bulk wreathed in white vapour.

'No mummy, there's one there!' But to no avail. We walked past the engine. Sometimes it was simmering quietly, on other occasions steam roared from the safety valves. It made no difference to me; that creature signified the end of the world. I made no efforts to conceal my fear and buried my face in my mother's skirts until, having walked on some distance and finding myself still alive, I risked looking back.

There were times when these survival tactics caught the crew's attention. On at least one memorable occasion my face was gently but firmly disentangled from its place of refuge and directed towards a smiling driver and fireman who looked down from their engine cab at this most frightened child. Their smiles were anything but reassuring.

Nevertheless my interest in steam locomotives and railways gradually increased.

Around a year before my birth in 1936, my father Frank helped to form the Victorian Model Railway Society (VMRS) and trains were a recognized part of our family life.

My father was gifted in the area of railway sound effects. He could imitate a steam locomotive chime whistle so that if you didn't know where the sound was coming from, you would look around for the engine. Also, he could bring to life the sound of a locomotive's air compressor, the staccato of an exhaust and all the audio effects created by a steam train as it rolled into a station and came to rest. These sounds were put down on a W&G records 12 inch, long play 78 rpm disc and hence preserved for posterity.

In 1939 the Melbourne Town Hall hosted the All Models Exhibition. The Victorian Model Railway Society had an elaborate exhibit featuring the then rural railway station of Melton. All buildings, track layouts, signals and surrounding countryside were faithfully reproduced in O gauge scale and trains were run just as they would have been at the full size station.

My father provided the sound effects. These were superb and had people wondering how the Society obtained such excellent synchronized recordings to provide such realism. Listeners scoffed when it was made known that the sounds were not recorded but produced by a society member.

At the invitation of Melbourne's Lord Mayor, Frank Barnett mounted the Town Hall stage and proved beyond doubt that the chime whistles and locomotive exhausts heard at the model of Melton station emanated from a human being. Everyone was vastly impressed.

At about this time my father made a highly prized trip to Albury in the cab of the S class pulling the Spirit of Progress. Mr Bill Lewis, an engineer in the Victorian Railway's Rolling Stock branch, and also a member of the Victorian Model Railway Society, obtained an engine pass for him and accompanied him on the footplate.

The driver on the night was George Padget. He and his fireman were based in Wodonga.

It is worth mentioning that the two most prestigious trains in Victoria, the Overland to Adelaide and the Spirit of Progress to Albury, were not operated by crews from Melbourne. The Spirit of Progress was handled by Wodonga men and the Overland by crews from Ararat and Dimboola.

At the end of this life-defining journey my father took water and helped clean the fire and coal the S's tender. It was then that Bill Lewis told the crew that Frank Barnett was an outsider and not a railway man. In recognition of his presence in the cab, George Padget removed the most recent portion of the engine's speed chart covering the trip for that evening and presented it to my father. It was most gratefully received.

The return journey to Melbourne was made in the cab of Victoria's only locomotive having a 4-8-4 wheel arrangement, H220. This pulled the Wodonga–Melbourne fast goods, loading up to 820 tons. The driver was Jack Collie and his fireman had the advantage of working on Victoria's only engine equipped with a mechanical stoker. The H made light work of running its train to Melbourne and there was ample time on the journey to boil the billy and enjoy a cup of tea. According to my father, they did this on three or four occasions while the H went along 'as if it had nothing behind it.'

As the years of the Second World War passed my fear of locomotives became less and my fascination increased. I made it my business to look closely at every engine within range. This meant being present, whenever possible, at the platform of country passenger trains departing or arriving Melbourne. I would walk along the train to whatever was pulling it and look respectfully into the cab. I spoke only when spoken to and never made any requests. In due course I would be noticed and nine times out of 10 one of the overalled figures on the footplate would say, 'would you like to come up and have a look?' 'Yes please,' and I would enter that wonderful space between engine and tender, soaking up the aromas of warm steel, hot lubricating oil and drifting steam that occasionally wafted back from the open cylinder cocks.

Sometimes a crew would put my railway knowledge to the test. 'Why do we have two gauge glasses to tell us the water level in the boiler?' I didn't know. 'Because if one fails we can use the other.' I caught on fast.

'Why do we have two injectors to feed water into the boiler?' 'Because if one fails you can use the other?' 'Right!'

I learned about the various locomotive classes in use on the Victorian Railways together with their wheel arrangements, technical details and principal areas of use. Of particular interest were the safety features built into the boilers.

These centred around a fusible plug, screwed into the crown of the firebox. This melted when the boiler water approached a dangerously low level, discharging the remaining steam and water into the firebox warning the engineman that the water level was too low and that the feed water injectors must be turned on and the fire knocked out into the ash pan.

A boiler explosion was thus averted. I found this knowledge greatly reassuring.

When it was time for the train to depart or the engine to move I would step smartly onto the platform with a sincere, 'Thank you very much!' 'That's all right, you're welcome.' And there were warm smiles all round. At times I had been in the company of some really hard-bitten characters but not one ever failed to appreciate politeness and good manners.

2 Escaping Steam

In January 1949 my parents rented a house in Emerald, 30 miles east from Melbourne, and my sister and I spent some of our summer holidays there. Emerald is on the 2 foot 6 inch gauge now preserved line from Belgrave to Gembrook. In 1949 the narrow gauge commenced at Upper Ferntree Gully. This was home to both broad- and narrow-gauge rail yards and a small locomotive depot servicing three or four Na class, 2 foot 6 inch gauge tank engines, having a 2-6-2 wheel arrangement. The Na's were nuggetty little machines which although lacking superheating are remarkably good pullers for a locomotive having a roadworthy weight of only 30 tons.

By the late 1940s trains to Gembrook no longer ran daily. There was one train on Tuesday, one on Thursday and two on Saturday, one in the morning and one in the afternoon.

I rode to Gembrook and return as often as I could. While progress was not rapid, the Na's exhaust was worthy of many a larger locomotive and it, together with their high-toned steam boat whistle, made the trip very worthwhile.

So it was on a sunny Saturday I boarded an eight-car afternoon train to Gembrook at Emerald. Its on-time arrival bade well for the future and I looked forward to an enjoyable outing. When engine requirements were completed we were on our way. The driver was large and affable and did not seem to mind his rather cramped and hot surroundings on a day on which most other people were not working.

We stopped at Lakeside and rolled pleasantly along in the afternoon sun. The clickety clack of the short wheel base bogie cars jogged in and out of rhythm, sometimes giving a pleasing rendition of the more lively portions of Liszt's 'Hungarian Rhapsody No. 2'. We made a spirited climb into Cockatoo where the beats of the air compressor gave way to the locomotive's sharp exhaust as it brought the train smartly into the station. Just the stuff for the grades ahead!

After about a minute the fireman came walking back from the engine requesting that everybody get out. Descending onto the platform with the other passengers I noticed a rather high-pitched sound coming from the front of the train, which now without passengers began to set back. As the engine approached the high-pitched sound got louder. I walked alongside the engine cab and observed the driver at the throttle, still affable, still smiling and, wonder of wonders, inviting me in. In the cab were the typical footplate aromas and the sound was loud. It came from somewhere inside the firebox, and as the door to this was swinging open I peered in. A few lazy tongues of flame were all that remained of a fire which was now mostly ash. Then the steam gauge caught my eye. It was showing 120 lbs per square inch, well down on the working pressure of 180. The driver backed the train past the turnout into Cockatoo's number two road. The guard was on the points, pulled them over for the diversion and signalled the driver to come ahead. He opened the throttle with the steam gauge now showing 100. The little tank engine used its steam well and we were soon clear of the main line. With the throttle now closed the air brake brought the train to a stand with the steam gauge slowly falling past 70. As the steam pressure fell so did the intensity of the sound from the firebox, thus leaving no doubt that it came from a blow of steam, and initially water as well.

The driver applied the hand brake, threw the reversing lever into mid gear, opened the cylinder cocks and turned off the air compressor. Satisfied that everything was in order he picked up his bag and joined me in walking across to the station. We addressed the issue of what had gone wrong and discussed the possibilities. I pondered on why he seemed interested in the opinion of a 12-year-old boy, but decided that was not a major concern. Either a boiler tube had burst, discharging steam into the firebox, or the fusible plug had melted. I regretted not noticing whether either of the gauge glasses, which register the boiler's water level, had any water showing. We decided it was unlikely that a burst tube would have such a detrimental effect so quickly, so centred our thoughts around the melting of the fusible plug.

There was a pause, then the driver said, 'What do you think it is?'

'I think it's the plug,' I said. 'I think it is too,' he replied. And we were at the station.

He went into the station staff area and appeared at an open window, talking on a telephone to someone in authority. His conversation, which anyone could hear, shed considerable light on what had happened. He explained to the party at the other end that shortly after leaving Upper Ferntree Gully he and the fireman noticed that one gauge glass showed a higher boiler water level reading than the other. They dealt with this unsatisfactory state by taking the minimum level as the true reading and this enabled them to reach Cockatoo, where the fusible plug had melted and the train became disabled.

No one seemed to mind the delay and it was soon announced that buses would transport everyone to their destination.

Then someone produced a bottle of wine. The engine crew used their glass tea-drinking cups to consume some of it, generously lending one of these to the guard for his share. Having given his report to a higher authority, and with the day's work all but done, the driver imbibed more than was advisable and became more jovial than ever, causing the fireman to 'hope that my mate sobers up by the time we get to Ferntree Gully.'

The buses duly arrived and we travelled in good company back to Emerald, where I and some other passengers were dropped off. I thanked the enginemen for their hospitality and made my way to our holiday house to relate the afternoon's adventures. My grandparents had come to spend the weekend with us, having come on the morning train, and my grandfather was considerably amused when I told them of my conversation on the technicalities of steam blows on disabled locomotives.

The driver lived to fight another day and escaped from that afternoon without discipline.

An unidentified Na on a train near Nobelius in 1949, rolling down grade towards Lakeside. (David Barnett)

3 Shelbourne Passenger

Easter Monday 1949 was significant. The Victorian Railways were going to run a passenger train from Castlemaine to Maldon and Shelbourne. Passenger trains to Maldon had long since given way to buses and no passenger transport, train or bus, ran to Shelbourne. My father joined a party made up of members of the Victorian Model Railway Society who were taking advantage of this rare opportunity to go to Shelbourne by train and I was included.

Motive power was short and our express to Castlemaine and Bendigo was hauled by a C class 2-8-0 freight loco, recently converted to oil firing and pressed into passenger service for that day. It did well despite its 60 inch driving wheels restricting it to 60 mph and we arrived at Castlemaine in good time. Here we joined a mixed train comprising about a dozen four-wheel trucks, two old but very comfortable passenger cars and a guard's van. It was drawn by $D^3$653, a light-line, long-funnelled 4-6-0. I made friends with the crew and on arrival at Maldon, before lengthy shunting took place, was invited into the cab. The temperature was higher and the oil, steam and steel mix was reassuring. After lunch I resumed my position of privilege on the fireman's seat while the mixed train to Shelbourne was assembled. Only one passenger car was included but this was ample to accommodate the few railway enthusiasts travelling. Before departing Maldon, I joined them. Line speed was 15 mph and with the engine running tender-first our trip under an overcast sky, through gum leaf scented bush was most pleasant.

Shelbourne did not possess a platform and the passenger car and guard's van remained on No. 1 track while wheat trucks were spotted and removed from the bank of silos. After travelling in the train I was quickly back in the cab on arrival and in the course of the yard work had my photo taken leaning out of the fireman's window.

Everything was done at a leisurely pace. People explored what there was of Shelbourne—no houses, mostly the railway yard—took photos, drank tea from thermoses and generally enjoyed the afternoon. With the engine now about to run funnel-first at the head of a short train we were ready to tackle the eight mile trip back to Maldon. Any figure of authority was miles away. The passengers were on the train, the guard was in his van and I was in the cab, hoping. The fireman put a generous sprinkling of coal on the fire and we were ready to depart. The driver looked at me in the fireman's seat. 'Now you sit there,' he said. I affirmed that I would. The whistle sounded and we were away. I waved knowingly to my father who was leaning out of a window in the train and he waved knowingly back. All was well.

With a light load and a 15 mph limit the fireman had a picnic firing 653. Even though grades of 1 in 50 were encountered there was nothing to it and the train made easy and enjoyable progress throughout its short journey. Speed dropped to 7 mph as we surmounted the grade on the outskirts of Maldon but the D3 soon rose to the occasion as the driver nudged open the regulator and the exhaust beats became firmer and we came cheerfully into Maldon yard.

Here the engine was cut off and moved ahead to the turntable where I marvelled at how it had to be so carefully balanced before it could be pushed around to face in the opposite direction. I assisted with this and was fascinated at how it just fitted on to this turning device, with both

Sporting a Preston Technical School cap, the author presents a picture of contentment leaning out the cab window of $D^3$653 at Shelbourne on Easter Monday, 1949. (W.F. Barnett)

the front and rear couplings sticking out in mid air. The fire was cleaned, the ash pan flushed and water taken.

Then began the final shunting for the day. With the tracks affected by recent light rain the engine slipped from time to time to the accompaniment of some beautiful sound effects, delighting all onlookers. The two passenger cars were marshalled next to the guard's van at the rear of the train and an assortment of four-wheel freight vehicles stretched towards the engine, which backed its consist into the platform.

The crew explained that they were unable to let me ride with them to Castlemaine because 'you never know who might be around'. So I said my farewells and 'thank you' and joined my party on the train. We reached Castlemaine in good spirits and picked up a late afternoon express from Bendigo to Melbourne hauled by an X class booster-equipped 2-8-2 heavy freight loco. This made light of the load and even though limited to 50 mph made good time with much whistling. It had been an excellent day and I had ridden for some distance in the cab of a D3.

4 No Water Showing

Having been frequently in locomotive cabs at stations, ridden briefly on a narrow-gauge engine and experienced a full-size cab for about eight miles at 15 miles an hour, I longed for what seemed the real thing — a cab ride on the main line. I reflected on how I might get one.

The year was 1949 and I lived in Melbourne, second city in Australia. Melbourne possessed an impressive steam locomotive depot located just outside the city's central business district. The suburban station of North Melbourne provided easy access to the depot via a meandering footbridge over a small freight yard. This location, I thought, was definitely worth investigating.

At thirteen I was tall for my age and had persuaded my parents to provide me with the two items I considered necessary for being on a locomotive – a pair of dark blue overalls and an engineman's cap of similar colour. Wrapping these in a tight bundle, together with a couple of railway sweat cloths provided by my father, I set off one Saturday afternoon to visit the North Melbourne locomotive depot, hoping to pick up a cab ride.

From the engine shed came a slowly rising pall of smoke coupled with occasional chime whistles as locomotives came and went.

I strode manfully onto the footbridge trying to look like I belonged there, deciding that in order not to say anything I would keep out of everyone's way and hence not be approached.

Engineman, generally in twos or threes, came and went across this elevated walkway. Imagining I was the centre of their attention I always looked away. Finally, after taking 20 minutes for a four-minute walk, I proceeded down the ramp to the engineman's sign-on lobby. I gave this a wide berth and with head down hurried along by an outside wall to where some tracks converged on one of the depot's two front entrances.

There was no one around, and slipping inside I found a convenient spot between a wall and a stabled engine where I donned my overalls and cap. I felt slightly more confident. Positioning a sweat cloth to casually trail out of a pocket, I surveyed my surroundings.

The rectangular brick depot was huge. In all, it could accommodate 60 engines of various sizes and wheel arrangements.

Of the three turntables under its roof, two were employed to receive and dispatch engines while the tracks radiating from the third were home to locomotives undergoing repair. Connecting rods and valve motion lay round about some engines here, others had their tenders either beside them or wrong way round on the same track, and a few were stabled awaiting attention; the faint wisps of steam from their cylinder cocks silently indicating they had arrived that day.

The air was slightly acrid and carried what was to me a therapeutic wafting of steel, steam and hot oil. Smoke continued to rise and the chime whistles, confined within four walls, were a sound to be reckoned with. Air compressors, both single and double stage, thudded out a rasping rhythm that echoed back from the roof and made conversation difficult if not impossible. When an engine nosed on to a turntable its immense bulk was enveloped in steam from the cylinder cocks whose noise was surpassed only by the thunder of each axle transferring its weight.

The whole place was terrifyingly wonderful!

Inside the depot, near the sign-on lobby, was the office of the depot foreman. Close by were two large blackboards whose ruled columns and stencilled headings announced what engines were going where. One board was for freight, the other for passenger. Details of engine numbers, departure times, train information and destination locations were written in chalk for each day.

On the passenger board, engine 177, on turntable B, was rostered for the 5.50 pm Leongatha, a town 73 miles to the south-east of Melbourne.

177 was one of 70 K class, light 2-8-0s, designed as low axle load freight haulers and limited to 45 mph. This limit was of little consequence when running to Leongatha because the line speed for passenger trains to there was only 50, traffic on that line being light.

I made my way to K 177. It was standing quietly on a B table track and I paused quietly beside it. A small, rather scruffy looking middle-aged man with tousled hair came toward the engine. He was dressed in dark trousers and something that had once been a luxurious suit jacket. This latter would now barely have made the wardrobe of a scarecrow.

He was unsteady on his feet but his speech was sharp. 'Don't just stand there, get the kit and oil up!' I had been mistaken for the fireman and this man was the driver. He was intoxicated and this accounted for his uncertain gait. I was staggered that any roster clerk in his right mind would sign on a man in his condition, particularly when he was to be in charge of a passenger train. But here he was.

The fireman now arrived carrying his kitbag and the tools and supplies for 177. Acknowledging the driver and nodding to me he got busy. There was a hiss of steam as he tested the gauge glasses, then the blower went on and a clang of fire irons announced the fire was being prepared. This done, he filled the oil feeder and in accord with Victorian Railways' regulations began oiling the motion, this being one of the fireman's official tasks.

Meanwhile the driver had made it into the cab, and more by instinct than coordination was filling the sight feed lubricator that fed the air compressor. After this, he rested.

The fireman was still oiling up and I knew my fate hung in the balance. I climbed into the cab and spoke to the driver. 'Excuse me, sir, would you mind if I came with you?' He looked at me without seeming to have heard; then said in a voice barely audible above the noise of the blower and the now operating double stage air compressor, 'Come where?' I spoke up. 'On the trip to where you are going.' He really had no idea who I was or where I'd come from. Fortunately this did not seem to matter and his slowly sobering face exhibited a half-smile accompanied by the words, 'All right, you can come.'

The fireman was well built and affable. His overalls were clean and his cap pressed. He finished his preparation, checked the water in the tender and returned to the cab.

'He's coming with us,' the driver said to him. This brought a casual nod of acceptance as he surveyed the now rising steam gauge, together with, 'You can sit there,' pointing to his seat. I said a genuine 'Thank you,' but it was some years before I realized just what a privilege I had been granted.

Both injectors were tested and one left on to bring the boiler water up to about three-quarters of a glass. It was now around 4.30 pm. The fire was bright, steam around 175, brakes fully charged, cylinder cocks open. Time to move.

Three short whistles and B turntable had us lined up. We eased engine first on to the table, steam from the cylinder cocks immediately blocking the view from each side of the cab while thunder claps from the axles announced our progress. The fireman said something to the man on the turntable, its electric motor ground into action and we were lined up to proceed to table A. Here we departed through one of the front 'doors' and began threading through the points and turnouts that led past the Spencer Street passenger yard, over the four-track viaduct, to our departure point at Flinders Street station.

Sound levels now dropped 50%, the air was cleaner and conversation easier. The sparse conversation between the crew revealed that we would head south-east until meeting the late afternoon passenger train from Leongatha a bit after 7 pm, changeover on to that train and run it home.

Running between platforms at Flinders Street

we passed our short train, stopped, then backed slowly down on to it.

All this time I had been watching the driver out of the corner of my eye, wondering just how he was going to run the engine, read signals and generally avoid disaster. Since leaving North Melbourne he had obeyed every signal, kept within speed limits and his generally faultless performance was highlighted by his easing up gently on to the train. This was short, five passenger cars in front of a luggage van; a mere 210 tons.

At 20 minutes before departure time I realized that my parents should be notified of what was happening. Loose change in my pocket from purchasing a train ticket to North Melbourne was just what was needed for a phone call and I swung down from the cab explaining why.

Walking back along the train in overalls and cap was a joy in itself. I was one of the engine crew, one of the privileged, a being on whom these other beings, for a while at least, were dependent. This deserved respect.

I called my parents. They were out. I called next door and asked if they would be kind enough to deliver a message. They would, and everything was satisfactory.

Back in the cab the driver looked more awake than before and said, deadpan, 'I rang your mother and she said you couldn't come.' That was the most he ever said to me for the whole evening. I graciously disproved his statement and looked forward to what was ahead.

It was a pleasant evening. The last rays of the sun streamed onto the platform as the train examiner completed the brake test. The guard came up with the train details, checked time-pieces and exchanged pleasantries. The fireman built up the fire, easing back the blower and putting the firebox doors on the half notch to prevent blowing off. Water was three-quarters of a glass. Using the cab hose he washed down the deck, swept up wayward coal and gave the smell of steel, oil and steam a hygienic flavour.

Departure time came. The three position upper quadrant departure 'Home' signal pointed skywards, the driver acknowledged the guard's 'right away' on the whistle, opened the throttle and we were moving. Our first 100 yards, enveloped in steam from the cylinder cocks, took us over some points and on to a long right-hand curve through the yards. The cylinder cock lever was on the fireman's side and at a nod from him I pulled it closed.

Speed picked up to 25 mph as we passed rows of stabled suburban electric trains, their bulk echoing our progress. Everywhere there was noise. Everything rattled and banged and vibrated with a cacophony that defies description. Communication was by gesture or bellowing into an ear at close range. And this roaring symphony produced not one sound from the exhaust, which was so far drowned out.

Speed increased to 30 mph and we swung around the sharp left-hand curve leading out of South Yarra. The driver opened the throttle wide and ran the train using the cutoff. The fireman proved an expert with the shovel—the funnel varying from clear to dark as he pressed the foot pedal controlling the air-operated firebox doors; coal shot into dancing flames and the safety valves lifted.

Climbing a short 1.25% grade the driver wound the reverse out a little and with wide open throttle the engine whisked its light train effortlessly along, speed increasing to 35, then 40 and still on the rise.

A staccato exhaust echoed back in classic style over the train. Whirling valve motion and 4 foot7 3/16 inch drivers added their own roller-skate rhythm making our journey down the four-track main line a first-class adventure.

Upper quadrant automatic signals displayed clear normal speed and we soon reached our first stop at Caulfield, six and a quarter miles from Melbourne.

The driver brought the train to a smooth stop. Having no experience of water consumption on main-line steam locomotives I vaguely thought that if we started with about ¾ of a glass in Melbourne there should be not much less where we were now. With the engine happily blowing off, I noticed that the fireman's side injector was on. Without bothering to look at a gauge glass, I promptly turned it off. Whether he saw me or not I don't know, but the fireman then crossed from the driver's side of the cab and, pointing to the injector, said 'Did you turn that off?' 'Yes,' I said. He shook his head in rebuke and pointed to the gauge glasses. I was staggered to see the water level was barely one-third, and this was with that injector on for at least half our short journey. He accepted my apology graciously.

We were soon on our way and the driver made sure 177 accelerated smartly to 45 mph and stayed there. The whistle warned each level crossing of our approach and upper quadrant signals beckoned us on.

The driver sat impassively at the throttle, responding to the whistle boards and obeying the signal indications and paying no attention to what else was going on in the cab.

Each time the train got under way the water surged back in the boiler and the gauge glass level rose accordingly, only to fall back when the brakes were applied and the water in the boiler surged forward. Sometimes it disappeared out of sight altogether, then reappeared when a water surge stabilized. I didn't like it disappearing. While all Victorian Railways locomotives were fitted with fusible plugs thus removing the threat of a boiler explosion due to low water, why not run with water well up in the glass and remove all chances of a mishap? If water disappeared in a gauge glass, how did you know what damage had been done to the firebox crown when it was out of sight? And how did you know that this damage wasn't cumulative, causing the plug or the firebox crown to suddenly let go?

These thoughts began to come and go and I experienced a vague sense of unease. Even when I later fully understood the facts of feed water treatment, water carryover and priming due to a boiler being too full, I still advocated a gauge glass showing a higher, rather than a lower, water level.

Meanwhile we had been steaming down the double track to Dandenong, our next stop and end of the electrified suburban network. Evening closed in gently. The turbo generator was turned on, gauge lights illuminated the cab and the atmosphere was warm and snug.

Signal lights stood out and the cooler air meant exhaust beats were clearer.

Right away! Again 177 got smartly away, water surged up in the glass and the suburbs were gone. The fireman picked up the staff for the now single line and darkening fields formed the passing scenery. Now when the fire doors swung open a white hot glare embraced the cab and was reflected overhead on the trailing exhaust — one of the world's truly great sights!

One more station stop and we were heading toward our changeover location at Clyde, 31 miles from Melbourne.

Clyde is in the middle of a three mile, 1.1% grade favouring trains heading towards Leongatha. Holding the main line, we rolled into the station past our changeover, already in the passing track; the illuminated headlight numbers showing 895.

The crew off 895 were on the platform and we joined them. 177 was handed over with a bright fire, steam issuing cheerfully from the safety valves, one-third of a gauge glass of water and a swept clean cab. Conversation was brief. 'What time do you want make it?' 'Seven o five ?' 'Yeah, righto.' 'You've got six for 210.' 'You've got six for 220.' They climbed aboard and the train departed. Treading carefully, we made our way to engine 895. It stood quietly at the head of its train, its single-stage air compressor breathing with a reassuring rhythm to the background serenade of the turbo generator.

895 was a sturdy 10-wheeler of the class known as A2. Although of an old Stephenson valve gear design and near the end of it's life, it had excellent adhesion, a free steaming boiler and 73 inch driving wheels.

We entered a clean footplate. Steam was near 200, the fire bright, even and ready to perform and water a shade over half a glass.

The driver answered the 'right away', snapped on the headlight and opened the throttle. The fireman picked up the staff and after the first few turns of the wheels I closed the cylinder cocks and we headed out on to the main line.

Helped by the grade 895 was climbing, water surged up in the gauge glasses and the fireman stepped onto the deck and got busy. The manually operated drop-down firebox door banged open, the shovel clanged and coal went expertly on to the fire. The throttle was wide open and with the headlight showing the way 895 whisked its train easily up the 1.1% grade. Speed rose from 25 mph to 30, then 35. The safety valves lifted and each time the fire door was opened their trailing white feather was captured in a white hot snapshot of light.

The strident beat of the 10-wheeler's deep-throated exhaust echoed across the countryside. Speed continued to rise and occasional short-lived live embers entered the air, having escaped the spark arrestor.

The speed recorder showed 45, then 50. We had topped the grade and on the now undulating track the driver wound the reverse back a few notches to limit speed increases. This had little effect and we were now doing 55. The notched-up reverse reduced the demand for steam and the safety valves continued to roar, the fireman responding, much to my relief, by putting on the injector on his side of the cab.

After one station stop we were approaching Dandenong, back in the suburban area. The classic sound of the air compressor punctuated the night air as we stopped at the brightly lit platform and I watched a gauge glass. It showed nothing. Then, after what seemed a very long time, water appeared, about three-quarters of an inch of it, dancing in the bottom. I would have put the injector on immediately, but not these gentleman. The driver wasn't looking and the fireman wasn't interested. I was concerned. Supposing the firebox crown sheet was uncovered for long enough to overheat? Would this be taken care of by the fusible plug? If so, why didn't it operate just then, when the glass registered nothing for such a long time? What if the plug was defective?

Right away!

The big wheels began to turn, the exhaust sobbed skywards and green over red signals ushered us out on to the double-track electrified main line.

The water mocked my concern and surged well up in the glass which now showed over half full. Speed soon reached 50 mph, the staccato exhaust sweeping back over the train. With the headlight now on dim, the beautiful chime of the whistle announced our presence to each approaching station which soon passed and was replaced by another.

The fire door clanged open and the fireman took hold of the shovel, his action caught now in full, now in silhouette, in the powerful glare of the firebox. The engine made light of the load, speed sat around 55, safety valves lifted and the fireman turned his injector on. For how long it was on I don't remember, but it was off when we stopped to set down passengers at the major suburban station of Oakleigh.

Approaching this station the safety valves lifted and we came into the platform with the engine howling its head off. Coming to a stand, the gauge glasses emptied themselves of their previously healthy water reading. Knowing there was water in the boiler and that it was bound to reappear, I waited; and waited, and waited. Nothing! I became frightened, cowering away from the firebox while at the same time watching in fascinated horror to see what would happen. After what seemed an eternity, a tiny wisp of water appeared in the bottom of both glasses. To see it, you almost had to stand beside one and peer down into it. And there the water remained, bobbing more out of sight than in, a frail and pathetic diminishing hope against some major mishap.

Apparently the fireman thought so too. He knocked open the water valve of his side injector and turned on the steam. But it was steam, not water, that issued from the overflow. The injector would not pick up. He tried again, again steam. The thing was overheated and, right now, useless.

Meanwhile the engine was howling even louder and the driver, oblivious to the prevailing crisis, was looking back along the train. Outside, all was normal, with people milling around the station's three platforms, unaware of their impending doom through what I perceived as a near certain boiler explosion.

The failure of one injector and the disappearing luxury in the bottom of the gauge glasses heightened my fear. The end seemed close. Suddenly the idea of riding on steam locomotives lost all appeal. If I escaped from what was going on here I would know to never again entertain crazy notions of travelling in engine cabs.

Leaving the overheated injector the fireman moved to the other one, ambling across the cab at a pace that would have made a snail impatient.

Predictably, the injector was stiff. He picked up the hammer from its bracket on the tender, knocked open the water valve and administered a sharp tap and twist to the steam valve. There was

$A^2$984 eases the morning Yarram–Melbourne passenger train out of Nyora while $A^2$995 waits to follow with a freight. With no oil refuelling facilities on the south-eastern line, oil-burning A2 and C class locomotives ran from Melbourne only as far as Korumburra. (ARHS Victorian Division Archives)

a throaty hiss followed by a gurgling discharge as water streamed out of the overflow. With a cheerful flourish he adjusted the water valve and a cool refreshing stream shot into the boiler. My prayers of thanksgiving were heartfelt and sincere.

The driver, who had paid not the slightest attention to what had been happening, now announced his presence by sounding the whistle and opening the throttle. 895's beautiful, throaty exhaust echoed around the station buildings as we pulled away. We had spent two minutes at Oakleigh.

Bowling along through the suburban stations we soon arrived at Caulfield, our final stop before Melbourne.

Caulfield ushered us back on to four-track main line and with a string of green over red signals in our path we pounded up a slight grade, the fireman having an easier time now as you can roll for about three miles soon after leaving Caulfield. This we did, steam on 200, speed around 35 to 40, no roar from the safety valves only the wonderful song of the injector. It had been on for over 10 minutes now and while running down grade the water appeared not to be rising; however, as soon as 895 was on the level it appeared at well over half a glass. The night was cool and clear and all was well with the world. Rounding a long left-hand curve brought us into the Flinders Street passenger yard. We picked our way deftly through rows of stabled electric trains, obeyed the reduce to medium speed yellow over green and rolled easily into No. 1 platform on time at 8.30 pm.

The fireman slipped out of the cab, uncoupled the engine from the train, waited till the driver moved 895 a few feed ahead, then came back. A bucket of hot water was produced, I took off my overalls and cap and with the aid of some communal soap used my sweat cloths to get as much coal dust off my face and hands as possible.

The trip was over. Disaster had been averted. What disaster? Was there really any? I wasn't sure. The main thing was we had completed a turn of duty and everything was fine. The crew knew nothing of my fears and I saw no reason to mention them.

Things were certainly different now.

$A^2$895 sat quietly at the platform, air

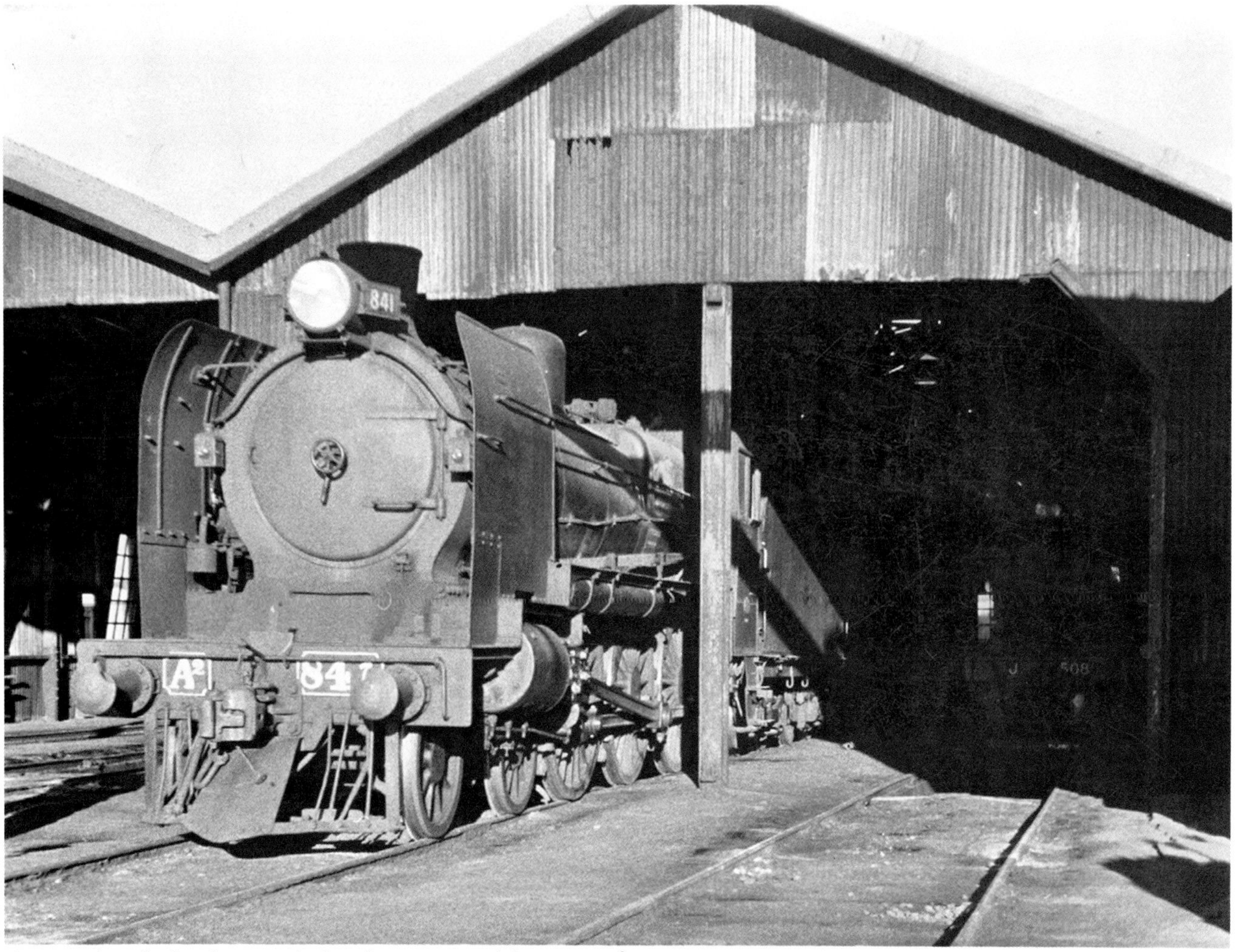

Equipped with Stephenson link valve gear, coal-burning $A^2$841 sits at Korumburra loco depot. It was on a similar locomotive that the author rode from Clyde back to Melbourne when the water kept disappearing in the gauge glasses. (ARHS Victorian Division Archive)

compressor breathing regularly, turbo generator sounding a credit to the Pyle National Company, cab bathed in a pleasant orange glow from the half-open fire door, blower barely on, steam around 190 and water three parts of a glass.

And that was how I left it.

I had just experienced the thrill of a lifetime and I was grateful. I thanked the crew very much for having me and I meant it. Their congenial response formed a fitting farewell as I swung down on to the platform, and with one lingering glance I made my way to the suburban train that would take me home.

I had tasted main-line locomotive running and longed for more

In the electric train journey home to Rosanna after leaving $A^2$895 I discovered I had a headache. On arriving home I fortified myself with two aspirin and glanced at my face in the bathroom mirror. I had coal dust round my eyes, in my nostrils, in and around my ears, around my neck, under my fingernails and as I later found, around my ankles.

It took quite a while and more than one face washer to become reasonably clean. After this my mother provided a much needed warmed-up meal. My overalls and cap went into the soiled linen basket in the laundry and I went into bed. The day's events had been wonderful but exhausting. I was asleep in five minutes.

But my headache had gone in the morning and I was alive and well and thankful. What a day yesterday had been. It must be repeated as soon as possible!

5 Firing the Spirit

I kept frequenting North Melbourne as often as I could and while I got one or two cab rides that were worthwhile it was to be some time before anything like the experiences of K177 and A^{2}895 were repeated.

Nevertheless the intervening time was not without interest. The Spirit of Progress to Albury was still hauled by one of the four three-cylinder S class 4-6-2 steam locomotives. Late one Saturday afternoon I found myself standing beside the engine rostered for the Spirit of that evening. I was invited into the cab and immediately soaked up the distinctive aroma of oil, steam and steel. Everything was on a big scale, signifying the importance of the task the locomotives performed; for the Spirit of Progress was very much a world-class train.

I knew I could not expect to go far on this engine, but the crew were most hospitable and invited me to travel with them to Spencer Street station where they would couple on to their train, and this was an experience in itself.

A little after 5 pm the mellow chime whistle sounded and we backed away from the depot and onto the loop. We soon arrived at the TR point where we stopped and the fireman telephoned the signalman to announce our presence.

There was a brief delay before we were signalled

A wet Sunday afternoon in 1942. S302, Edward Henty, and an unidentified sister engine at North Melbourne. One will take out the 5.0 pm Albury Express, the other the 6.30 pm Spirit of Progress. (W.F. Barnett)

to proceed. I asked could I do some firing. 'Go ahead!' I stepped on the treadle that activated the air-operated firebox doors. They swung smoothly open revealing a yawning firebox. I fastened the doors open, turned round, picked up a shovel full of coal and did my best to swing it into the fire. I had done some firing on other locomotives and this stood me in good stead because the coal shot cleanly off the shovel and dropped neatly onto the fire bed. I repeated the process eight to ten times, trying, with some success, to put each delivery where it would do most good. At this point we were signalled to move and my firing came to an end. However, I can genuinely claim to have fired an S class that pulled the Spirit of Progress, although sadly I did not note its number.

The driver guided us through a myriad of signals to Spencer Street's No. 1 platform. He stopped short of the 11 car consist. The fireman coupled the engine to the train, checked that the couplings were secure, coupled up the brake pipes, opened the brake pipe cocks and returned to the cab.

The driver signed the speed recorder chart and all was ready. Departure time of 6.30 pm approached and it was time for me to leave. With the steam gauges nudging the working pressure of 200 psi I thanked the crew for having me and stepped off the footplate.

Shortly after this occasion, my father's fire protection firm transferred him temporarily from Melbourne to Ballarat.

6 R Class to Maryborough

With my father temporarily in Ballarat, our family spent an autumn school holiday break there. I was now 15. Wearing overalls and engineman's cap I blended in well with the surroundings of the Ballarat loco depot. It was large, had two turntables and accommodated around 35 engines. There was plenty happening. Wheat was still being moved and there were three or four trains daily that transferred this commodity from Ballarat to Warrenheip, four miles 'Distant' at the top of a 1 in 52 grade. The trains would be placed in sidings and later hauled to Geelong, from where the grain was exported overseas. A2s were the principal motive power. Trains were marshalled in one of the Ballarat station platforms and would typically weigh 685 tons, the load for two A2s to Warrenheip.

The engine crews were friendly and in one day I made three trips to Warrenheip and return; once on a coal burner with Stephenson valve gear and twice on an oil burner with Walschaert's valve motion. We made a vigorous start through Ballarat East where the grade was 1in 91 for about a mile before stiffening to 1 in 52. The exhaust from each engine blasted back over the train in a satisfying symphony of steam and steel. Once on the 1 in 52 the pace was around 10 mph, firing was easier and conversation possible, with the purposeful exhaust beats providing a delightful background rhythm.

Mr Tom Hardy was one of the drivers. I learned that on the next day he was to run the 12.40 pm goods to Maryborough, returning on the same day with the 4.10 pm Maryborough to Ballarat. This was a mixed train, carrying both goods and passengers and popular with school students.

The next day I kept away from the engine shed but presented myself at the head of the 12.40 pm Maryborough, which fortunately departed from an insignificant portion of the goods yard.

The engine was an R class.

The R's had been in service for some months but my contact with them had been minimal.

As expected, Tom Hardy was in the driver's seat and he invited me into the cab.

His fireman on this occasion was Laurie. He was a well built and clean cut figure who looked friendly and capable.

The footplate was swept clean and washed down, accentuating the engine's roominess. The layout of controls was impressive. An arc of shining turret valves near the cab roof spanned the steam and brake gauges, while the brake valves above the reversing wheel on the driver's side and the stoker gauge and valves on the fireman's side were equally striking. Each crew member had his own injector and the gauge glasses were mounted to conveniently display the boiler water level. Overall, the scene was dramatic and awe-inspiring, added to by the beat of the single-stage air compressor and the aroma of oil, steam and steel.

The train examiner completed the brake test, the guard delivered details of the load and departure time approached. Laurie supplemented the stoker's delivery of coal to the firebox by wise use of the shovel and steam sat on the red mark of 210.

'If there's no one around, I'll take you,' said the driver. It turned out that there was no one around and I was on the footplate for the return trip.

I stood behind the driver.

Our progress out of the yard and through Ballarat station was smooth and we were soon approaching Ballarat North. The driver spoke. 'Is the water on, Laurie?' 'Yes, the Water's on.' I immediately looked at the water level in the gauge glass. Not a drop was showing! The R class firebox is fitted with two Nicholson thermic siphons, which among their other benefits circulate water over the most vulnerable portion of the firebox — the crown sheet — in circumstances where the boiler water level may be low. And they worked well on this occasion. After a short time there came a bob in the bottom of the glass and all was well.

With one exception, the big 4-6-4 made light of its load. The exception came when ascending one of the well-known grades between Ballarat and Maryborough — the Great Australasian Bank. Here, the engine pulled to a stand. There was no shortage of steam and no slipping.

The driver set back, purposefully opened the regulator and after a spirited approach we sailed over the summit in confident style.

On arrival at Maryborough, we took coal and water, turned the engine and had a meal. Suitably nourished and refreshed, we coupled on to our return load. This was the 4.10 pm Maryborough–Ballarat mixed. It comprised several four-wheel goods wagons, two passenger cars and a guard's van, having an all-up weight of 325 tons. This was a full load for an A2. An R could take 15 tons more.

Promptly at departure time the 'right away' came from the guard and we blasted up the 1 in 48 grade out of Maryborough and were soon rolling down the 1 in 50 for a stop at Daisy Hill. Leaving here, we faced 25 miles of generally rising grades with some as steep as 1 in 50.

R class cab, driver's side. (David Barnett)

Laurie had the steam and water well under control. As the coal rumbled in the stoker trough on its way to the firebox, Mr Hardy opened the regulator wide, adjusted the cutoff and sent us pounding up these undulating grades with the most spectacular of staccato sound effects. The speed limit for trains with four-wheel vehicles is 45 mph but at times we rattled along at 50.

The passengers were all but gone by the time we left Creswick, and with the turbo generator now adding the warmth of its lighting to the cab atmosphere our arrival at the Ballarat passenger platform heralded the end of a most enjoyable day.

R class cab, fireman's side. The stoker jet manifold sits beneath the stoker throttle and booster valves. To the right is the injector steam valve. Steam and stoker gauges are also visible. (David Barnett)

7 Thirsty Work

My father's temporary transfer to Ballarat came to an end and our family continued living in Rosanna.

This meant that as often as possible I resumed my Saturday afternoon visits to the loco depot at North Melbourne. With perseverance I met some interesting people.

One was Andy Donohue.

Andy was the quintessential engineman. A senior driver on the passenger roster, he was 6 feet 2 inches tall, of heavy build with thinning grey hair. His benign features included a slightly prominent nose and thick, grey eyebrows, while his relatively husky voice carried with it a ring of authority. Along with blue overalls and cap his attire comprised a well-tailored blue denim jacket with a breast pocket, distinctive lapels and two side pockets. Whenever he appeared on the footplate these items were freshly laundered.

He enjoyed working on steam engines and was not averse to giving politely spoken persons a ride in the cab.

One trip I had with him stands out. It was on the weekday 9 am Melbourne–Yarram passenger. I had arranged with him to travel in the cab and arrived at North Melbourne loco depot at the appointed time of 7.05 am. The fireman was Frank Melbourne. He was slim, pleasant faced and most capable. Motive power was a coal-burning J class.

Preparations got under way with the banked fire being pushed down, the tender tank water level checked and oiling up soon completed. As usual, the interior of the depot was steamy, smoky, and alive. Men shouted, hammers clanged, wheelbarrows rattled, safety valves hissed, air compressors thudded, turntables shuffled into position, whistles sounded and cylinder cocks wheezed. As engines came and went there was a vigorous contest between each axle and its turntable, resulting in minor thunderclaps as each protested against the other.

We left this spectrum of steam and sound at 7.55 am and made our way in sunny weather to where the 9 am Yarram would depart at Flinders Street station. Here, by mutual agreement, the station staff boiled the 9 am Yarram engine crew's billy, thus affording them the opportunity of a cup of tea prior to departure. On this day, the boiling water arrived in the cab close to departure time. With the fire in good shape and brake test complete, the tea was made but there was little time to enjoy it. We each had a few hurried swallows; then it was time to go.

The hot billy with its precious contents was placed on the metal shelf above the firebox doors. The six-car, 200 ton load gave the engine and its crew little trouble. However, approaching South Yarra the fireman took a look in the firebox and decided things could be improved. He took up the shovel and was soon sending coal expertly onto the fire, making good use of the air-operated firebox doors. Meanwhile, as we rounded the left-hand curve out of South Yarra and onto the 1 in 60 upgrade, Andy Donohue eased the regulator wide open and adjusted the cutoff. With a delightful reverberating exhaust the J rose to the occasion and was soon whisking its light load up grade at 35 mph. Frank Melbourne continued firing. 'It'll be alright when we get to Caulfield,' he said. And then added, 'when it gets going!'

All this time the billy remained on its shelf. As speed increased the cab rocked a little and this rocking caused the tea to slop in increasing amounts out of the billy, pushing up its lid and cascading onto the shelf. This went on for three of four minutes as the fireman continued his efforts.

Then from across the cab came an agonized cry. 'Isn't that bugger ever going to stop shovelling? Here am I dying of thirst with the tea spilling all over the place and I can't get to it!' The fireman promptly paused in his labours and the driver retrieved the billy and refreshed himself. Cab harmony was thus restored.

Frank Melbourne was right about the fire. On reaching Caulfield it was near enough to being white hot.

We made good progress to our changeover point at Nyora. Here we surrendered our J, and took over the oil-burning A2 at the head of the morning Yarram–Melbourne passenger. With a load similar to that for the J class, the A2 had no trouble keeping time on the homeward journey and each billy of tea was shared equally by the three on the footplate.

8 Fireman for an Afternoon

While at North Melbourne one day during a school vacation I noticed a D2 shunting near the car repair workshop. The day was fine and I walked over to where it was standing. I was on the driver's side and a smiling face called down from the cab, 'What are you doing?' 'Just having a look around.' 'Well, you'd better come and have a look around up here.' I gladly accepted this invitation and in doing so commenced a long friendship with driver Arthur Reginald Adkins. Arthur was of slim build, with pleasant features and a strong bias for cleanliness. This was in evidence in the clothes he wore and the way he kept cab items clean to the point where some bordered on the hygienic. His fireman always swept the footplate and washed it down, removing any coal from the floor and attending to floor grease with kerosene and cotton waste. Cab windows were washed and cleaned and handrails groomed till almost spotless.

I thus learned, and was able to put into practice, all that was needed for good cab housekeeping.

Arthur was also active in union affairs.

I explained I was interested in locomotives, had been fortunate to have some main-line footplate trips, and was seeking to have more of the same whenever I could. He was sympathetic and so was his fireman, who was nicknamed 'The Admiral.'

Shunting movements soon resumed and in due course I sought permission to do some firing. This was granted. Watched closely, I dropped down the firebox door, took a look at the fire, picked up the shovel and placed about 14 shovelfuls of coal on the fire bed where I thought it was most needed. Straightening up, I used the shovel to close the fire door, replaced it in the tender and adjusted the blower. Lastly, I swept up the small amount of spilled coal and replaced the banister brush in its holder under the fireman's seat. These actions meet with silent approval. Soon after, I was able to demonstrate familiarity with an injector and for the rest of the day I did the firing.

At around midday we moved through the Melbourne yard to the Dudley Street signal box, entered a short siding and 'tied up' for lunch. Halfway through the meal an engineman appeared from somewhere, climbed into the cab, and engaged Arthur in conversation about union matters. You never heard anything like the language this man was using or the emphasis with which he used it! The conversation went on for some time. Finally, after a meal break of over 30 minutes, the disc signal for departing our siding was pulled off, signifying that we were to resume yard duties. Still the conversation went on.

The Admiral saw what was happening and interrupted in a deferential tone with, 'We'd better be going, he's been pulling that disc off for about five minutes.'

The reply from our visitor not only entered one's body through the normal auditory channels, but violently permeated the very fibre of one's being.

With the most vitriolic vituperation he rasped out, 'Let him pull his f---n' ar-e!' Fortunately, however, he took the hint and left. With a soft whistle we moved out into the yard where a shunter was waiting. He coupled us on to a string of wagons which were destined to be placed in an unloading dock near Macaulay station on the line to Coburg. With signals beckoning, we went through North Melbourne station, rolled over the complex of tracks that make up North

Melbourne Junction, diverged from the main line and arrived at our destination. Here the shunter, who had been riding in the cab, swung to the ground, set some points and waved us back to the location where the vehicles were required. Here we were uncoupled and signalled ahead. More changing of points and a move that brought us to the head of some empty trucks to be transferred back to the Melbourne yard.

We were now set to run tender-first. The single-stage air compressor charged the brakes and after these were tested a disc signal was soon pulled off and we retraced our steps to the Melbourne yard.

The D2 used very little steam and firing was easy. Our light load was placed on an appropriate track and some hand brakes secured. We were then uncoupled and ready to move elsewhere.

It was now a little after 3 pm. The Admiral moved to the driver's side of the cab, said something to Arthur Adkins, and received a nod in agreement. He then came across to me and said in a matter of fact manner, 'I'm going, you're the fireman now.' With that, he picked up his kitbag, swung down from the engine, made his way across some adjacent tracks and disappeared behind one of the rakes of trucks being assembled for departure that afternoon.

Arthur Adkins took all this in his stride, saying, 'He's rather a funny fellow.' For the rest of the afternoon I assumed the duties of fireman. I was 16. In overalls and cap I looked the part and fortunately had been around locomotive running long enough to be familiar with the various hand signals given to initiate train movements.

The rest of the afternoon, however, was short. We made a few moves, followed by the shunter saying, 'We're finished, so you can go over the pit.' The fact that we were finished was somehow communicated to the appropriate signalman and in due course a series of signals were placed at 'proceed' and the D2 threaded its way on to the main hostling road at North Melbourne.

Here, I helped take coal, rake out the grate and bank the fire, and took water. The engine then moved into the depot proper and onto B

A D2 class locomotive on shunting duties. It was on this class of engine that the author was fireman for an afternoon. (PROV, VPRS 12800 P4 RS/1333)

turntable, which obliged by lining up a vacant track where the D2 was stabled. The blower was turned off, regulator closed and cylinder cocks opened. The reverse was placed in mid-gear, the air compressor turned off and hand brake turned on. The bucket, shovel, tool kit and oiling implements were collected and returned to the store. Pleasantries were exchanged with shed staff and other engine crews as we made our way to the engineman's lobby where Arthur signed off. I was taken for granted as his fireman and walked away from the depot as if fulfilling this role.

Arthur was kind enough to give me his phone number for future contact; contact that was to be both fruitful and enjoyable!

9 Making up Time

The years advanced to February 1954 and B class diesel electric locomotives had taken over the early morning paper train to Seymour.

Timetabled as the 'Fast News Goods', this departed from the Melbourne yard goods depot and reached via Flinders Street extension at around 1.40 am on Monday to Saturday.

In Victoria, the passing of each day in February 1954 gave rise to mounting anticipation and excitement. The long awaited tour of Queen Elizabeth and the Duke of Edinburgh was about to take place, with the royal couple scheduled to arrive by air and touch down at Essendon airport on 24 February.

But supposing there was fog on that day? Contingency plans stipulated that the Queen's aircraft be diverted to Mangalore, with the journey to Melbourne being made by Royal Train. It was thus necessary to have two B class diesels on standby.

One of the runs from which they were removed was the 1.40 am paper train to Seymour.

The driver rostered for this was Arthur Adkins. I had kept in touch with Arthur after firing for him on a D2 some time previously, and had been invited to join him on this early morning trip to Seymour. His fireman for this job was Allan Smith.

Arthur liked goods trains. Speed was not his forte. While always running to the timetable, he welcomed any signal displaying 'caution', often remarking, 'There's money in those yellow lights.'

A little after midnight on the 24th I met the crew at North Melbourne soon after they had signed on. They, and I, had been expecting a diesel. However the driver greeted me with, 'We've got a steam engine, 754 on B.' We proceeded to B turntable and R754 sat quietly on one of its stabling roads.

We prepared the engine. Following this, three short whistles brought B table around to our track. We moved on to it and were dispatched tender-first down to and across A table and out of the depot into the cool morning air. A series of disc and dwarf signals guided us through the Melbourne yard towards our train.

Despite it being February, the air was crisp. Stars shone in a clear sky and noises were distinct. From time to time fragments of conversation became audible and the delightful crunch of footsteps on unsealed surfaces accompanied railway men going about their lawful occasions.

R754 backed slowly through the yard with the air compressor providing a bass accompaniment to the twanging treble of the turbo generator. Presently a lamp appeared, dimly silhouetting its owner. He turned out to be the shunter in charge of putting us onto our train.

He signalled us to stop.

The conversation between him and the driver was lively and explicit.

Precise movements were needed to move the engine onto its consist. These needed to be carefully executed according to exact distances. Thus, the major item of the driver's genitals would be used as the uniform unit of measurement!

This proved satisfactory and the 1.40 am and its locomotive were gently united.

The guard arrived, climbed into the cab and announced that our relatively short train weighed 397 tons. He took the driver's name, exchanged pleasantries, left the engine and disappeared into the darkness towards his van. Next came the train examiner. He inserted his key into the regulator quadrant, and with a 'put 'em on, will you please' stepped down and went back along the train. On receiving his hand lamp signal, Arthur released the brakes and the examiner came back to the engine, checking the opposite side of the vehicles. He retrieved his key, affirmed that all was in order and bade us good morning.

With visitors no longer present, the billy was boiled and a cup of tea revived and invigorated our mental alertness.

A long whistle was sounded at 1.40 am and this was promptly answered by a green lamp from the guard. With all brakes released, the regulator was eased open and with steam paving the way from the cylinder cocks the train moved towards the first fixed signal. This was green. We moved on, navigating carefully over numerous sets of points that led us behind the hoardings at North Melbourne and onto the suburban tracks to Broadmeadows.

Speed increased to around 30 miles an hour and the exhaust began to make its presence felt on the slight rise through Newmarket to Ascot Vale and on to Essendon. The streets were dusty and silent and passers-by few. The big 4-6-4 was steaming well and while nothing was said in the cab, the mood was cheerful.

The long sweeping curve down to Pascoe Vale saw speed increase to 40. I had hoped for the maximum of 45, but remembering who was driving was not surprised. The regulator was eased wide open at the bottom of the grade, and with a relatively long cutoff 754 went blasting past a sleeping population, all too unaware of what they were missing. In the cab it was different. Everyone was listening. The sound was that of exhaust steam, orchestrated into a strident rhythm rushing back over the train and echoing from passing houses.

One of the occasions I was on the footplate with Arthur Adkins was on transfer duties around Tottenham yard on C11. At an opportune time, the engine was stopped and I was photographed oiling up. The year was 1951. (David Barnett)

Speed dropped to 35. The cutoff was wound out a little, and the exhaust sharpened.

We were pulling a very heavy 397 tons! Through Jacana, 754 was labouring along at 10 mph, with the exhaust beats now much more distinctive and the cutoff wound right out on the link block.

The fireman had the steam gauge needle on the mark and nothing more could be done. 'Didn't he say we had 397?' It was the driver speaking. 'I don't know where he got that from,' he said, with the clear implication that the progress we were making was due to something more than the guard's figure.

There was little wind and the rails were dry. We plodded on in a clear 'I think I can, I think I can' mode past Jacana and on to Broadmeadows. The engine never lost its feet and topped the slight rise at the down end of the station that marks the end of the Glenroy Bank at a sedate but steady pace, with the speed recorder needle still on 10.

Things began to improve. The driving wheels began to turn faster and the exhaust became more strident. A pale moon shone on the grassy fields of Somerton, casting shadows around the trailing vapour and picking out sheep looking in the direction of this early morning intruder.

Despite the rising grades through Beveridge we bowled along effortlessly, as if some restraining force had been overcome as we left the suburbs. Wallan was bathed in fading, misty moonlight as we rolled into the platform prior to stopping to deliver newspapers. This took about five minutes. With the starting signal at 'clear' and a green light from the guard, the driver whistled off and opened the regulator. There may have been some dew on the curving track, or perhaps the opening was a little too rapid. However, whatever the cause, the engine slipped. Steam shot skyward and as the driving wheels rotated the whole locomotive shuddered and vibrated in protest. The regulator was immediately slammed shut. Nevertheless, a whole pipe full of steam went into the cylinders and slipping continued for at least another five seconds.

'When they slip, they won't stop, will they!' said Arthur.

He eased steam into the cylinders a second time and we pulled smoothly away. The moon had discovered some cloudless sky and illuminated the grade ahead towards Heathcote Junction. Not wanting a repeat performance of our earlier experience ascending a grade, the throttle was opened wide and the cutoff adjusted to provide a near 45 mph approach to the final climb over the dividing range. The staccato exhaust sounded highly professional as we pounded up the 1 in 50, and as speed fell back the cutoff went out on the block. 'I'm giving her the lot,' came from the driver's side of the cab. As if on queue, the safety valves lifted.

Things were different this time. We went blasting triumphantly over the summit at 20 mph, with three parts of a glass of water and the safety valves sizzling!

R754 rolled gleefully through Wandong and rode smoothly around the curves leading to the undulating switchback on the way to Seymour.

Making use of momentum, steaming was only required from time to time as we crossed the predominately down grade alignment to our destination.

This was reached just after sunrise. We were signalled into No. 1 platform road. Here we left the fast news goods and took the engine to be hostled down at the loco depot, handing it over to a relieving crew with the brief dictum, 'She's going alright, there's not much wrong with her.'

A visit to the roster clerk revealed the crew's next assignment. In a matter of fact, early morning sunrise manner, they were told to 'take that C class over to the new yard and run the Melbourne goods, due away about now'. 'Due away about now.' That sounded fine! The oil-burning C had been prepared and was standing on the departure road. After entering the environs of the Seymour station, we backed along the 'down' main line (i.e., away from Melbourne) towards our train.

The new yard was a World War II addition to Seymour's marshalling and storage tracks, built about half a mile from the station on the way to Mangalore. It was accessed by crossing over the 'up' main line (i.e., towards Melbourne) from which it diverged, and entering a series of well laid out parallel tracks.

The Melbourne goods was standing on the nearest of these, with a train examiner leaning against the leading vehicle. He gave an 'ease up' and we were soon coupled on. A brake test

After taking water, C11 sits in Tottenham yard waiting for a shunter to announce its next move. Standing in the cab gangway is Arthur Adkins, while in the fireman's seat is his fireman, Bernie Bewick. (David Barnett)

was promptly initiated. This was satisfactorily completed in about 15 minutes. The driver sounded a long whistle and all eyes focused on the dwarf signal that would enable us to depart. It remained at 'danger' and stayed that way for well over an hour.

The atmosphere in the cab went from warm and reassuring to hot and soporific. Seven o'clock came and went. So much for 'Due away about now'! Finally, some time after eight that morning, the dwarf went to yellow. Everyone was dozing, but soon roused and got busy. A long whistle brought a green flag from the guard and we were away.

After eight hours on duty, the prospect of getting home was enough to inspire the most conservative of engineman to get the most out of their engine. So it was that the oil-burning Consolidation got hold of its load in a businesslike manner and with an up tempo exhaust slowly accelerated around the curve into the Seymour yard. It was a waste of time. The departure home signal was at 'danger'. Some heavy braking ensured we stopped short.

It was February. The summer heat began to make its presence felt and the cab was soon sweltering.

Then, there was the sound of an engine on the adjacent track and a fully prepared R class stopped with its cab parallel to our own. Its crew came aboard. 'We're relieving you. You take our engine and run the "up" Goulburn Valley pass. It's 20 minutes late.' A prompt changeover was made and Allan Williams got busy with the shovel and stoker while we waited for the passenger train.

At that time, diesels had not yet reached the Goulburn Valley. The 6/240 tons consist of the 'up' morning passenger came in behind a trim and tidy D3, which soon relinquished its charge, enabling us to back down and take over. While the rhythm of the air compressor heralded a modified brake test, Arthur dispatched me to the platform to buy some barley sugar to sustain us on our journey. This was liberally handed round and our spirits and energy levels rose.

Departure time was near. The run to Melbourne was to be non-stop. 'I'll give you a fast ride,' Arthur said to me. 'Seventy miles an hour?' I asked. 'Damn near it!' was the response.

'Right away!' The water was a couple of studs from the top of the glass and the red mark at 210 on the steam gauge was obscured by the needle. The regulator was opened and steam hissed briefly from the cylinder cocks. We were away. The time was 9.18 am.

Two hundred and forty tons was not a big load for an R. Speed soon rose. The 1 in 50 grade from the wartime sidings at Dysart, up to Tallarook, was topped at 55 miles an hour and with the co-acting arms of this station's advance starting signal showing 'proceed' we swept around the right-hand curve with the speed recorder showing 65.

With a few exceptions before Broadford, the gradient profile onwards to Heathcote Junction is constantly climbing. Through a series of rising switchbacks, with frequent pinches of 1 in 50, there is no respite until Heathcote Junction at the top of the dividing range is reached.

Storming towards the 1 in 50 away from Tallarook it was noticed that steam dropped to 190. An immediate investigation revealed that the stoker trough was empty, with coal failing to gravitate to where it was needed. To save the fireman moving, I used the pricker, stowed diagonally across the back of the tender, to restore the coal supply. In the seconds that this took, the driver did not take his eyes off the track or ease the working of the engine. The regulator was wide open and Arthur was using the cutoff to control steam to the cylinders. The speed recorder needle remained on 65. And on we went! Sixty-five was a good speed to maintain, with many of the curves set at this limit. A grand polonaise of sound from the funnel accompanied our progress, shooting back over the train, now waxing, now waning as the driver wound out or wound back the cutoff.

Broadford went by in a flash.

Then the coal again stopped feeding. Using the same method as before it was quickly restored, but a glance into the coal bunker indicated more was needed. Coal was forming a kind of bridge across the stoker trough, falling to each side rather than in the middle. Unfastening the bunker doors, and clutching the diagonally stowed pricker and the shovel, I stepped into the tender and got busy. I climbed the mass of coal and, ankle-deep in it, pushed and shovelled so that most of it would find the stoker trough. It took two or three minutes and was exhausting.

Arthur Adkins, at right, and his fireman Bernie Bewick beside an oil-burning A2 at an unidentified location. (David Barnett)

Turning to rest, I got a snapshot view into the cab. It was exhilarating.

On the driver's side:

The regulator remained wide open and both brake valves were in the running position. Arthur's left arm leaned on the window ledge while his right hand adjusted the cutoff, mostly by sound, as his eyes rarely left the track. The speed recorder needle was glued to 65, where it had been for the past 15 minutes. Steam was just over 170 and water was a shade under half a glass.

On the fireman's side:

The steam gauge and gauge glass readings were the same. Having adjusted the stoker jets to an optimum setting, the fireman responded to the exhaust sounds by opening, and easing back, the stoker throttle as required. 170 seemed a little low for the steam pressure until I realized that the engine had been running constantly at 65 mph uphill for over 15 minutes with 240 tons behind it. And at no time did the boiler water fall below its present level. So much of the firing was against at least one injector, with coal that comprised at least 50% of small powdery pieces, slack and fines. A commendable effort to say the least!

All the while the exhaust was blasting back over the train in a blurring staccato, marginally rising and falling as power was adjusted to keep the speed constant. This was railroading! Meanwhile, the scenery, framed in the gangway on either side of the cab, was at once overtaken and left behind in a blur.

Throughout the whole journey, the big 4-6-4 rode like a palace.

Kilmore East went by at a steady 65 mph and the train was on its way to the summit. On the steepening grades, the same driving and firing techniques kept the speed constant, the water level steady and enabled the steam gauge to creep up.

On the final 1 in 50 approach to Heathcote Junction speed began to fall. Arthur wound the reverse out a little, lessening the decline. We went blasting over the top at just over 50. The accompanying prize-winning sound effects had every kangaroo within earshot bounding away in the opposite direction, with the goannas and blue tongues bringing up the rear. A signal check at Wallan cost approximately five minutes. However, we were soon once again up to 65. Nevertheless, the approaching suburban area meant that opportunities for making up time were strictly limited.

We rolled into Spencer Street at 10.35 am, five minutes late, having made up the 20 minute deficit but being denied an 'on time' arrival because of the delay at Wallan.

Coming into the platform, Arthur remarked, 'We knocked spots off the timetable!'

And he was right.

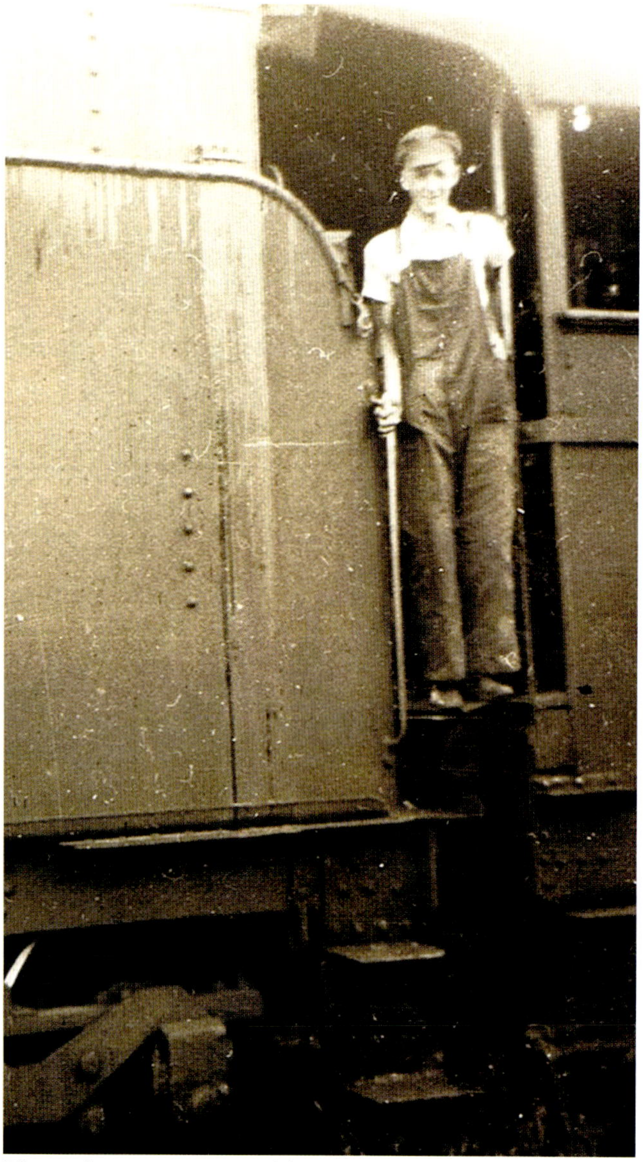

The author at 15 on an oil-burning A2 on the Maribyrnong River line. The crew picked up the staff, engraved 'Maribyrnong River Line', from the South Kensington signal box and were signalled onto the diversion after crossing the Maribyrnong River. (David Barnett)

10 As Far as Bacchus Marsh

Whenever possible, I continued my Saturday afternoon visits to North Melbourne loco, as I now called it. On one of these I noticed an R class come into the depot with a familiar figure in the fireman's seat. This figure was Alwyn Thomas Marshall. I had met Alwyn while staying at Ballarat. He was the fireman on one of the engines I had travelled on to Warrenheip and return. We had struck up an acquaintance and kept in touch by letter. He was 28 years old, of slim build and 6ft, 3½ins tall. He fired on Ballarat's passenger roster and was close to going for his driving exam.

He was a committed Christian, a strict Methodist opposed to alcohol and gambling, a dyed in the wool railway man and a gentleman in every sense of the word. He was responsible for some of the most enjoyable footplate days I ever experienced. On this Saturday he had fired a passenger train from Ballarat to Melbourne and was going back firing on the 6.15 pm Melbourne–Ballarat passenger later in the afternoon. We spent some time talking and he introduced me to his driver, Mr Tom Keating, who gave permission for me to ride with them in the cab when they took their engine from North Melbourne to Spencer Street. Dressed in my usual overalls and engineman's cap, I blended in well with the depot personnel.

The engine for the 6.15 pm Ballarat was the same R class the crew had brought to Melbourne. Coal and water had been taken and the fire cleaned. I assisted Alwyn with the oiling up and at around 5.20 pm we left the depot. Our departure was via the Arden Street loop. This being the same loop used to turn the Spirit of Progress S class. We were thus running tender-first and soon arrived at the TR point, where Alwyn swung down, informed the signalman of our presence, swung back into the cab and attended to the fire. This was even, of sufficient body and correctly sloping from back to front. The shovel was used to place coal down each side of the firebox, in each back corner, and under the fire door. Then, with a stoker jet pressure of approximately 80 psi, and a stoker engine pressure of 50 psi, the stoker was used to give a brief overlaying fire. The blower was adjusted and fire doors cracked open to admit sufficient secondary air over the fire bed to minimize the smoke, now in evidence from the funnel. Later, the fireman's side injector brought the water level up to three parts of a glass.

Meanwhile, the TR point signal went to 'proceed' and we were lightly steaming tender-first through the points and crossovers that led to where the train was waiting in No. 1 platform at Spencer Street station. I was given the privilege of coupling up, connecting the brake pipe hoses and opening the brake pipe cocks. Back in the cab I swept up some stray coal and gave the footplate a tidy appearance.

The train examiner's key went into the regulator quadrant and while the brake test was under way, I casually asked whether they crossed any 'up' (i.e., Melbourne-bound), passenger trains on their way. The answer was in the affirmative. They crossed an 'up' passenger at Ingliston. The crossing arrangements were such, however, that they would not stop; the 'up' train being scheduled to be there well before them.

Nevertheless, in my mind at least, all was not lost. Both trains stopped at Bacchus Marsh. The 'down' before the 'up'. A return journey was thus possible. Time ticked by. With the brake test complete, the guard appeared. He took the driver's name, furnished the load, 'six for 240,' and walked off to his van. The cab was relatively quiet. The blower was at a minimal setting; the fire being in good shape, steam nudging 200 and water at three parts of a glass. The air compressor's rhythmic tharn, tharn, contributed to this restful scene. I was preparing to step down on to the platform when Alwyn approached Mr Keating. Would it be alright if I came with them to Bacchus Marsh? His reply was positive. I was placed in the fireman's seat and, under supervision, carried out the firing.

With station signals at 'proceed,' a green flag from the guard heralded 'right away.' This was on the fireman's side and was relayed across the cab to the driver. He blew the whistle, then with brakes released, cylinder cocks open and the regulator slightly raised the big 4-6-4 strode away from the platform. The evening was mild and the signals to North Melbourne and beyond, green. The needle on the steam gauge continued to hover around 200. Alwyn stood behind me. On passing North Melbourne Junction I received a tap on the shoulder and my attention was directed toward the mechanical stoker valves. 'Put the jets on first, at about 75 psi.' I opened the valve controlling steam to the stoker jets and watched the jet needle swing up to 75. A distinct hiss came from behind the firebox doors. 'Now turn on the stoker. Let it run between 50 and 75.' I opened the brass valve of the stoker throttle. Steam went to the small two-cylinder engine mounted beneath the footplate and connected to the stoker screw. Coal rumbled along the screw and up to the firing table. Here the stoker jets sent it evenly over the fire bed. Smoke appeared at the funnel. A tap on the shoulder indicated that the stoker engine should be eased back.

By now we were steaming through South Kensington. With the cutoff adjusted, the regulator was wide open and the exhaust made its presence felt as speed rose above 30 mph.

Use of the stoker brought the steam pressure to the maximum of 210. Approaching the stop at Footscray the safety valves lifted and at a nod from Alwyn I put the injector on. Starting from Footscray was made easier by the short down grade and we were soon bowling along at 35 mph with the speed increasing. The regulator was wide open and the cutoff adjusted to an optimum setting. With plenty of water in the gauge glasses the injector was turned off.

Once again the stoker went on. Jets first, then the throttle. This time, with a period of constant steaming, the stoker was kept on. The engine steamed well. Smoke, though present, was kept to a minimum and steam stayed between 200 and 210. Speed rose and the speed recorder soon showed 50 mph, the limit between Footscray and Sunshine. The regulator was eased, the blower increased, the fire doors opened to reduce smoke by giving the fire secondary air and as the safety valves lifted the injector went on.

Coal had spilled out over the stoker trough and into the cab. Deft use of the shovel placed this in the back corners of the firebox and brought approving nods from both sides of the cab. Leaving Sunshine, Alwyn picked up the staff for the single line section to Rockbank. We got away in fine style with speed rising to 55 mph before the stop at Deer Park. The good thing about stopping trains is that they offer the opportunity for great sound effects accelerating away from stations. And this one didn't disappoint! The big Hudson picked up its light load and stormed up the rising grade. With good supervision I was getting the hang of firing with the stoker as well as knowing when to use the injector.

Speed on the western line at this time was still limited to 60 mph and this was reached and maintained for about a mile before the stop at Rockbank. Here Alwyn exchanged the staff and called 'Rockbank, Melton' as he handed it to the driver. We made good time to Melton. Alwyn again did the honours with the staff and this time the call was 'Melton, Bacchus Marsh.' While standing at Melton, I scooped up the spill of coal from the stoker trough and saw to it that the back corners and sides of the firebox were well filled. This took a while and we were under way before I'd finished. We were on the level and the water showed two-thirds of a glass. After rounding the 45 mph curve just west of Melton station, the cutoff was wound back and the regulator opened wide.

I quickly had the stoker on and the staccato exhaust whipped the products of combustion up in the air and back over train. We were now crossing the impressive Melton viaduct and the speed recorder needle was sitting on 60 mph. The engine enjoyed this treatment. Steam remained at just over 200. With coal rumbling into the firebox Alwyn pointed to the needle on 60 and called, 'You're doing 60 miles an hour uphill now.' And we were. Leaving the Melton viaduct the grade rises at 1 in 50 for about a mile, then eases to 1 in 85 for another mile before levelling off into Parwan. We did 60 mph all the way and as scheduled went through Parwan non-stop before braking heavily for the 20 mph curves that brought us into Bacchus Marsh. Alwyn delivered the incoming staff in exchange for the one from Bacchus Marsh to Ingliston.

The journey from Spencer Street had taken 55 minutes. It seemed no longer than a quarter of an hour! With grateful thanks to Alwyn and Mr Keating I took a final look around the cab. Steam was at 180, water just over ½ a glass, the fire in good shape and the footplate swept clean. I stepped onto the platform and was enveloped by the cool evening air. A green light from the rear of the train signalled its departure. There was a brief whistle and a powerful, quickening exhaust echoed from the surrounding buildings as it negotiated the left-hand curve away from the station and pounded up the grade towards Ingliston. Penetrating into the darkness the exhaust lingered in the air for two or three delightful minutes before finally fading into the distance.

I purchased a second-class single ticket to Melbourne. The 'up' train also had an R at the head end and its sight and sound were a fitting conclusion to a rewarding afternoon and evening.

Driver Tom Keating and fireman Alwyn Marshall at Spencer Street on the 6.15 pm Saturday pass to Ballarat. The author rode with them in the cab to Bacchus Marsh, circa 1953. (David Barnett)

11 Yea and Seymour

Soon after the trip to Bacchus Marsh, Alwyn Marshall passed his driving exam at Ballarat and was temporarily transferred to Yea. This was an outstation of the major depot of Seymour.

I was now 17 and studying Mechanical Engineering at the Footscray Senior Technical School. Alwyn invited me to spend time with him and when the autumn holidays came I caught the Monday evening rail motor to Mansfield and detrained at Yea. I was met by Alwyn who had arranged accommodation for me at Beaufort House, the boarding house where he was staying.

At the station I also met Alwyn's fireman, a delightful 20-year-old Irishman named Billy Eldon.

As we walked the short distance to Beaufort House Alwyn explained that for the time I would be at Yea he would be running the 7 pm Yea–Tallarook goods and return. While this required signing on at 5 pm to relieve the crew who had brought the train from Mansfield, there was usually a sufficient lull in the proceedings to have the evening meal at our boarding house.

Depending on the shunting needs of the three intermediate stations, the journey to our destination could take anything up to two hours. At Tallarook the engine would be turned, the crew have a meal, and the return train assembled. This could also take up to two hours. Time for the return journey was dependent on whether shunting was required at any stations along the way.

The landlady at Beaufort House was hospitable and I was soon settled in. Alwyn now related his latest dealings with his employer. At Yea, he worked mainly day and afternoon shifts. These were convenient and acceptable. However, as engines were stationed here for long periods, this outstation possessed a sand-drying unit to supply loco sand boxes. This unit had to be supplied from a nearby sand mound delivered by a contractor. To achieve this, the Seymour roster clerk booked Alwyn on at 5 am on certain days to shovel from this mound. Alwyn declined. 'I mean, you've had no breakfast,' he said. The railways insisted. 'I told them I wasn't going to shovel it!' Still they insisted. Finally, the Seymour roster clerk began receiving time sheets from Alwyn showing: 'Sign on 5 am, sand dryer'. This was satisfactory, until someone thought to check on what should have been in the sand dryer. It was sadly lacking. The upshot of it was that Alwyn was fined £1 1s. 0d., for 'falsifying time sheets'. He was now complying with this rostering, which thankfully was infrequent.

The next day we were at Yea station at around 4.30 pm. Here we met up with Billy Eldon, the fireman. The train from Mansfield with a K class in charge soon came along. Although not required until 5 o'clock, Alwyn and his fireman promptly relieved the incoming crew. This accomplished, I could now move more freely and was soon in the cab. It was decided that before the engine was serviced, whatever shunting was needed would be carried out and the consist for Tallarook made up. At the Melbourne end of the Yea yard was a major road crossing equipped with a set of hand-operated gates. Four long whistles advised the gate keeper that the gates needed to be closed against road traffic.

Shunting took some time. With the 7 pm departure made up, coal and water could now be taken and the fire cleaned. It was approaching 6.30 pm when these necessities were completed.

The fireman had brought his tea with him, so leaving him in charge of the engine, Alwyn and

I made our way Beaufort House for a hasty, but enjoyable, evening meal.

As we arrived back at the engine, evening was closing in. The air was crisp, sky clear and later the moon would rise. The atmosphere in the cab was warm and reassuring and we felt snug and cosy in its protected environment. While the brake test was under way, I got busy with the banister brush. Spilled coal, and there was plenty of it, was cleaned up and placed in the back corners of the firebox so one could negotiate one's way around the cab without the danger of slithering to the floor. The stationmaster had delivered the staff for the single line over which we would be travelling. It was inscribed Tallarook–Yea. At almost 24 miles, this was the longest single line section in Victoria Alwyn appointed Billy Eldon to drive, me to fire and himself to supervise. We were an interesting trio, or quartet if you included, Martin, the guard. Alwyn was a fireman qualified, acting driver; Billy Eldon was an engine cleaner qualified, acting fireman; Martin was a shunter qualified, acting guard and I was a student acting as a trainee and not qualified at all! 'We are all acting,' was Alwyn's cheerful observation.

It was just past 7 pm and time to go. I got busy with the fire. One long whistle brought a green light from the guard's van and four long whistles saw the level crossing gates swing open. A final short whistle and with a surge of steam from the cylinder cocks we were moving. The first two miles were relatively flat and speed soon rose to almost 40 mph. Unlike many drivers, Alwyn believed that if you could run at the maximum line speed, then run at that speed. And with this I heartily agreed. Speed soon began to drop back as we tackled the two miles of 1 in 40 grade leading to a summit before dropping down to Homewood. With the regulator wide open and a lengthening cutoff the light consolidation made purposeful progress as it wound around the numerous curves that characterized the line to Tallarook. I, however, had little time to appreciate any aesthetics. The cab lightened and darkened as the fire doors opened and closed to accommodate each shovelful of coal. The injector went on near the top of the grade and the near full reading of water in the gauge glass fell away to almost nothing as the 1 in 40 up became 1 in 40 down.

It was non-stop through Homewood. The next station, Kerrisdale, was six miles 'Distant' over terrain featuring a series of short, sharp pinches of up and down 1 in 40 combined with sharp curves often restricting speed to 20 mph. And the sharpest curves were generally at the bottom of a grade so it was not possible to get a run at any incline. The result? Spectacular sound effects as the throttle was opened wide on a long cutoff, and with a thick, specially prepared fire, the engine pounded around the curve and blasted its way up half to three-quarters of a mile of 1 in 40. It then fell over the top with the injector singing, the water a faint bob in the bottom of the gauge glass, smoke from the now silent funnel swirling around the cab, the speed recorder showing about 10 mph and the crew heaving a sigh of relief that they didn't stall and preparing for the next encounter.

Alwyn knew the track well enough to be able to scrounge a few miles an hour around the curve at the bottom of certain grades. Thus, there were times at the bottom of a pinch of 1 in 40 when the speed board read 20, that we would roll around the curve at 25 mph with a wide open throttle and storm the ascent with sufficient momentum to reach the top at 15 rather than 10 mph. Doing this certainly avoided a stall but could also mean that coal spilled out of the bunker as the engine lurched one way, the tender the other, and you were clinging to whatever was within reach. As speed soon dropped below the designated curve limit, even a close look at the speed recorder chart would fail to detect any irregularity.

This was a track where stalling was an ever present threat. Risqué movements such as that described were common to all crews and contributed to event free running. The occasional alternative was for the train to pull to a stand and divide and proceed with the first half to the next station, secure that portion of the train there and return and pick up the second portion before continuing. Or, set back to the bottom of the grade, back up away from the curve, ensure the boiler water level was adequate and the fire in first-class shape, and let her rip. If the curve speed was exceeded it was not by much and the end result was satisfactory. What Head Office didn't know wouldn't hurt them. The second alternative was the one generally used. Nevertheless, Head Office did not like engines stalling.

This was set down on the driver's record as 'bad management'. So it was that when an engine did come to a stand on an adverse grade, various circumstances were called into play. It might be that there were 'sheep obstructing passage of train', or 'brakes on vehicles 4 and 5 found to be defective and sticking', or 'burst brake hose between vehicles 10 and 11'. All legitimate possibilities in the everyday life of an engine driver.

Kerrisdale was passed without stopping and the five miles to Trawool, were even more arduous and tricky than the six that preceded them. I was therefore kept busy. Meanwhile, under Alwyn's tuition Billy Eldon was making a good fist of keeping us moving with minimal exceeding of the speed limits and no hint of stalling. This was his first driving experience and he was proving to be a dab hand at it. And as he readily agreed, 'it's much better than shovelling!' Trawool was passed without incident and we were soon climbing the final one and a half miles of 1 in 45, stiffening to 1 in 40, into Tallarook. Here, we detached from the train and reversed from the yard over to the turntable.

It took a while to get the engine balanced so that the table would move. Tallarook lacked watering facilities of any kind so it was not possible to add water to the tender, which would have provided the turntable with a more even distribution of weight. Finally, after about 10 minutes of moving the K back and forward about an inch at a time, the thing balanced and the engine was turned. Alwyn explained that if the turntable had refused to move, he would have separated the engine from the tender and turned each separately.

At my suggestion that this was well nigh impossible he pointed out that he had done this a few weeks ago when no other option remained. The turntable would not budge when supporting both the engine and tender, so the engine was positioned so that the tender would be roughly in the centre of the table when left on its own. Then, having ensured there was plenty of water in the boiler and adequate coal on the fire, and by the lights of the engine cab and that of a kerosene slush lamp, Alwyn and the fireman, 'cut her in half'. The tender wheels were chocked, the engine moved out of the way and the tender turned. By some means or other it was pushed onto the turntable extension and the wheels chocked again. The engine was then moved onto the centre of the turntable, the hand brake applied and the loco turned. Both items were now facing in the right direction; however, the tender was in front, not behind, the engine. This was moved forward and coupled on to the tender. The brake pipes were connected and cocks opened. At a whistle, the disc signal giving entry to the Tallarook yard went to 'proceed' and the engine and tender moved into the station area with the cab and crew leading. Understandably, the look on the stationmaster's face had to be seen to be believed. Arrangements were soon made for the engine to run around its one-vehicle 'train', and with the aid of some platform lights engine and tender were recoupled, hose pipes reconnected, relevant cocks opened and electrical circuits secured. The engine and tender had been apart for about 20 minutes. Fortunately, water and steam had remained adequate.

While on the subject of the Tallarook turntable, Alwyn related another recent incident. The turntable area was unlit and placing the engine accurately on it not easy. One night he over ran the short turntable extension and the K class's leading carrying wheels, the pony truck, dropped into the wet earth while the rest of the engine and tender ensemble remained on the track. Fortunately, the pony truck wheels remained aligned with their rails. The engine was placed in reverse, the regulator eased open, and the wheels lifted back onto the track. The loco was then turned and no one was any the wiser. There was, however, a pair of deep furrows at the end of the turntable track that were unmistakably from a locomotive. Some time later, while Alwyn was turning his engine at Tallarook on day shift, a foreman from nearby Seymour appeared and drew attention to the evidence of the obvious derailment. 'There's been an engine off the road here,' he said. 'Why so there has,' replied Alwyn, looking mystified and offering no further detail. 'You don't know anything about it?' 'I haven't really noticed it before,' Alwyn answered. 'We've only been here at night recently, and even with the headlight on, you can't really see anything.'

This last statement was true and no further enquiries were made.

Having digested these incidents, it was now time to digest some food and the three of us set off on the short walk to a milk bar. The engine was left in the textbook manner. Regulator closed, cylinder cocks open, reverse in mid-gear and hand brake on. Water was about ¾ of a glass, steam at 160 psi and the fire adequate for a short absence. As we would be returning soon, the air compressor was left running. We were away for some 15 to 20 minutes. On coming back, it was obvious something was not right. The air compressor exhausted through the chimney and with each sluggish, slow beat, a mixture of steam and water ascended into the night air. Why? The fireman's side injector had been left on and the water was well out of sight in the top of both gauge glasses. With the injector turned off, the steam gauge revealed we still had 70 psi left. The boiler blowdown valve was opened and only closed when the water showed less than ¾ of a glass. Seventy psi of steam severely reduced the effectiveness of the blower. Nevertheless it was turned hard on and the fire laced with as much coal as was advisable with the reduced draft.

Who had left the injector on? Thankfully it wasn't me and I forget who the culprit was. What mattered was raising the steam pressure and with so much cold water in the boiler this took time. When the steam gauge had risen to 80, the disc signal giving entry to the Tallarook yard went to 'proceed'. This meant our meal time was over and we were required to make up our train for Yea. We moved into the yard. 'We can shunt with 100 pounds of steam,' Alwyn said. And this we did.

I was given the driver's seat. It took about 30 minutes to make up our train and I was surprised at how well the engine responded with only 100 psi of steam. When ready to depart, the steam gauge needle was over 150 and Alwyn took over at the regulator. With a load of less than 300 tons we rolled easily out of Tallarook and down the grade leading to Trawool. Here we discharged van goods. It was a beautiful, clear night and the warm cab atmosphere made an interesting contrast to the fresh scent of gum leaves in the countryside. We were soon on our way to Kerrisdale, where we set out one truck and unloaded more items from the guard's van. Our stay here was about 20 minutes. The engine was performing well and the cab conversation, as always, most convivial.

The railway line to Yea at this location followed a similar route to that of the road, but was much higher, giving a vastly superior view of the surrounding country. So it was that on leaving Kerrisdale we came upon a never to be forgotten sight. Stretching ahead on the driver's side of the engine and diverging from our path was the broad, shimmering expanse of the Goulburn River. It was both mystical and magnificent. Illuminated by a rising full moon, a gossamer like mist rose from the water, enlivening and rearranging the patterns of moonlight reflected on the surface. There was not even the faintest breeze and this captivating display went on uninterrupted. Thickly wooded gums, shrouded in their own faint mist, swept down to each side of the river, with moonlight creating spontaneous areas of misty light and shadow as it explored each tree's leaves. A starry firmament added its own signature of wonder to this ethereal scene. It took your breath away. No one in the cab spoke as we took in this magnificence of God's creation. The view lasted, on and off, for about three minutes, so one could attend to the running of the engine and then return to this captivating setting.

Arrival at Homewood was, understandably, something of an anticlimax. Van goods were again unloaded and I put on a good starting fire in preparation for the final one and a half mile climb at 1 in 40 that would take us over the hill, down the other side and on into Yea. Leaving Homewood, the K's exhaust shot unimpeded into the clear night air and the rhythmic staccato soon had us rolling down the final section of track toward our destination. Arriving at Yea, we left the bulk of the train in No. 2 road, carried out some shunting and proceeded to take water. This done, the engine was moved to the coal stage and in the early morning hours the three of us manhandled a barrow of coal up into the tender. During these activities, the turbo generator hummed its melody and the air compressor thudded out its rhythm. With minimal movement, the engine was now placed over the ash pit and the ash pan slides opened. The fire was thick and took some time to be shaken out. Sufficient hot coals were left at the back of the firebox to enable the fire to be banked. The hot ashes in the pit were quenched with a hose provided for that purpose. Acrid odours, the inevitable consequences of fire cleaning, swirled up and around the cab and were exacerbated as much as they were dissipated by the application of water. Finally, the fire was banked, the ash pan slides closed, the damper shut, the blower turned off and the hand brake applied. This latter allowed the air compressor to be shut down. Steam was at 150 and water well up in the glass. With everything as it should be, the turbo generator was turned off and we went home to bed.

Refreshed from our day's rest, the three of us arrived at Yea station at 4.30 pm the next afternoon. The train from Mansfield arrived a few minutes later. It had two K class at the front. The first was in steam while the second was 'dead'. The dead engine was being towed to Seymour for repairs to its grates, these having become defective at Mansfield a few days earlier. The incoming crew were soon relieved and Harry, the stationmaster, came up to the engine to advise on the shunting. There was quite a lot to be done. As on the previous day, the fireman had brought his evening meal so Alwyn and I arranged to eat in shifts to accommodate the yard work. In Alwyn's absence, Billy Eldon would drive and I would fire. As it turned out, it was the fireman and I who did nearly all the shunting. Both the guard and stationmaster were involved, with the latter working at the 'up' end of the yard. 'We'll go ahead, set back into three, pick up in two and then back on to the train' was a typical instruction. No mention was made, however, of whether we would need to pass over the 'up' end level crossing. Billy Eldon therefore called out in his beautiful Irish brogue, 'Wul aye bloo fur tha gaets, Harry? Wul aye bloo fur tha gaets?' 'Yes, blow for the gates.' The ensuing four long whistles sounded superb in the cool evening air and 'tha gaets' obligingly opened. We moved well forward over the level crossing and then carried out the required moves, finally setting back onto the train allowing the gates to close. At each move, the engine exhaust produced its beautiful, distinctive sound, while air escaping from the exhaust port of the brake valve assured us that all was well in stopping. Another shunting instruction required the same question to be answered, 'Wul aye bloo fur tha gaets, Harry?' 'Yes, blow for the gates.' Another four long whistles and the gates swung in our favour. More sharp exhausts and short whistles, more setting back, moving forward then setting back again. From time to time there was the measured crunch and clang of the shovel as I sent coal into the firebox. Intermittently, the injector added its own sound effects to anyone within range. No one bothered about why the crew was so young or who they really were.

The train for Tallarook was now made up. Alwyn arrived shortly before 7 pm and, following a brake test, four long whistles saw the crossing gates open and a green light appear from the guard. We were away. The crisp night air enhanced the exhaust's sound and good progress was made to Homewood, where we stopped to pick up van goods. Billy Eldon was driving and I was firing. The relatively easy run to Kerrisdale was completed without incident and again we stopped for van goods. It was here that Alwyn decided he would like to ride on the engine being towed. 'You can manage, can't you, Dave?' 'Yes, I can manage, Alwyn.' 'And you can handle things, can't you, Bill?' 'Yes, but are ya shure it'll be alright, Alwyn?' 'Yes it'll be quite alright.' 'But are ya shure, Alwyn?' 'Yes, I'm sure!' So Alwyn went back to the second engine, leaving the fireman and me in charge of this one. Kerrisdale was our last stop before Tallarook, so we would be running the train to its destination.

'Right away', and we were off. The fireman's nervousness about driving soon evaporated and we made excellent progress. The exhaust shot skywards and trailed back over the train, regularly illuminated by the glow from the firebox as, using the air-operated foot treadle, the fire doors opened and closed with each shovelful of coal. Steaming was good and keeping the water at around half a glass was not hard. We had just passed Trawool and were rolling down a short stretch of 1 in 40 when Alwyn left the cab of the second engine, made his way forward along the running plate to the smokebox, stepped across the couplings onto the tender of our engine, climbed up onto the water tank, walked along and slithered over the coal into the cab. He explained that the boiler filler plug on the second engine had been removed, and that if you wound the valve gear into reverse, you got excellent sound effects as air whistled through this empty fitting.

Being happy with the crewing arrangements, he stood in the gangway on the driver's side and reflected on the enjoyment of his experience.

By now we were on the final 1 in 40 climb into Tallarook. After thundering past the home signal displaying a green light, steam was shut off and we rolled into the yard. The dead engine was placed in a convenient siding and we were soon on our way to the turntable. Turning was easy and in only a few minutes shunting to make up the train for Yea commenced. It was now just after midnight. As Alwyn brought the engine to a stand after one of our numerous moves, an irate stationmaster appeared and called out, 'You're making too much noise. You're talking too loudly. My wife can't sleep. If you go on making this noise I'll send you over the pit!' Then he was gone. For a moment in the cab there was silence. Then laughter, followed by whispered reproofs all round, reminding each other that laughter might keep the wife awake and we would find ourselves over the pit. Fortunately our train was nearly complete and it took only one or two more moves to have it ready.

Making too much noise. Talking too loudly. What did the man expect? Music of the spheres? We were operating a steam locomotive, not a library!

With the brake test complete, I was placed in the driver's seat. Billy Eldon was firing and Alwyn, standing behind me, supervising. With apologies to the stationmaster's wife, I sounded one long whistle. The guard responded with a green light and I eased the train out of the yard. We rolled down grade and around sharp curves for the first two miles, with moderate to severe brake applications needed to keep the speed in check. The K class rattled and banged and rocked and vibrated until I opened the regulator to negotiate the grades up into Trawool. We did not stop here, but continued on over the switchback 1 in 40s to Kerrisdale. The exhaust was now fierce, now silent, now muted, as we sometimes steamed, sometimes rolled, and sometimes drifted around the curves. We stopped at Kerrisdale to discharge van goods. It was again a calm and still night, although cloudy rather than moonlit. Leaning out of the cab brought one into contact with the gum leaves scented air. Our stop was lengthy. A green light from the guard announced its conclusion and I accelerated the train away, up a short pinch of 1 in 40 and on towards Homewood. Speed was not an option as many of the curves were no more than 20 mph. Nevertheless, I opened her out when I could and we pounded up the concluding grade that saw us sweeping into Homewood. Here, we came to a smooth stand and began the process of once again discharging van goods. The guard advised that this would take some time so Billy Eldon went back to assist. 'Stay in the van, Bill,' Alwyn said as he left. 'Dave and I will run her home.' 'Righto, Alwyn,' and he was gone. 'Drop the damper, Dave; that'll keep her warm while we're here.'

Accordingly, I lowered the damper, eased back the blower, and placed coal in the back corners of the firebox and under the fire door. We were there for a little over half an hour. Now on the fireman's side, I kept the water at ¾ of a glass and steam at around 150. At last we received a green light from the guard. While Alwyn acknowledged this with a whistle, I raised the damper, opened the blower and quickly shook the grate on each side of the firebox. With air now flowing through the fire, I placed some 24 shovelfuls of coal on it, making sure the sides and back corners were sloping towards the front. A cloud of smoke darkened the sky, confirming combustion was taking place. Alwyn got us smartly away and steam pressure stayed close to 175 psi as we climbed the one and a half miles of 1 in 40 to the final summit before rolling down the other side towards Yea. At the bottom of this grade the track levels out and curves permit running at 40 mph. Alwyn kept us moving at this speed and after putting on what I knew would probably be the last major fire for the trip, I turned on the fireman's side injector. It would not pick up water. I tried again. Still no water. I tried the driver's side injector. Same result. Turning on the tap from the tender water tank revealed the problem; we were out of water. The gauge glass was showing just under half. Not

Alwyn Marshall and Billy Eldon at Yea on K152 on the 7 pm 'up' goods. The second K is being towed 'dead' to Seymour for repairs. On the right is the sand dryer building that required Alwyn to be an early riser. (David Barnett)

enough, I thought, to get us home. I promptly drew the driver's attention to our plight. He had been keeping an eye on proceedings and when both injectors failed to deliver had anticipated what I told him. Looking at the gauge glasses he said, 'We'll be right, we're almost home.' The water in the gauge glasses, however, continued to fall. At a mile from our destination it was down to one-third and when we at last stopped at the water crane it was barely a bob in the bottom. I lost no time in swinging the crane into position and climbing up on the tender. Alwyn had spotted the engine correctly and water was soon flowing into the tank. After about two minutes, Alwyn put an injector on and the boiler received its own life-saving stream. The drama was over. After a minimal amount of shunting we were able to take coal, clean the fire and put the engine to bed. Having done this, we headed for the same location ourselves.

That was the end of my brief stay at Yea. Sometime later Alwyn was transferred to Seymour and when holidays allowed I went to stay with him there.

His assignments at Seymour included yard pilots, pusher engines and main-line freight.

The Seymour day shift pilot was an E class tank engine. One day on the pilot, Alwyn became dissatisfied with the operation of the driver's brake valve. When things quietened down around lunchtime, and with the engine sitting in a platform road, Alwyn began to dissemble this item in order to find what was wrong with it. With pieces lying around the cab, who should come along but Mr Magnay, one of the depot foremen. The fireman was elsewhere but as I looked the part he ignored me completely. Bill Magnay made a living, in part at least, by always being ready to tell some engineman what he was doing wrong. And today was no exception. 'What are you doing, Alwyn?' His tone was blunt and curt. 'Oh, hello Mr Magnay, I'm fixing the driver's brake valve, I think the feed valve is faulty.' 'What do you mean, you're fixing the brake valve, Alwyn?

The Vintage Train visited Yea in September 1970. Alec Stevenson captured K184 and its train in the Yea yard before its return to Melbourne. (Drawing, Alec Stevenson)

You don't touch the brake valve, you know that! The fitters in the shed are the ones who fix brake valves. Just leave it alone and book it for them to attend to!' Alwyn carefully put down the items he was inspecting and turned his benign features toward the foreman. He spoke calmly, politely and firmly. 'I'm the driver, I'm in charge of this locomotive and I can do whatever I like. If I want to work on anything, I can, because the driver is in charge.'

This caused extreme irritation in the foreman. 'I've told you not to touch it, so leave it alone!' And he went off fuming. In due course the brake valve was reassembled and all was well.

On night shift, a number of heavily loaded goods trains would depart from Seymour, travelling north. In this direction they faced two miles of 1 in 75 upgrade. As loads often exceeded the tonnage for one engine, a pusher was provided in the rear to ensure stalling did not occur. Alwyn was on one of these pushers one night and the rostered engine was a K class. The procedure was to buffer up to the guard's van of the train being pushed and leave the regulator slightly open. The assisting engine would thus move off with the train, the movement alerting the crew that they were under way. The pusher was not coupled on, nor was the air brake connected. This arrangement enabled the rear engine to push to a required location, shut off, and drift back down to the Seymour yard.

In line with accepted practice, we eased up to the van of our train and Alwyn left the regulator a fraction open. It was around 3 am and the atmosphere in the cab was warm and reassuring. We had been sitting there for some time when Alwyn decided that, with plenty of water in the gauge glasses, it would be a good idea to blow the engine down. There were a number of vacant tracks on the fireman's side, that is, the boiler blowdown valve side, and this valve was now partially opened. Boiling water shot away from the blowdown discharge and the fireman's side of the engine was enveloped in steam. When the

The fireman on X46 has some second engine assistance as the double-headed X and R stock train leaves Seymour over the Goulburn River bridge heading towards Tallarook. This is a valuable record as X and R combinations were rare. (ARHS Victorian Division Archive)

gauge glass water levels had dropped about an inch, the blowdown valve was closed.

No sooner had the steam dispersed than a shadowy figure came hastening across the tracks. 'What's going on here?' said a severe voice. It came from a senior Traffic branch yard official. Alwyn rose to the occasion. 'I'm making mud pies,' he called down to the man on the ground.

'Oh, its you, Alwyn. What are you doing blowing an engine down in the yard? You blow engines down in the shed, not in the yard!' 'I'm making mud pies. I like making mud pies. We don't blow engines down in the shed. You can't make mud pies in the shed.'

'Well you're making a mess here!' 'No, I'm making mud pies.' The yard official could see that anything further would be fruitless, and as the 'mess making' had concluded he left the scene.

'Fancy saying we should blow an engine down in the shed,' said Alwyn. And with that, the matter ended. The rest of the shift passed without incident.

An interesting assignment for Alwyn on early morning shift was the 5 am Melbourne goods. This was headed by an X class, booster-equipped, 2-8-2 Mikado. The train load was 600 tons. The Seymour to Melbourne through load for an X was 650 tons. This required the use of the booster.

Without a booster, the big 2-8-2s were allowed 555 tons. So a 600 ton load was within that needing the booster to be used. The fireman was a young man in his twenties named Jack Canty. I was eager to try my hand firing an X and he was happy to let me do the work.

I swept the footplate of the big cab clean and put on a good starting fire. This brought the steam around and I was able to fill the boiler to ¾ of a glass. A few more scoops of coal around the firebox and all was ready. Sometime after 5 am the starting signal dropped to 'proceed.' A long whistle brought a green light from the guard,

Alwyn Marshall holding the signal operating lever beside the Seymour new yard signal relay building. (David Barnett)

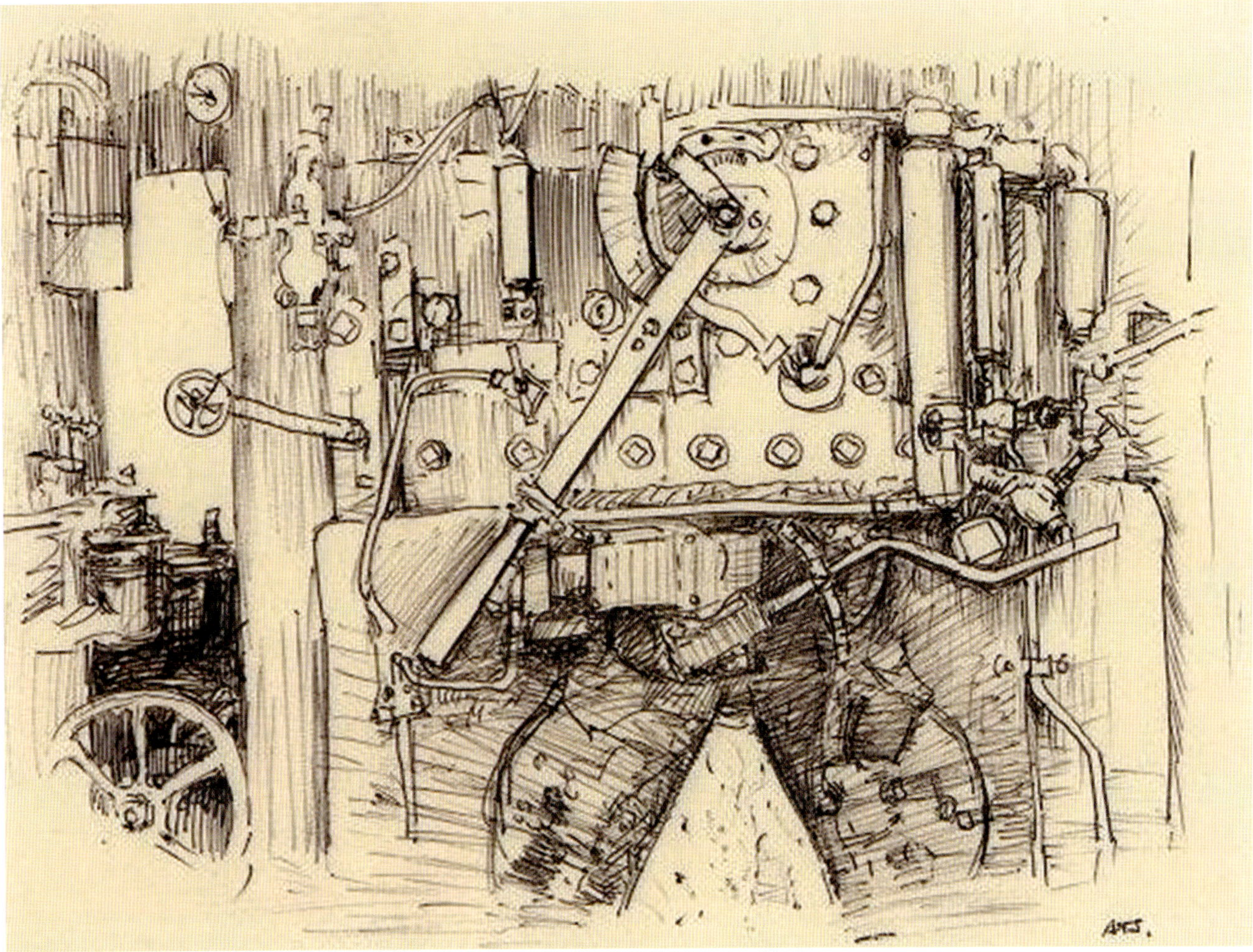

In the cab of J500. This is the engine in which Alwyn Marshall is shown at the throttle overleaf. (Drawing, Alec Stevenson)

acknowledged by a shorter whistle, and with steam hissing from the cylinder cocks we were under way, heading into the dawn. I occupied the fireman's seat and the fireman stood behind the driver. The X class grate, at 42 square feet, was 65% bigger than a K class and felt like it. On starting, the safety valves were sizzling at the maximum boiler pressure of 205 psi. After a mile on the road I was battling to keep the needle on the steam gauge at 190. We were soon on the two mile climb to Tallarook, much of which was at 1 in 50. Keeping the steam respectable came at the expense of the water. I was loath to use the injector, but when the gauge glasses showed just under half, I had no choice. Steam went back to 175, the grade was 1 in 50, and the big Mikado was labouring.

Meanwhile, with the regulator wide open, Alwyn was making some adjustments to the items in front of him. These resulted in a series of hisses from the booster cylinder cocks and the needle on the booster steam gauge swung up to 170. With the booster cut in, the cab floor vibrated slightly. Speed had dropped to 10 mph, and taking advantage of a smooth firing platform I left the fire doors open and placed about 30 shovelfuls of coal at what I hoped were strategic locations on the fire bed. Heading upgrade, the water level showed about two-thirds and I risked turning the injector off. Steam rose to 180.

Then Alwyn spoke. 'I shouldn't be doing this.' 'Shouldn't be doing what?' I asked, after sweeping up some loose coal. 'Running this engine.' 'Why not?' 'Because I haven't been instructed in the operation of boosters.' 'Yes, but you know what to do,' I replied. 'It doesn't matter,' Alwyn affirmed, 'I should have received official booster instruction.' The fireman and I silently agreed. Official instruction or not, the booster was certainly making a difference. Speed had risen

J class — Alwyn Marshall at the throttle. (David Barnett)

to 14 mph and by dint of perseverance the steam gauge needle was nudging 190. We were now nearing the top of the 1 in 50. The speed recorder needle showed 16 mph and with every turn of the wheels the exhaust beats strengthened. A muffled clank and a noticeable Ssshht announced that the booster was no longer cut in. Rolling down the short grade into Tallarook, the steam rose to 205 and with the injector on I got busy with the shovel. A liberal lacing of the firebox saw smoke appear at the funnel. This was soon trailing back over the train as the regulator was eased wide open and the cutoff adjusted to tackle the switchback grades to Broadford. With the exhaust now a purposeful staccato, the fireman was ushered into the driver's seat. Steam again dropped to 190 and I had no choice but to turn off the injector. Using the foot treadle to open the fire doors, I fired little and often; although on this engine, 'little' usually meant 8 to 10 shovelfuls!

Under Alwyn's watchful eye the fireman did a good job in keeping us moving. With the booster required on the approach to Tallarook, it was something of a surprise, and a relief, to find that the engine made steady progress on the first of the 1 in 50 switchbacks, with no sign of needing the booster. Nevertheless, I rarely had the steam over 190 psi. And when I did, the injector soon brought it down. Rolling down the other side of the grade speed rose to 45 mph, giving valuable momentum for the next encounter of 1 in 50. This we handled in fine style, pounding upgrade beneath a strident exhaust, glinting in the penetrating rays of the rising sun.

Down the other side. Steam on 205, the injector on and speed approaching 45 mph. Another major effort with the shovel had the fire in good shape for the two and a half miles to Broadford.

The fireman made good use of momentum, keeping us rolling at over 30 mph without pushing the engine hard. While steam was down to 180 through Broadford station, the water was sitting on ¾ of a glass, allowing some much needed breathing space. On towards Kilmore East. Although the grade was gradually steepening, the engine seemed to be steaming more freely and with careful use of the injector steam sat on 190. Kilmore East was passed in good time and from here we settled down to the six mile climb to Heathcote Junction. The regulator had been wide open for some time and I watched out of the corner of my eye as the cutoff was gradually wound out to cope with the stiffening grade. The exhaust sharpened and if nothing else the big 2-8-2 certainly sounded like a locomotive! Speed slowly fell away. The gauge glasses gave an up grade reading of over two-thirds, and with the injector off I continued with the little and often pattern of firing. It kept us moving, but the needle on the gauge would not move past 190. Nevertheless progress was steady. During the final two miles of 1 in 50, speed remained at 15 mph, and with over half a glass of water and 185 pounds of steam we sailed over the crest at Heathcote Junction in fine style. With the injector on I relaxed in the fireman's seat as we rolled towards Wallan. Here we were brought to a stand and soon after the morning Melbourne–Seymour rail motor arrived, bringing with it a North Melbourne crew who were to take our train on. We handed the X over with a clean footplate, a good fire, and plenty of steam and water. We travelled back to Seymour on that same rail motor, enjoying the morning and satisfied that a worthwhile job had been done.

Whenever his work roster allowed, Alwyn attended church on Sunday. His Christian views were in line with mine and thus we had much in common. His private means of transport was a motorbike, a Panther, 600 Single. From time to time I was a pillion passenger on this machine. One Sunday morning we set out for church at 10 am, and as the service did not commence until 11 we had time to spare. We headed a short distance north from Seymour on the motorbike, on a road that ran parallel to the double track railway line on the way to Mangalore. This brought us opposite the new yard, which was still in use at that time. Entrance to the new yard was via a crossover from the 'up' main line, with Seymour informing Mangalore when to hold trains there if anything was coming or going from this group of sidings. However, as an indication to 'up' through trains that all was well at this crossover, a 'Distant' signal was set about 900 yards from it in the 'down' direction. This 'up' direction 'Distant' was a pair of co-acting arms, provided to give far off and close up vision of the signal, which was set on the up side of an over-bridge. Apart from exceptional circumstances, these signals were always set to 'proceed', and this is how we found them on this particular morning.

Control of these semaphore arms was from a small signal relay unit close to where we were standing. The unit was at ground level and featured an operating lever padlocked parallel to the ground. Adjacent to this small unit stood a one-roomed brick building housing more signalling equipment. During his railway career, Alwyn had acquired a variety of departmental keys, one of which fitted the lock to this building and another which unlocked the outside signal operating lever. He unlocked the building and we went inside. Signal relay equipment was grouped neatly against the back wall and in front of this were two levers, one for signal operation and the other for locking. These levers set the signals at 'proceed', while the outside lever restored them to 'caution'. As the Victorian Railways always promoted cautious operation, it was decided to give them some assistance. The outside lever was unlocked and operated through 180 degrees. The semaphore arms promptly went to horizontal, indicating 'caution'. And that was as far as it went. After placing the arms at 'caution', the lever used for this movement moved loosely back and forward, doing nothing. They could only be reset by the levers in the building. We tried them but they refused to move. They were locked and only qualified signal fitters had the means to move them. Alwyn locked the door and also relocked the external lever in its original position. It was now about 10.15 am and a distant air horn heralded the arrival of the Melbourne-bound

On the Monday of our revisit to the new yard signal relay building, the morning 'down' Goulburn Valley passenger train came by. It was 1955 and D^3 644, still with its original cowcatcher, makes a fine sight at the head of its 7/280 ton train. (David Barnett)

Spirit of Progress. There was a long blaamp from the B class air horn as the driver challenged the signals at 'caution'. However, seeing nothing ahead he kept the train rolling and it swept past at around a mile a minute. It was now time for church.

Monday morning was free and we retraced our steps to our location of the day before. The signals had been reset to 'proceed', the relay building was open and two signal fitters were in attendance. 'We heard something happened,' said Alwyn. 'Yes, the up "Distants" were at "caution",' a fitter said. 'How did that happen?' Asked Alwyn. 'Well, we don't know,' came the reply, 'we found everything alright in here; and the external ground lever was locked in position.' 'Mmm, fancy,' said Alwyn looking mystified. At this point I added my own look of wonder, contributing to the gravity of the situation. With the fitters still pondering the movement of the signal levers, we wished them well and left. And the secret remains to this day.

Soon after this, Alwyn was transferred to Toolamba, the junction of the Tocumwal line to Kyabram and Echuca. It was here that I also spent many rewarding footplate hours with Alwyn at the throttle, travelling towards, and from, stations on the way to Echuca.

It was here that his footplate career came to an end. Travelling in the 'up' direction one afternoon, his goods train was brought to a stand by the Toolamba home signal being against him. After a challenging whistle, he waited some time for the signal to be lowered to 'proceed'. It remained at 'danger'. Another challenging whistle. Still at 'danger'. Leaving the engine in charge of the fireman, he walked to the station to investigate the delay. Here, he found the stationmaster, who was also the signalman, inebriated. In order to expedite matters Alwyn went to the signal box, with which he was familiar, set the points to bring his train into the yard, pulled off the appropriate signals and went back to the engine. Now with a clear road, he moved the train into Toolamba, deposited the staff, restored the points, placed the home signal to stop, and set the roads to enable the engine to be stabled. When stabling was complete, he signed off. The infuriated stationmaster reported the matter to the Superintendent of Locomotive Running and a few days later Alwyn was demoted to hostler's mate at Seymour.

He remained here for some months until the Railways established a board of enquiry. This was really more of a witch hunt than an inquiry. His past 'record' was trotted out as proof that he should be permanently removed from the footplate. He had once sent a number of trucks over a set of buffer stops while shunting at Wallan. He had stalled on a few occasions while at Yea. One of these, unfortunately, was on a passenger train. He had accidentally touched an item of brake equipment on the K class he was driving and the train stopped before he could correct things. This greatly upset Mr Magnay at Seymour and in reply to the report he submitted detailing the incident Alwyn was deemed to have 'exercised poor locomotive management' and 'better management is expected from driver Marshall in future.'

His dissembling the brake valve on the E class pilot engine, while not an offence, would have been noted and added to the list of his 'misdemeanours.' Not long before the signal box incident, he had a young boy in the cab, sitting in the driver's seat. His fireman promptly reported this as his 'having a boy driving the engine'. Of course the youngster was doing no such thing, but a few feathers were ruffled and the name Alwyn Marshall was again mentioned unfavourably in management circles. The fact that he was conscientious, always strictly sober, always available for work, rarely took sick leave and did his best to run to the timetable was completely ignored. His polite independence was annoying to some, but to those who knew him he was not only a through gentleman but also a truly gentle man. In the end management prevailed. He was reduced to the rank of labourer and transferred to North Melbourne workshops. In his defence, he pointed out that the signalman/stationmaster was intoxicated and in no fit state to be on duty, let alone operate points and signals. Also, that in bringing his train into Toolamba he had assisted in avoiding delays and the possible bank up of traffic. Management, however, maintained that a signal box was sacred ground and not to be profaned by some upstart engineman. The intoxicated condition of the employee who made the initial complaint was repeatedly ignored.

Alwyn spent some time at North Melbourne before resigning to join Australia Post. Here he worked in Melbourne as a mail sorter for some 12 months. He was, however, a railway man at heart and through connections he had in the VR Traffic branch obtained a position as a guard on Melbourne's suburban system. When asked how he liked it, he said, 'I'm lapping it up like ice cream!' He died and went to his heavenly home on 4 February 1989.

12 Working at North Melbourne

At age 17, studying Mechanical Engineering at the Footscray Senior Technical School, I needed some income over the Christmas holidays. As the end of the academic year approached I wrote a letter to the Secretary of the Victorian Railways. I explained my interest in railways, what I was studying and enquired if I could obtain temporary employment at the North Melbourne locomotive depot during the Christmas–New Year vacation.

My letter was passed to the Rolling Stock branch and in due course I was invited to attend an interview with the chief clerk of that department. I was told that my suggestion that I be employed as part of a hostling crew dealing with steam engines was not possible because 'we have men trained to carry out hostling duties'. However, I could be employed as a Lad Labourer. This would mean I was nobody's boss, but if I had an interest in steam locomotives I should find it worthwhile. I agreed and on a Monday morning early in December 1954 reported to the depot foreman at 8 am for duty. I was assigned to work under the supervision of the engine cleaner foreman.

He decided that the first thing I needed to learn was how to operate a turntable. The depot possessed three of these, tables A, B, and C. A and B turntables were in daily use, handling the arrival and departure of locomotives. C table saw only occasional use. It was home to engines undergoing repair and it was common to see tenders separated from their engines and standing alongside them on an adjacent track. Engines would be jacked up, wheels removed, boiler parts replaced, pipe work repaired, welding carried out, super-heater elements attended to and brake equipment maintained. When all was complete the loco would be returned to service.

B table had its own arrival door, but when dispatching engines it usually sent them out via A table, which had both arrival and departure doors. It was not hard to operate a turntable and after a couple of hours instruction I was deemed capable of handling things alone. It was remarkable how soon one became accustomed to all the noise. Being on the end of a turntable when a steam engine came onto it subjected one to a series of thunderous crashes that tended to test your auditory channels to the limit. And this was in addition to a variety of other bangs, hammerings, scrapes and grinds that were the result of a host of other everyday activities that made up the depot's daily life. Add to this the sound effects from engines entering and leaving B turntable and you are in the middle of a most interesting audio mix.

The next day was largely occupied unloading firewood from a row of trucks parked on a siding near the track providing entry to B turntable. Five engine cleaners and I were assigned to this task.

Some of us threw the three foot logs to the ground and some stacked them up. They were thus conveniently available to be wheeled to whatever engine required lighting up.

One of the depot's highly amusing characters was the blacksmith in charge of a small smithy forge located adjacent to C table. His name was Michael. He had a burly frame, a smiling face and a husky voice. We would exchange pleasantries relevant to whatever happened to be going on, on that day.

From time to time I would be sweeping the shed floor, a never-ending task in a place constantly deluged with soot. In order to make a noticeable impression on this sooty environment,

I applied myself to the task with vigour. On one of these occasions I was sweeping vigorously along near Michael. 'Hello Michael'. 'Hello David'. A pause; then, 'No, not like that. You're going at it too hard! You get no thanks for it. Just sweep the bastard along!'

Steam engines need water, and there were a number of waist-high stand pipes at various locations around each turntable to provide it. These had canvass hoses attached so that water could be delivered into the filler opening of a tender. Stand pipes were also positioned adjacent to a number of stabling tracks outside the depot enclosure. To get water into a tender you had to lug the hose to the engine, and the hoses were heavy, somehow manoeuvre it up onto the tender tank, drag enough of it up onto the tender so that it didn't just fall down again, open the tank lid, then feed enough of the hose into the tank so it didn't fly out under pressure, climb down, go to the stand pipe and turn on the water. Up on the tender again to monitor the rising water level. When nearly full, down to the stand pipe to turn it off. Then retrieve the hose, close the tank lid and coil the hose ready for further use. It might sound easy but in fact it was a real pain in the neck to carry out and I seemed to be doing it too frequently.

One engine made things particularly awkward. This was pulverized coal-burning X32. Instead of being at the back of the tender tank, the water tank lid was in the narrow space between the enclosed coal bunker and the side of the tender. This made the tank lid extremely difficult to access, and when it was open there was barely any room to feed a hose into. Also, when accessing the filler lid there was practically nothing to hang onto, so you had to balance yourself perilously in this elevated area, dragging a heavy hose and trying to get it far enough into the tank to prevent it flying out when water was flowing. It was a loathsome task, made all the more difficult by X32 always being stabled in some remote area out side the depot, with no one to give assistance or watch you fall to your demise. And the thing always seemed to be needing water at the most inconvenient time.

One morning, approaching lunchtime, the depot foreman handed me a piece of paper. It was an Engine Repair Card of the type given to fitters who are going to carry out some specified engine repair. Under the heading 'Engine Number', was S300. Then came 'Description of Repairs'. No water taken. 'S300', he said, 'that's the blue. She's out beside the water crane. Do you know how to take water?' I replied in the affirmative and went outside to where S300 was standing. Steam still pulled the Spirit five days a week, with B class diesels running it on the weekend. I pulled the spout of the water crane around to make it accessible and climbed up on the big 4-6-2's tender. It had been well positioned and the spout lined up exactly with the tank lid. I looked into the tender. The water was far away and after turning on the crane it was only after 20 minutes of inflow that the tender was full. I closed the tank lid, swung the water crane back to its previous position and went back into the depot. On the Engine Repair Card was the heading 'Description of Repairs Effected'. Under this I wrote, 'Water Taken' and signed my name above the line 'Employee Effecting Repairs,' then delivered the completed documentation to the office of the depot foreman.

Cleaning locomotives was a regular part of the daily routine, and this included cleaning diesels. With the introduction of the X class locomotives, an eight-track stabling facility had been constructed for them outside the depot building, adjacent to the wall of C turntable. This area was known as the Burma Roads. When diesels arrived, four tracks of the Burma Roads were requisitioned and on these were built a modern diesel locomotive depot. It was here, under cover, that hand cleaning of these locomotives was carried out. A mechanical wash plant took care of the overall body appearance of a B class, but failed to remove dust and grime near ground level. The fuel tank and associated fittings got filthy with dirt and grease and had to be cleaned by hand. The diesel depot had below-ground walkways which gave access at eye level to these items. Kerosene and cotton waste were put to work and in due course this portion of the loco looked like new. The other side then received similar treatment and soon looked the same. The foreman who supervised diesel cleaning had grey hair, wore a blue dust coat and engineman's cap, had a rather gaunt appearance and was known as

R class were a familiar sight when operating one of the turntables at North Melbourne. R750 reverses off B table past sister engine R751. It was received on to A table, lined up with the correct exit door, and departed for its next turn of duty. (Geoff Oliver)

Grumps. This was probably a bit harsh, because despite his looks he was always fair when dealing with me.

Steam engines were cleaned inside the shed. Kerosene and cotton waste were used on the tender, valve motion and buffer beams. The boiler was done with cotton waste and tallow and this produced a glistening shine. A team of up to six cleaners would work on a single loco and in four hours its appearance could be transformed. Wheels were generally left untouched. They frequently had layers of grease that defied kerosene and hence required scraping. To scrape and clean every spoke of every driving wheel on any engine was at least a day's work in itself.

Other items on steam locomotives, besides tenders and boilers, were also cleaned. On arriving at work one morning I was immediately assigned, with an associate, to a Y class. This was standing over the inspection pit on one of the shorter turntable roads. Its valve gear had to be dissembled and the fitters involved had refused to touch it until the valve motion involved was cleaned. The Y class is an inside-cylinder engine with Stephenson valve gear so the only way to clean the offending items was to squeeze between the boiler and frames and get to work. It was an uncomfortable and unpleasant job. But you couldn't blame the fitters. There was grease an inch thick on the connecting rods and the eccentric sheaves and straps. When scraped off, this curled up into a kind of 'industrial ice-cream' shape before the vile concoction fell into the pit below. It was not a five-minute job. Morning tea time came and we were about to extricate ourselves and have a welcome break from these confined surroundings when a voice beside the engine spoke. 'Are you blokes having morning tea?'

C22, K180, J515 and $D^3$691 stabled on North Melbourne's B turntable in June 1956. The absence of steam and smoke indicate that the photo was taken on a Sunday. $D^3$691 was then the regular engine for the evening Monday to Friday passenger train to Lancefield. The engine crew would rest there overnight and bring 691 and her train back to Melbourne the next morning. 691 would then sit with a banked fire in the shed until required that afternoon. (National Library of Australia, vn3411310)

'Yes, we're just getting out now,' I said. 'Oh don't worry,' said the voice, 'we'll bring it to you. Do you have tea?' 'Yes.'

'Milk and sugar?' 'Yes please.' 'Biscuits?' 'Yes please.' 'Alright, wait there.'

We waited. As usual, much of the noise around the shed faded away as men downed tools for their mid-morning break. We listened for the footsteps that would herald the arrival of our morning tea. None came. So we continued to wait. It was not long before the shed noise began to pick up again, indicating morning tea was over. We had been had! Somewhere, someone and their associates were laughing at the two wet behind the ears cleaners still waiting for their morning tea. We never found out who the culprits were, but never made the same mistake again. Meanwhile, we scrambled out of our grimy little den, had a quick wash, made some tea and retired to a secluded location to enjoy it. By the end of the day the valve gear on the Y class was not exactly immaculate, but certainly clean enough to be worked on by the most discerning of fitters.

It was at this time that the Victorian Railways experimented with treating locomotive smokeboxes with a particular kind of paint. When an engine was being cleaned, it was not only the wheels that were generally left untreated, for the smokeboxes were never touched. So it was that I, and others, were given the task of 'trying out' this new paint. It was terrible! Equipped with a large brush and a bucket of paint, the requirement was to climb up on top of the boiler, proceed to the smokebox, straddle the boiler barrel and paint

Pulverized brown-coal-burning X32 parked outside the rear of North Melbourne loco depot — its regular resting place when at North Melbourne. The tender water tank was filled through a tank lid located between the pulverized coal hopper and the edge of the tender — a most inconvenient arrangement when watering the engine with a standpipe and heavy rubber hose. A water standpipe can be seen to the left of the engine. (National Library of Australia, vn3411253)

the smokebox from top to bottom. This was easier said than done. The paint was black in colour and of the kind used for facing male urinals. It had an extremely pungent odour that threatened to overcome your senses unless you kept out of its way. This was not easy as most of the engines being worked on were in steam, meaning their smokeboxes were very hot, and when applied the paint immediately started evaporating, sending fumes everywhere. On coal-burning engines a surprising amount of cinders and ash were piled up behind the funnel and had to be swept away before applying the paint. In addition, many of the engines worked on had banked fires and smoke from these oozed out of the funnel, often swirling around the person with the paintbrush. Things improved somewhat when the top portion of the area to be painted was done. However, on engines fitted with smoke deflectors, one had to paint the area covered by the deflectors, and this presented its own difficulties, particularly when an air compressor entered the picture. The easiest part of the task was standing on the front buffer beam and painting the smokebox door. The one advantage of the engines being in steam was that the paint dried almost immediately, allowing the overall effect to be readily assessed. Generally, this was satisfactory. So it was that the treatment continued for about a week, until the supply of paint ran out. Fortunately, in my time at least, it was not reordered.

After the painting I was back operating turntables. One afternoon on A table, just after 3 pm, an E class blew three whistles, the standard code for access to a turntable. Once ready to be turned, I called to the driver, 'Which door do you want to leave by?' 'I don't know,' came the reply, 'you'll have to ask the box.' 'Alright, what are you?' 'The 3.15 pm pilot.' The telephone to the signal box that handled engine departures was

Y108 was a regular feature of Monday to Friday operations at North Melbourne, performing duties as the truck shop's pilot. (Ian Scutt)

close by. I spoke to the signalman. 'I've got the 3.15 pm pilot here, what door should I put him through?' 'The 3.15 pm pilot?' 'Yes.' 'The 3.15 pm pilot going where?' 'I don't know,' I said. 'Well, what do think I am, a clairvoyant?' came the brisk reply. I assured him I had no expectations in that direction and hung up the phone. I went back to the E class. 'Where exactly are you going?' I asked. 'Melbourne goods receivers.' And with a 'thank you' I again picked up the phone.

'I've got the 3.15 pm pilot for the Melbourne goods receivers here, what door should I put him through?' 'That'll be B door.' 'Thank you.' And hanging up the phone I swung A table round to B door, gave the 'alright' hand signal, and with a short whistle the 3.15 pm pilot departed.

On another afternoon, at about the same time and also on A table, I was approached by a worried looking man. He was of slight build with a rather dark olive complexion. His clothes were rather nondescript and he wore a hat. He thrust a piece of paper under my nose, and pointing to something on it, said, 'Whata dis one mean?' I took the paper from him. It was an 'Application for Sick Leave' form. He had filled in his personal details and the date he was ill. The part that was giving difficulty read: 'I hereby apply for sick leave on — and the date was inserted — when I was suffering from_______.' I pointed to this. 'Yah, whata dis one mean?' 'It means they want to know what was wrong with you,' I said. He didn't quite cotton on. So I said, 'what was it that made you sick?' 'I hada da hatage.' 'You hada da hatage?' 'Yah, Yah, da hatage!' Now it was me that didn't cotton on. I had no idea what a 'hatage' might be and was at a loss at what to do next. Finally, I said, 'when you were sick, where did it hurt?' He straightaway pointed to his forehead. 'So you had a headache,' I said. 'Yah, Yah, I hada da hatage.' I wrote headache on the appropriate line, and he went away grateful and smiling.

Every day brought the chance of something different, and at times, very different. After signing on one sunny morning the foreman said to me, 'you might like to go and help him,' indicating a nearby gentleman in a grey felt hat

With afternoon shadows lengthening, Y108 organizes a long rake of trucks at North Melbourne. (Ian Scutt)

and a dark blue dust coat. He was a Westinghouse Brake inspector. 'What are we going to do?' I asked. 'Well,' he replied, 'we're going to have a dirty big hose, and we're going to connect it up to some trucks, and do some brake tests.' 'Oh, and bring your lunch,' he added. Grabbing my kitbag with my lunch and tea-making items in it, I followed him down past C table and around to the remaining steam portion of the Burma Roads. On the way, we stopped to pick up the 'dirty big hose'. This was a long brake pipe hose, equipped with brake pipe connections at each end. It was both big and dirty, and also very heavy. We each shouldered a portion and struggled towards our nearby destination. This was an X class. We were to travel in the cab to Tottenham yard, about three miles 'Distant', and there carry out our tests. These were due to finish about 3.30 pm, after which we would return to North Melbourne. With the help of the crew we got the hose onto the back of the tender and were soon under way. The X ran tender-first around the Arden Street loop and, now engine-first, headed towards Tottenham. A polite request to the crew received their permission to do some work with the shovel and I kept the needle close to the mark for our short journey. Our route was via the freight line and through the Bunbury Street tunnel at Footscray. Passing Middle Footscray and West Footscray, we were diverted into a siding adjacent to two long rows of four-wheel trucks. Each row comprised 75 vehicles.

After coming to a stand, there was universal agreement that the best way to tackle our assignment was to first have a cup of tea. Accordingly, the billy was boiled and morning tea enjoyed. The hose was now delivered from the tender to the ground and dragged to the rear of the first rake of trucks. Meanwhile, the engine moved forward over a set of points and set back to couple on to this rake. I now learned the purpose of the tests. The Victorian Railways maintained a policy of running goods trains with a maximum length of 75 four-wheeled vehicles. A bogie vehicle was countered as two four-wheelers. The South Australian Railways, however, with similar brake equipment ran goods trains up to 140 four-wheel vehicles long.

Our tests were to assess the length of time taken to recharge brakes on trains of various lengths, after a 20 lb reduction in brake pipe pressure had been made. The hose was connected to the last vehicle on the first rake and its other end connected to an additional 10 vehicles in the second rake. A check was made to ensure that all the relevant brake pipe cocks were open and the driver of the X then signalled to put air through the 'train'. When the train line brake gauge in the cab showed 70 lbs, a 20 lb brake reduction was made. When this had stabilized, the automatic brake valve was placed in charging release for 17 seconds, the equivalent of one second for every five vehicles. Air was now flowing into the auxiliary reservoirs on each wagon. From the time charging release was selected, the time taken for the brake gauge to return to 70 lbs was noted. On completion of the 85 vehicle test, the hose was used to add a further 10 vehicles to the 'train' and the test repeated. This went on, with a break for lunch, until a train of 140 wagons had been evaluated. As each set of 10 vehicles was added, the engine's automatic brake valve was placed in charging release for an additional two seconds to preserve the 'one second for every five vehicles' ratio. As the 'train' length increased, the time to fully recharge the brake pipe increased to the point where the brake inspector deemed it was not viable to increase goods train lengths in Victoria. It was thus well into the diesel era before longer trains were run in this State.

With testing complete, the hose was rolled up and lifted once again on to the tender. A final boiling of the billy brought another cup of tea and the X returned to North Melbourne.

An enjoyable and worthwhile time had been had by all.

I also worked at North Melbourne in the Christmas/New Year break in 1955 and had a number of similar experiences to those recently described.

13 Head Office and Newport Workshops

The final year of my Mechanical Engineering Diploma course was 1956. Toward the end of this year I made contact with the Rolling Stock branch of the Victorian Railways, seeking employment, with a view to commencing early in 1957. I would be a few subjects short of a full diploma, but for the moment at least this was not a major issue. My representations brought me in contact with the departmental Rolling Stock Engineer, Mr Alf Hughes. Mr Hughes ranked close to the Chief Mechanical Engineer. He was in his early sixties, a most capable engineer and a thorough gentleman. He greeted me behind a polished oak desk in a very well appointed office. On the wall behind him was a large, framed, coloured, builder's photograph of an R class. I shared with him my enthusiasm for railways. He was sympathetic. I also purposefully pointed out the advantages of steam locomotives over diesels and developed this theme for quite a few minutes. He listened graciously, then gesturing to the photo behind him said, 'That'll beat the diesel to Bendigo, but it costs too much to run, needs all the ash disposed from it, and is too often a dirty mess.' Despite this gentlemanly rebuke, he did think I was worth employing and I was assigned to the Investigating Engineer's Office. This was located in room 140A, on the second floor of the VR's Head Office building at 64 Spencer Street. It was next door to the office of the Assistant Chief Mechanical Engineer, and just two doors away from the Chief Mechanical Engineer.

I commenced work in January 1957. The Investigating Engineer was Mr W.H. (Bill) Chapman, a most capable and likable person. The office comprised six technical staff and one typist/secretary. It was from here that the dynamometer car tests on new motive power, such as R and J class, were carried out. Also, tests on Wonthaggi State Mine coal were carried out annually. Dynamometer car graphs of tractive effort and horsepower for all Victorian locomotives were thus within easy reach. Sadly, locomotive testing was all but over. My first job was drawing up a rack for plate storage for Jolimont Workshops. This assembly used boiler tubes from scrapped steam locomotives as rack supports. It is putting it mildly to say that I found this job less than inspiring.

The things I thought would further my railway career proved, in the main, to be more like obstacles than assets. These were: my conscientious attitude to work, my enthusiasm for railways and trains, and my strong liking for steam locomotives. I soon learned that to many railway employees, anyone who liked trains was looked upon with suspicion. This suspicion deepened if the person concerned was enthusiastic about their work. And if their liking embraced steam engines, best give them a wide berth!

A highlight of the daily correspondence and memos circulated was that titled 'Items of Information'. This was a summary of events from around the system that happened the day before. It included things such as train delays and their cause, reports of hot axle boxes, locomotive failures, signal faults, derailments, suburban train defects, equipment failures and anything that affected the normal running of trains. It generally arrived early in the day and made privileged and interesting reading.

A major cause of concern at this time was the frequency of hot axle boxes on fast goods trains to Adelaide. I spent some time investigating these, both in the office and in the field, checking the history of offending items of rolling stock. It was thought that incidents such as derailments or damage through rough shunting may have resulted in misalignment of journal bearings with their axles, leading to reduced bearing surfaces, increased bearing pressures, and hence hot axle boxes.

The Spencer Street passenger yard possessed a foot warmer plant that boiled up metal containers holding sodium acetate. When boiled correctly, this became a supersaturated solution and when cooling gave off heat. The containers were placed on the floor of non-air conditioned carriages to warm the feet of passengers. The passenger yard plant was located at the Dudley Street end of the sidings and needed to be relocated. I was given the task of revamping the place. This entailed reviewing the existing site, including the location of services such as electricity, water, drainage and sewerage. Then measuring nearby areas to determine their suitability as relocation sites, and fitting these measurements with the equipment to be moved to ensure everything matched. Drawings were prepared of the existing and proposed locations, and a report written setting out the means to achieve relocation. These tasks took me four months. To my knowledge, however, no action was taken and the foot warmer plant remained where it was.

A more enjoyable and interesting task came about when the price of steam locomotive fuel oil suddenly rose dramatically. A few simple calculations revealed that if the current program of converting coal-burning engines to oil firing was halted, and the oil burners converted back to coal, savings of between £200,000 to £300,000 could be realized. N class were the principal engines involved. Accordingly, I received the job of surveying the ash pans on oil-burning N class to determine what fittings were available, should they be converted back to burn coal. Checks were made for the following: ash pan slides three-way air operating cock, ash pan slides air cylinder, air cylinder linkage, linkage lever, linkage lever bracket, left and right grate shaker brackets, tender 'W' number, and the ash pan sprinkler cock. The presence of any, and hopefully all, of these fittings on an engine would make it much easier to convert back to black coal firing.

N class at depots other than North Melbourne were inspected by the respective depot staff and the details passed on to me. A list of the fittings on each engine was prepared and made available for the Chief Mechanical Engineer.

After a few months in room 140A I came to a couple of conclusions. The first was that the railways could function quite satisfactorily with half their present administrative staff. The second was that the railways' technical personnel had plenty of modern ideas to improve the system but lacked the financial wherewithal to implement them.

Some of the administrative staff had to be seen to be believed. They represented a selection of the sorriest specimens of humanity alive at that time. Men who were overweight, had pockmarked complexions, balding hair and big noses. Men who shuffled around in suits threadbare with age, over shirts yellowing with the same complaint, whose voices were like gravel and whose chief occupation seemed to be making prolonged pilgrimages from one office to another, trudging along dark corridors with some finger-marked piece of meaningless paper. Years of indulgence in alcohol and tobacco were obvious in many and it was only their seniority that kept them 'employed'.

In the first half of 1957, the Investigating Engineer's Office carried out a series of tests evaluating the use of non-metallic brake blocks on multiple-unit suburban trains. The New South Wales Railways had recently completed a comprehensive series of tests using these brake blocks and had made their report available to their Victorian counterparts. Following its review by the Chief Mechanical Engineer and Rolling Stock Engineer, the Investigating Engineer was commissioned to carry out tests to determine if Hardie Ferodo VG2 formulation non-metallic brake blocks were suitable for use on Victorian Railways suburban rolling stock. Non-metallic brake blocks cost three times as much as their cast-iron counterparts, but lasted six times as long, giving a 50% overall cost saving. Cast-iron blocks, however, had a proven track record in safely stopping trains. No alternative would therefore be considered unless its performance was proven to be equal or better than that of cast iron. A series of stopping distance tests were devised to ensure that the non-metallic material met this strict criterion.

It was at this time that the new series Harris trains were being introduced on to the Melbourne suburban network. With improved riding qualities, sound insulation and acceleration, they were nevertheless unsatisfactory. The buffing gear between each car was found to bind on curves and when negotiating points, making cars prone to lift and derail. The offending items were promptly removed from all of the 10 new trains in service. This solved the problem of derailments but left the connection between each car without any shock absorbing capability. Acceleration and braking could thus be rough and noisy. The problem received further attention and the next train to come into service, No. 11, was fitted with modified rubber cushioned draft gear. It was also fitted with non-metallic brake blocks, having been selected as the train to evaluate these on test.

Level track was required. The Seaford–Frankston section was thus selected, being without grades and having few curves. To ensure accurate stopping distances, portable train trips were installed on 'up' and 'down' tracks at a calculated distance on the 'down' side of Seaford station. When set up, they would operate the trip gear on the train's leading motor car, sending the brakes immediately into emergency. The first series of tests were conducted with the train empty. Initial speed was 20 mph. With the train rolling at this speed, it was tripped and its stopping distance measured in the 'up' and 'down' directions. Speed was then increased to 25 mph and the tests repeated. This sequence continued at increments of 5 mph until the final test speed of 50 mph was reached. Drivers were instructed to have the train rolling accurately at each test speed. After each 'down' direction test, the train would continue to Frankston and, subject to timetabled services, return to Seaford for the 'up' test. It would depart from here and immediately cross over to the 'down' track.

On completion of the 'Train Empty' tests each car was filled with a known weight of cast-iron brake blocks, equivalent to that of the vehicle being crush loaded with passengers. We now had a crush loaded train and this was tested in the same manner as when it was empty.

When all 'Train Crush Loaded' tests had been carried out, the seven-car Harris set had the non-metallic brake blocks removed. It was then fitted with new cast-iron blocks. These were tested first with the Train Crush Loaded, and finally with the cast-iron blocks removed from all cars, in the Train Empty mode.

Results from all tests were compiled, graphs of Stopping Distance vs. Speed drawn for each braking material, and a report prepared describing their performance characteristics. It was found that in the higher speed ranges, non-metallic was superior to cast iron. However, as speed dropped, cast iron was better. Overall, the stopping distance for each material was the same. Non-metallic brake blocks were thus approved for use on the Victorian Railways.

Following the evaluation of non-metallic brake blocks, it was decided by the Chief Mechanical Engineer to carry out similar tests on the cast-iron brake blocks used on 102 hp, 153 hp, and 280 hp Walker rail motors. These were conducted on the Laverton–Werribee section, which was then single track. A device was fitted to the rail motor driver's brake valve handle, and when the brake valve handle was placed in emergency it activated an electrical circuit connected to a revolution counter operating on one of the rail motor's wheels—this measured the number of revolutions the wheel turned until the vehicle stopped. The known circumference of the wheel enabled the stopping distance to be accurately calculated.

Steam locomotives, although loathed by many, still handled the bulk of the railway's traffic and from time to time their needs were addressed. A consignment of washed Lithgow black coal was received and distributed to a number of depots including North Melbourne and Bendigo. When an engine was bunkered with this coal, the driver was informed and at the end of the trip was required to write a report on the engine's performance in relation to this fuel. I was given the job of collating these reports and summarizing their findings. Reports were received from drivers of both passenger and goods trains. The driver of the R class on the 5.04 pm Spencer Street–Woodend pass was particularly complementary on the performance of this coal, as was the driver of the X class on the 8 am Bendigo–Korong Vale goods. In general, engine crews thought the coal's steaming capability varied from satisfactory to good. Ash content, however, was reported as fair to heavy. A report was prepared and forwarded to the Chief Mechanical Engineer.

While in the midst of a variety of railway happenings, I still had one major interest, steam engines, and if possible riding on them. I knew it was unlikely that this would take place in work time and approached Mr Chapman with the idea of my being granted an engine cab pass to be used in my own time at the weekend. He was sympathetic and agreed to approach the Chief Mechanical Engineer on my behalf. A day or two later he was summoned into the chief's office and on his way said, 'I'll fix up your request, my boy'. The matter he had been called in to discuss was of minor importance and I waited eagerly for his return to give me some good news. Twenty minutes went by. Thirty. Forty. Fifty. Finally, after over an hour in the chief's office, he returned. The look of dismay on his face said it all. Mr Chapman apologized. My request had been rejected. It had attracted attention from all quarters. A vigorous discussion had taken place between Mr Chapman, the CME, his clerk and other senior departmental figures who bought in to a topic that was nothing to do with them. One senior personage said it shouldn't be allowed on matter of 'procedure'. Overall, the general consensus was, 'If we let him do it, everyone else will want to.'

However, not to be outdone by departmental bureaucracy, Mr Chapman organized something else. About a week later I was informed that I would be provided with an engine pass the next day and to come prepared. Accordingly, I arrived at work at 8.30 am armed with a sweat cloth, an engineman's cap and a grey dust coat. I collected the engine pass and was told to pick up the 9.25 am Melbourne–Seymour goods in the Melbourne yard at Dudley Street signal box. The engine was X42. I found the air in the Melbourne yard most therapeutic! The 9.25 am Seymour was easy to find and I swung up into the cab just as it was leaving Dudley Street. Introducing myself to the crew I found that they were brothers. Driver Prentice and fireman Prentice. Departing the Melbourne yard at 9.30 am, our route was via the Bunbury Street tunnel at Footscray and on to the Tottenham yard. The guard had reported the load as 34 vehicles for 655 tons. We were delayed at Tottenham for about an hour and didn't leave until 10.45 am. During our wait I had sounded out the crew to see if I might do some firing. Their response was in the affirmative. The engine appeared to be steaming well and on passing through Sunshine, with the water near the top of the gauge glass and the safety valves just lifting, I got busy. The fire was in good shape and it was relatively easy to keep the steam gauge needle on the mark as we proceeded towards Broadmeadows. The cab reflected the fragrances of steam and steel mixed with hot oil, and rolling along at around 35 mph I spilt very little coal as the big 2-8-2 rode well. The fireman had generously given me his seat and there were a few occasions when I was able to enjoy the scenery from the cab window.

We stopped at Broadmeadows to change crews. Frank McCarthy was the new driver and Wally Tonge his fireman. With the approval of the relief crew, I continued firing. Frank McCarthy soon had us under way and I kept the water boiling. On the rising grades through Somerton and Craigieburn speed dropped to around 20 mph but picked up on the relatively level stretch through Donnybrook and we were soon on the 1 in 50 of the Beveridge Bank. Speed fell away to 10 mph and with a few deft movements the driver cut in the booster. Aware of the extra steam needed, I made sure the boiler could supply it. The gauge glasses displayed a satisfactory reading, steam was healthy and the exhaust a steady and purposeful beat. With the footplate swept clean, we jogged along at a steady 12 mph. With things in this supposed satisfactory mode, I handed over the firing to Wally Tonge. He stepped into the deck and got busy. 'I was waiting for him to have a go,' said the driver; and promptly wound out the reverse one turn forward. The exhaust soon changed from a beat to a blast! Speed increased to 18 mph and I realized I'd been given a carpet slippers ride while firing. With a professional on the job the driver could now get the best out of the engine. Passing through Beveridge the booster was disengaged and we made easy work of the level run to Wallan. Here, water was taken and it was time for me to leave. A Melbourne-bound rail motor soon came along and shortly after 1 pm I was heading home. It was a pleasant journey, with plenty of time to enjoy a home-made cut lunch and reflect on the events of the past few hours.

One afternoon, on returning to Room 140A after lunch, I noticed a memo on Mr Chapman's desk. It was from the CME and of immediate interest. There being no one else in the office, I joyfully devoured its contents. It read:

> **Warrenheip – North Geelong Section**
> It is proposed to increase the load for R class locomotives on the above section from 1250 tons to 1400 tons. J class loads will be similarly increased.
> For your comments, please.
> G.F. Brown
> Chief Mechanical Engineer

Surely this *would* mean road testing. I made a few mental calculations. Checking running times with existing loads for R and J class between Warrenheip and North Geelong, say one week. Then another week for similar tests with the increased loads. Plus one week to prepare and another to consolidate results. Four weeks of sheer bliss!

In due course, Mr Chapman also returned from lunch. He observed the memo with a rather disinterested look and turned to a filing cabinet. Withdrawing a file, he spent 15 to 20 minutes going through it and making notes. This done, he replaced the file and spent a few minutes drafting a reply for typing. Attracting my attention, he said, 'There you are, David, I've just solved an enquiry on engine loadings without even leaving the office.'

What he had done was to refer to the load tables that are prepared as part of the final report when a locomotive undergoes road testing. These tables set out the maximum load for any given gradient, together with the speed the engine will sustain with that load on the specified grade. Using this information, he was able to endorse the proposal and my four weeks of bliss evaporated.

Another major task involving the Investigating Engineer's Office was the annual wheel census. This was an inventory of every 'spare' wheel set on the system, including those lying around at depots, and in sidings, workshops and outstations. Each pair of wheels was categorized by its journal size and wheel seat diameter.

After nine months in the Investigating Engineer's Office, I was transferred to the Locomotive Design Section of the Rolling Stock Drawing Office. I disagreed with this transfer but had no control over it. One engineer explained to me that, 'you've got to learn to draw.' I found the whole idea distasteful, as engineering drawing was the last thing I wanted to do. As the junior in the Drawing Office, I sometimes substituted for the officer responsible for ordering and delivering blueprints.

I worked on drawings for both Walker and diesel electric rail motors. Diesel electric rail motors were referred to as DERMs. DERM assignments included the fitting of Oerlikon Brake equipment to a DE rail motor, including the design of under frame brake pipe support brackets, to accommodate brake pipe runs beneath the vehicle's body.

It was at this time that two M class, 150 hp, diesel hydraulic, 0-6-0 shunting locomotives were being constructed at Newport Workshops. Their prime mover was a General Motors diesel obtained from a former military tank. I drew the air horn mounting installation, and the engine instrumentation, for these locomotives.

An interesting design project, although I was not associated with it, was the preparation of drawings to enable the fitting of automatic staff exchanging apparatus to T class diesel electric locomotives. This project had occupied a senior design engineer for over 12 months and was ongoing during my time in the Drawing Office. Despite all this effort, no T class was ever fitted with automatic staff equipment.

One steam oriented assignment was the comparison of N class and J class front end dimensions, with a view to providing a standard front end design for these two locomotives. The front end designs were similar. A tracing was made of the front elevation of the J's front end, without the smokebox door, looking into the fittings of the smokebox. Using the centre line of the blast pipe, and the top of the blast pipe cap as the reference point, a tracing of the N's front end, with its blast pipe cap positioned over that of the J, was superimposed over the J's tracing, enabling an accurate assessment of what modifications were required to achieve a standard design. Not a lot needed to be done, but nothing ever came of this investigation.

The railways of Australia and New Zealand maintained an exchange of information through the Australia and New Zealand Railway Conference. One item discussed by this body was the fitting of Laidlaw Drew oil-burning equipment to a steam locomotive.

The conventional means to deliver oil into the firebox was via a weir type burner, set at grate level at the front of the box, and inclined upwards facing the rear. Oil from the tender tank flowed by gravity to the burner, which beneath its weir overflow had an atomizer nozzle supplying boiler steam. The steam emulsified the oil into a fine spray, making it burn easily. The induced draft of the locomotive's blower created a flow of air through the firebox, providing oxygen for combustion.

The Laidlaw Drew system, which had wide use in marine applications, was different. It used a swirl type burner placed in the centre of the firebox floor. The swirls were designed to deliver oil in a combustible pattern, and incorporated passages for atomizing steam. The system came in a kind of kit, with the burner installed in the middle of a floor that bolted on to the bottom of the firebox of the locomotive. The 'floor' was of a refractory material having angled holes for the entry of combustion air.

The Victorian Railways were nominated to conduct the Laidlaw Drew tests and J 546 was the engine chosen. It went to North Melbourne, where its weir oil burner and firebox floor were removed, and in their place was fastened the Laidlaw Drew equipment. This came with a small lever, moving through a horizontal quadrant, connected to a vertical shaft, at the base of which was the valve controlling the flow of oil to the burner. The lever and quadrant assembly was mounted at a convenient height in front of the fireman. The atomizer steam valve was unaltered.

Stationary tests were conducted, and providing air was used to atomize the oil, good combustion results were obtained. The results with steam atomization, however, could only be described as mediocre. After persevering to obtain an optimum position to secure the new firebox floor, a road test was performed.

Starting with a full load and full boiler pressure, the new equipment failed to deliver an adequate steam supply. Whenever the engine was worked hard, the steam gauge fell. Poor combustion in the firebox was to blame and this was thought to be, in part at least, due to an inadequate air supply to the burner. Deflector plates were welded in position in front of the firebox and angled so as to provide maximum deflection of combustion air. The burner was slightly repositioned to hopefully obtain a better air supply.

The next road test was from Melbourne to Seymour and return on 13 February 1958 and I was nominated as a member of the two-man test team. The train was a specially prepared goods, designated the 9 am Seymour, with a load of 18 vehicles weighing 395 tons. This was the maximum for a J class to Seymour. Tender water and oil levels were recorded before the trip commenced. Departmental test driver Dick Hall was in charge, supported by a fireman with the first name of Graham. We left the Melbourne yard at 9 am and with its full load, 546 ran to Broadmeadows via Sunshine and Albion and was soon slogging its way through Beveridge towards Wallan and Heathcote Junction. Despite a barely acceptable performance to Wallan, the engine topped Heathcote Junction blowing off, although this was at the expense of a very smoky funnel.

On arrival at Seymour, oil and water levels were again recorded and a slightly larger blast pipe cap fitted in an effort to improve steaming.

The return journey, however, proved disappointing. Leaving Seymour at 2 pm with a reduced load of 31 vehicles for 367 tons, the rising grades south of Broadford saw the crew involved in a three-cornered battle with the regulator, steam gauge and gauge glasses. The steam gauge was the first to wilt, with the engine pulling to a stand beside the Kilmore East up 'Distant' signal with 140 lbs on the clock. Here, opportunity was taken to raise the boiler water level, and after about 10 minutes with safety valves lifting, the train proceeded without difficulty for an

Spencer Street station as seen from Room 140A. (David Barnett)

uneventful run to Melbourne. On arrival, final oil and water readings were taken. It was noted that the engine had used 425 gallons of oil for the journey to Melbourne, while for the 'down' trip the amount consumed was 398 gallons.

There was no guarantee that further fine tuning of the burner's position would produce improved results, and the indifferent performance during the initial weeks of testing saw the project shelved.

J546 was converted back to weir burner firing, with the only evidence of the Laidlaw Drew experiment being a bracket on the fireman's side which guided the vertical shaft to the valve controlling the flow of oil to the burner.

The Victorian Railways shared information with other systems, and other systems, such as New South Wales, reciprocated. So it was that one morning one of the senior engineers gave me an intriguing task to research some steam locomotive information. New South Wales had fitted one of their C36 locomotives with a Geisel exhaust blast pipe which, according to reports, was providing a 20% saving in fuel costs. My task was to go through a number of editions of professional railway magazines to see if they carried any detailed information on Geisel exhausts for steam locomotives. I spent a fascinating morning, but found nothing. Nevertheless, subsequent details published years later in railway enthusiast periodicals, showed that the claim of a 20% fuel saving was well founded. During this literary research I came across a number of catalogues from overseas railway suppliers. These were some years old and dealt mainly with items relating to steam locomotives. One from America was of particular interest. This was the catalogue from the Franklin Railway Supply Company. It contained a wealth of information on locomotive boosters, power reverse equipment, air-operated fire doors, poppet valves and other, to me, fascinating items. I spoke of it admiringly to the engineer in charge of the Drawing Office who, without a moments hesitation, gave it to me. It dealt with steam locomotives and steam equipment and nothing new in this line was going to be ordered, so it was surplus to requirements.

Shortly after looking for information on

After leaving Broadmeadows, X29 accelerates away towards Seymour with a long freight. (PROV VPRS 12800 P4 RS/0977)

Geisel exhausts, one of the assistant engineers at Newport Workshops went on extended sick leave and I was sent there to replace him. This was a promotion. Previously, I had been classified as Draughtsman, Class 4. Now, my classification would be Assistant Engineer, Class 4 (Acting). The 'Acting' didn't matter because one's salary was automatically increased.

The work at Newport was generally administrative, largely attending to updating rolling stock drawings for various workshop locations including New Boiler shop, Steel Construction, Wheel Shop, Brake Shop, Car Shop, Erecting Shop.

Mr Gerald Dee, who had recently passed for driving, was the driver of the E class steam loco on the Newport Workshops pilot. I was introduced to Gerald by one of the more humane engineers at Newport and spent some enjoyable moments discussing railway matters with him. Our views on locomotives were just about identical and his company was like a breath of fresh air.

At this time some senior Rolling Stock branch management moves took place. Mr Bill Chapman, formerly Investigation Engineer, was transferred to Newport as Workshops Superintendent. The Chief Mechanical Engineer, George Brown, was promoted to Railway Commissioner, and the Assistant Chief Mechanical Engineer, Mr W.O. (Bill) Galletly became the CME.

Mr Chapman requested cab passes to enable me to ride on steam locos in my own time from the new CME. These were granted, 'providing he is possession of a rail ticket for the journey'. I was thus able to ride in the cab of the R class hauling the 12.20 pm Saturday, Melbourne–Woodend passenger, returning as a passenger on a scheduled train to Spencer Street. I also rode on the footplate of a K class hauling the Saturday morning Frankston–Stony Point and return passenger. While these were enjoyable occasions, they were in vivid contrast to what was generally not a happy time at Newport. I supervised four apprentices, who were given three months in the Drawing Office as part of their training. They were responsible for minor drawing amendments and distributing new drawings to various areas throughout the workshops.

My attitude was positive and conciliatory; theirs was unashamedly negative and I was given a hard, heartbreaking time.

Finally, I resigned. Mr Chapman called me into his office and when I arrived he removed a file from a filing cabinet drawer, selected a memorandum from it and handed it to me. It brought tears to my eyes. He had written to the powers that be in Head Office, summarizing my skills in relation to railways and locomotives and concluding with something like. 'I believe Mr Barnett would be better suited to a position related to locomotives and their daily operation.' His suggestion fell on deaf ears.

PART 2: OFFICIALLY ON THE FOOTPLATE

14 On the Way to Firing

Following my resignation from the railways, I worked in the administration of the Billy Graham Crusade in 1959 and attended Ridley Theological College (Anglican), studying Theology, from 1960 to October 1963.

The years at Ridley were difficult financially and this had taken a toll on my health. I was advised by my doctor to seek a change. I had attended theological college not to be ordained but to obtain a sound biblical foundation to be used for a Christian witness in the general community. I had achieved the biblical foundation so I asked my doctor, 'What about firing steam locomotives?' 'Ideal', came the reply.

Fortunately, I was favourably remembered at VR Head Office. When I contacted them I was told I was eligible to join as an engine cleaner/trainee engineman and my interest in steam locomotives would be accommodated by being placed at Ararat, the State's largest steam depot.

I passed the medical examination and near the end of October 1963 I reported for duty to Mr Jack Irons, depot foreman at Ararat locomotive depot. My first day task was 'cleaning shed floors'.

I obtained full board at Leslie House in Birdwood Street, Ararat, just across the road from the railway station. The wooden exterior of Leslie House looked a little dilapidated, but inside it was spotless. Also, the meals served were excellent. It catered for a variety of clients including bank employees, school teachers and railway men. Railway employees were catered for by having cut lunch meals supplied at all hours of the day and night — you put your name and time of duty on a chalkboard and your meal would be in the fridge with your name on it when required.

Ararat was a well designed depot. Its 85 foot turntable served a 28-stall semi-roundhouse, plus at least four other roads in an uncovered area. It was equipped with a drop pit for loco driving wheel changes, a small machine shop for manufacture and machining of minor rolling stock components and a well-equipped store holding a comprehensive collection of steam loco parts. Coal was supplied from a four-bin outlet overhead coaling plant, and a below ground ash road facilitated ash pit cleaning. Oil storage tanks, supplying fuel for oil-burning engines, were located at ground level and warmed by a system of steam lines supplied from a nearby, small, dedicated boiler.

After a first day of sweeping the shed floor, the Engine Cleaner Instruction class began. I was one of four in the class, with the other three members also staying at Leslie House. Instruction was carried out in a small on-site building, by Mr Allan Blatchford, instructor driver at Ararat and also a member of the local council.

The class lasted eight days and included the following:

Description of signals: their aspects, speed indications and their meanings; Train staff; Use of Disc signals; Point indicators; Train signals; Hand signals; Whistle signals. Stalls, disablements and obstructions; Wrong line orders; Walschaert's valve gear; Stephenson's valve gear. Fusible plugs; Gauge glasses; Steam locomotive fittings; The Blower, its use and abuse; Injectors, their theory and operation; Lighting up a cold boiler; Oil-burning locomotives; Washout plugs; Triple valves and air brakes.

On arrival at Ararat I prepared myself for life in a depot whose main function was to service, maintain and operate locomotives. And on the surface, this is what it was doing. However, after being there a couple of weeks I came to realize that this was only a secondary occupation. The depot's main purpose was to advise members of its work force on all aspects of their personal well being, with particular emphasis on their mental and physical health, their various emotional states, and all and any biological and reproductive issues. Being a 26-year-old, unmarried male, I came in for specialized attention.

In roundabout ways, I was questioned on my techniques for seducing women, what aspects of sexual intercourse I enjoyed most, how I went about it, how many broken hearts I'd left behind in Melbourne, how many women I'd slept with, and what arrangements I was making for my biological satisfaction in Ararat. I politely and truthfully answered in the negative to all these enquiries. Initially, this produced roars of unbelieving laughter. However, seeing that I stuck to my guns, their attitude changed. While still maintaining a degree of unbelief, the unbelievers took it upon themselves to perform a paternal role and advise me on those aspects of my behaviour that were failing to let me enjoy the intimate pleasures of the opposite sex.

So it was that every morning tea, lunch, and afternoon tea break, it would be likely that I would be the focus of attention and receive free, unsolicited and in depth advice on the mysteries of successful interpersonal relations. I received instruction on how to identify and select 'likely women'. Then, once selected, how to 'persuade' them to yield to intimacy. Then came details of the physical act—what to do and when to do it, how much and how long — what she'd probably like most, etc., etc. Having been instructed in these matters, I was now expected to act! The fact that I didn't caused more disbelief and a high degree of feigned disappointment. In vain did I assert

Taken in 1930 when the Ararat loco depot was barely one year old, $A^2$966 poses beside the below-ground ash pit road, with the wagons parked on it showing how it facilitated ash handling. The coaling plant is also shown. (ARHS Victorian Division / PROV/VR Collection)

that my Christian beliefs taught that sex was for married couples only, and that when I was married I would be pleased to enjoy it. 'No,' was the response. 'You want to get it NOW!' But I was unmoved and everyone could see that. In the end my attitude produced a degree of acceptance and admiration. Some grudging, some spontaneous.

From time to time the subject was revived, and again I would be assailed with advice on how to improve my 'technique' to ensure quick and satisfying success, as well as the best way to 'make up for lost time'. It should be noted that the 'advisers' considered themselves experts in the field and that this ensured that any information they supplied was of the highest clinical standard.

After eight days instruction, each person was given a comprehensive oral examination by a loco travelling foreman. This lasted about one and a half hours. We all passed. The next day was spent at the depot where, under supervision, we learned how to oil up and generally prepare the steam locomotives rostered for use on that day. Five engines were prepared.

Next came seven instruction trips.

A[2]966 takes coal from the Ararat overhead plant. The pipe from the side of the coal plant to the post beside the engine is for sand. Later, sand was available from overhead pipes accessible from the road beneath the coal stage. (ARHS Victorian Division / PROV/VR Collection)

Allan Blatchford. Engineman's instructor and a senior driver at Ararat. He was the Instructor for the class of four engine cleaners of which I was a member. He was also a member of the local Municipal Council. (David Barnett)

Leslie House, Birdwood Street, Ararat. While looking a little tired on the outside, it was spotless on the inside. The beds were comfortable and the meals excellent. (David Barnett)

Coal-burning, Newport-built N428 on Ararat loco depot's electrically operated 85 foot turntable. Although reboilered, N428 still carried its 'as built' front end, and had a slightly more throaty exhaust than its British-built counterparts. In the background is the 280 hp Walker rail motor that ran the Ararat–Portland service. (Geoff Oliver)

15 Instructions on the Road

As qualified trainees, we were each allotted an instructor driver to accompany us on seven rostered road trips. On these, we would learn the basics of firing, On their completion, provided we did nothing stupid or disastrous, each candidate would be passed to be rostered for regular firing duties. We were, however, confined to regular goods trains and yard pilots until completion of 520 firing hours. At the end of this time a locomotive foreman would ride with each person on a road trip, and if found competent they would be certified to fire on passenger and fast goods trains.

My instructor driver was Mr Robert (Bob) Quinlivin. He was in his early forties, a bachelor, rather taciturn and tending towards being phlegmatic. He was, nevertheless, friendly.

My firing experience on previous cab trips stood me in excellent stead and I was quickly at home on the footplate of each engine.

My first instruction trip was on the morning of 11 November 1963. I was rostered to travel from Ararat to Stawell, with Bob Quinlivin, on the 9 am Dimboola fast goods, and to relieve the fireman on the Stawell pilot for that day. Rather than travel by train, Bob Quinlivin arrived at Ararat station driving his Austin A30. This conveyed us to Stawell in a degree of comfort not found in the guard's van of a fast goods train. It was a fine, sunny day, with a gentle spring breeze.

The engine performing pilot duties at Stawell was $D^3$641. She had seen better days, being minus her cowcatcher and missing one of her headlight numbers. Nevertheless, her performance for the day was fine. Her driver was Claude 'Airgun' Dunn. Claude was in his sixties and being the senior driver in the district, had secured the plum, day shift, five day a week job of driving the Stawell pilot. Bob Quinlivin introduced me, then hardly spoke another word for the rest of the day.

I swept up loose coal on the footplate, noted the gauge glass water levels, put on a light fire and took over the fireman's seat. The single-stage air compressor sounded its reassuring tharhn, tharhn; tharhn, tharhn beat and we were soon positioning goods wagons in various positions around the Stawell yard. As well as shunting, the pilot provided rear-end assistance to goods trains proceeding to Ararat. At the height of the wheat season this often meant pushing out six trains a day. Today, however, there were only two, and both were steam-hauled. The train to be assisted would arrive in the yard on the track featuring the water column, and take water. This took some time because the Stawell water crane was notorious for its slow delivery. Meanwhile, the D3 would be signalled to ease up on to the guard's van of the waiting train. Before coupling it up, I aligned the auto couplers, then gave an 'ease up' sign. When coupled, I connected up the brake pipe hoses and opened the brake pipe cocks. Claude Dunn cut in his brake isolating cock, giving control of the air brake to the engine at the front of the train. The signalman from Stawell A box would then arrive with the bank engine key, together with the driver's Bank Engine Authority form. When withdrawn from its frame, the bank engine key left the electric staff instruments locked, ensuring that no staff was issued until the bank engine was back in the yard and the key replaced.

Once attached as a bank engine, I built up the fire. With the injector on, and the blower adjusted, coal was placed in quantity down the sides of the firebox, in the back corners and under the fire door, while the centre and front were treated sparingly. Two-thirds to three-quarters of a glass of water was ample, and at this level the injector went off. The fire door was left partly open to minimize excessive smoke, and finally, the banister brush was used to sweep up a few pieces of spilled coal.

On receiving the bank engine key, Claude Dunn blew a long, short, long on the whistle, notifying the crew on the leading engine that 'Driver has received bank engine key'. A sense of drama now pervaded the cab. In due course, from the front loco would come two long whistles — two engines coupled together move forward — and the bank engine driver would sound two long whistles in acknowledgement. A final short whistle from the leading engine and we were moving. The D3 moved off with long, characteristic sobs from its exhaust that gradually firmed into a coarse, strident beat as speed picked up to anything between 10 and 15 mph. This was railroading in the most classic style, and I was actually being paid to take part in it! With the regulator wide open and the cutoff wound out, Claude Dunn supervised things on the driver's side with a relaxed attitude and a watchful eye. He preferred a felt hat to an engineman's cap, and with his pipe in his mouth looked every inch a senior railway man.

It was easy to fire at 15 mph, and for most of our four- or five-minute journey to the 'Stop' board, the safety valves were sizzling in tune with the beat from 641's exhaust.

Trains were assisted in the 'up' direction out of Stawell as far as the 'Stop' board. This resembled a curve speed board, with STOP, written on it. It was placed at the top of the grade, and on passing it the driver of the leading engine was required to stop in a train length, thus enabling the assisting engine to uncouple and return to Stawell. On coming to a stand at the 'Stop' board, Claude Dunn would alter the setting of his brake isolating cock, once again giving himself control of the air brake on 641. I would swing down from the cab, walk to the front of the engine, give an 'ease up' sign and with the tension off the couplers pull the coupler pin on the engine and so uncouple

D^{3}641 simmers quietly on pilot duties at Stawell. (Ian Scutt)

With characteristic throbbing exhaust, D^{3}641 leans into the task of banking a long train up the 1 in 62 grade out of Stawell towards Ararat. (Ian Scutt)

This was the author's view from the fireman's side of D^{3}641 as she pushed a heavy train away from Stawell. (Ian Scutt)

us from the train. With the brake pipe cocks closed, I waved the engine back a short distance, and when satisfied all was disengaged returned to the cab. Claude Dunn then sounded one long whistle, advising the train engine crew we were no longer attached, and proceeded down the grade to Stawell A signal box, to hand over the bank engine key to the signalman. As this was my first day on the job, after completing our first push I was presented with the driver's Bank Engine Authority form for that series of movements. With bank engine duties over for the moment, we retired to a nearby siding waiting for our next assignment. So the day passed most pleasantly. It concluded with 641 being hostled and its fire banked, after which Bob Quinlivin drove us back to Ararat. Here, on signing off, I was credited with 10 hours and 51 minutes firing time.

The next day saw us catch the 9.25 am Ararat–Hamilton rail motor as far as Dunkeld. Waiting in the loop was oil-burning J542 with the 9.10 am goods from Hamilton to Ararat. We relieved the crew and ran the train home. Again Bob Quinlivin hardly said a word, leaving the running of the engine to the driver and me. Once under way, with the cooperation of the man at the throttle, I gave the boiler tubes a good sanding. Black smoke poured from the funnel and steaming noticeably improved. The consolidation steamed well, and with only a moderate load we made good time to Ararat. Leaving our train in the yard, we were signalled to the loco depot where we took water and oil, and with a near full boiler and the safety valves about to lift we ran the engine into the shed and left it there. This shift was short at just seven hours. Our job for the next day was to sign on at the shunter's cabin in the Ararat yard at 6.55 am, for the 7 am pilot relief.

The day was bright and sunny and the engine was my old friend J546. The yard was not busy and we sat around for as much time as we were shunting. Everyone found this agreeable and there were long interludes of pleasant conversation in the cab. At 3 pm our shift finished. We went over the pit, handed the engine over to a hostling crew and signed off. We were rostered for the 6.55 am pilot relief on the following day. Again the day was sunny and J546 the engine. Things were

In the mid-1960s, steam locomotive sound effects were plentiful on 'up' trains leaving Stawell. Oil-burning N class nos 459 and 460 provide a symphony of steam as they blast their way up the 1 in 62, with the plume of smoke from K174 indicating powerful assistance in the rear. (Ian Scutt)

a little busier than the day before and we were kept busy moving around, making up trains and removing vehicles from others. The cab of 546 had the characteristic smell of fuel oil. This was a little stronger than usual, there being no constant draft of air across the footplate, such as happens when on the road. Still, the engine was a picnic to fire and everyone enjoyed the day.

Next was a rostered day off. This was followed by travelling with Bob Quinlivin and the rostered driver on the 8.55 am fast goods to Stawell. In the yard, with the crew awaiting relief, was oil-burning N488. This was the engine designated to push and pilot for the day. It being a Saturday, things were rather quiet. When the yard work was complete, R763 arrived on a goods from Dimboola. After taking water, it pulled ahead and we coupled onto its train, as train engine. We returned to Ararat double-heading with 763. Climbing the grade out of Stawell, the engines produced excellent sound effects, with each producing a pounding staccato as it pulled its share of the trailing load. Being Saturday afternoon, everyone was in a hurry to get home, and this resulted in the engines being worked that little bit harder. The result? Beautiful exhaust sounds and a spirited run home! Once again, it was railroading at its best. The engines were hostled at Ararat and placed in the shed. It had been a short but enjoyable shift.

Monday, 18 November 1963 was a most beautiful spring day. In this ideal climate I was booked to sign on at the shed at 2.15 pm and take out and run the 3 pm Hamilton goods. Our return was to run the 8.45 pm to Ararat from Hamilton. R731 was the engine for the 3 pm. It had been prepared and was waiting in the shed with its fire banked. This was soon pushed down and three short whistles had the turntable lined up to take us out of the depot. Bob Quinlivin introduced me to the driver, an Irishman named Tom Finlay, then said very little for the remainder of the day, which turned out to be a long one at 10 hours. At the depot TR telephone post, I notified the signalman in A box of our engine number and driver's name. There was a pause, then, 'Okay, up to the disc.' Running tender-first, we moved up to the disc signal controlling movements into Ararat yard. This soon turned to 'proceed' and we set back onto our train. This weighed just under 400 tons. The train examiner who coupled us on was soon busy with the brake test and I turned my attention to the fire. Opening the blower to just over a quarter of a turn, I picked up the shovel and delivered generous quantities of coal down each side of the firebox, in the back corners and under the fire door. Three shovelfuls went down the front: one in each front corner and the third in the middle. The centre of the grate received a light sprinkling. Using the hinged wedge to leave an air opening between the fire doors, I turned on the fireman's side injector. As the water came up, I opened the stoker jets to 75 psi and eased open the stoker throttle. Coal rumbled through the stoker trough and went shooting onto the fire. When the smoke thickened, the stoker was turned off. Meanwhile, the water level in the gauge glasses showed almost three-quarters full and the injector was also turned off. It was close to 3 pm. The steam gauge needle was creeping up over 180 and a voice on the ground next to the cab was that of the signalman handing up the staff for Ararat–Maroona. A ground disc giving access to the main line to Hamilton came off, and at 3 pm a long whistle brought a green flag from the guard. With a shorter whistle and swishes of steam from the cylinder cocks, 731 rolled out of the yard. Passing over the final crossovers, the guard gave the final 'right away' and we were rolling along the main line. R731 was a delight to fire. The slightest application of the stoker saw the steam gauge needle zoom towards the red mark, and even long shots from the injector had little effect on steaming. From time to time I used the shovel to pick up coal that vibrated on to the footplate, and place it down the sides and around the back of the firebox. Positive movements on the steam gauge rewarded this practice.

The speed limit to Maroona was 30 mph for all trains and our initial progress was thus leisurely. Following the staff exchange at Maroona, Tom Finlay eased 731's regulator wide open and adjusted the cutoff. The exhaust erupted into a magnificent crescendo, with sharp, distinct beats sending a rhythmic serenade across the sunlit countryside. I couldn't help smiling. And strangely, I got smiles in return. A gentle use of the stoker, and the needle on the steam gauge attached itself to the red mark at 210 like a limpet.

Around lunchtime at Stawell and oil-burning R748 rolls into the yard at the head of No. 86 'up' goods. Here it will take water and later depart for Ararat with banking assistance from local pilot J542. (ARHS Victorian Division Archive)

The safety valves lifted and the injector went on. And on we went in effortless style to Willaura. Here, with the staff in hand for the section to Glenthompson, we sailed on, making light of the few grades and bowling along at between 30 and 40 mph. At the staff exchange at Glenthompson, the stationmaster called up that we would be crossing the rail motor at Dunkeld, the next station. Arriving here, we were signalled into No. 2 road and came to a stand opposite the station platform. We were informed that the rail motor was over half an hour away, and so had plenty of time to have our evening meal. I boiled the billy, and at the same time banked the fire. This done, the three of us climbed down from the cab and sat down comfortably on a nearby stack of sleepers.

Close to Dunkeld station, one of the outcrops of the Grampian Ranges sent its bulky outline rearing skywards in an impressive display of nature's handiwork. It was now around 6.30 pm and this stand-alone mountain was bathed in the rays of the evening sun, which also silhouetted our train. There was just the faintest breeze, and this carried the sound of the still running air compressor in our direction. It punctuated the balmy air with a rhythmic and beautiful tharhn, tharhn; tharhn, tharhn. There was never a more idyllic railway scene. We finished our tea and drank our fill from the billy, then whiled away a few minutes enjoying the evening. The sound of a rail motor air horn interrupted our reverie and we returned to our engine. With over half a glass of water and 150 lbs of steam, I pushed the fire down. This had a worthwhile effect on the steam gauge and we were soon ready to depart. The staff for the Dunkeld–Strathkellar section was duly delivered. This was followed by a long whistle, a green flag from the guard, and we were on our way. Once again it was fingertip firing. We made easy work of the grade into Mountajup and drifted along the seven miles of predominately down grade to Strathkellar. I kept the fire bright and the water level satisfactory, but the steam fell to 150. After the staff exchange for the final section into

Hamilton, the regulator went up to the roof and the cutoff was wound out as we encountered the 1 in 50 grade of the Strathkellar Bank. In a trice the stoker had coal rumbling into the firebox. The effect was remarkable and dramatic. With R731 blasting its way up the 1 in 50, in the space of about two minutes the steam gauge was sitting comfortably on 210, with the safety valves lifting. A slight widening of the stoker throttle and the engine was howling its head off. Meanwhile, the cutoff was being wound further out, and at a speed approaching 25 mph 731 went over the top in breathtaking style. The big 4-6-4 rode smoothly and we rolled the remaining three and a half miles into Hamilton, where a relief crew waited to take over our engine. They had also brought out the engine for our 8.45 pm return to Ararat. This was coal-burning N463.

We had an engine but no train. Finally, after endless delays, we were signalled to back on to some vehicles that had just recently arrived. This was our consist for Ararat, and it weighed 360 tons. When the brake test was finally complete and we had the staff in our possession, it was well past 10 pm. Leaving Hamilton, we faced the reverse side of the Strathkellar Bank. This was longer and steeper than what we had negotiated in the down direction, and I built up the fire accordingly. With plenty of water and the safety valves lifting, we pulled out of Hamilton. We made a spirited departure, storming up the short series of switchback grades that led to the final one and a half miles of 1 in 50. N463 steamed well, and with a very listenable exhaust topped the grade at around 20 mph. I was able to effect all the hand staff exchanges without incident and we made good time to Willaura, where we took water. The engine certainly performed well and was easy to fire. It might have been easier if, every time I put a fire on, Bob Quinlivin hadn't chosen to stand in the middle of the footplate, right in front of the firebox doors, and stare dreamily up at the steam gauge. So it was, every time I went to put on a fire I had to motion to him to politely get out of the way. However, in the overall scheme of things this did not have any adverse affects. On arrival at Maroona, a relief crew took over N463, and we travelled in the guard's van for the remainder of the journey into Ararat. It had been a truly wonderful day, the whole 10 hours and 3 minutes of it.

When servicing locomotives, distinctions were made in the terms used for what was being done. A 'preparation' was oiling up; a 'hostle' was cleaning the fire and taking water and coal or oil. However, when a preparation and a hostle were carried out together, this was known as a 'recondition.' For most locomotives, the time allowed for a recondition was 1 hour 5 minutes at the start or finish of a shift, and 1 hour during a shift. R class were different. To recondition an R you were allowed 1 hour 10 minutes at the start or finish of a shift, and 1 hour 5 minutes during a shift.

My final instruction trip was to sign on at the shed at 4.35 pm, recondition oil-burning N451, and use it to run the 5.55 pm goods to Hamilton, changing over with the 3.25 pm from Hamilton. We only got as far as Maroona on the 5.55 pm, and hence had little time to test 451's steaming ability. R763 was waiting for us, and in next to no time we were back in Ararat. We hostled 763 and then assisted in the preparation of a J class. And that was the end of our shift. We signed off with just 6 hours and 10 minutes to our credit.

In the days following the instruction trips, I was further examined by the Ararat depot foreman in boiler washouts and procedures for lighting up steam locomotives at outstation depots. On passing this exam, I was qualified to be sent away to relieve at other locations.

Soon after completing their instruction trips, the other members of my cleaner class were transferred to Dimboola. This meant I was the junior man in the shed and first in line to be sent away relieving at another depot in the Ararat district. This was my status quo for the next six months—there being no other trainee engineman classes during that time.

16 Mount Gambier

After a couple of day shift hostling and loco pilot jobs, I was called to the depot foreman's office. The roster clerk, Bob Finch said, 'I'm sending you down to Mount Gambier for a week, champ. D'you reckon you can handle it down there?'

'I'll do my best, Mr Finch', I replied.

I didn't want to go to Mount Gambier, or anywhere. I valued the comforts of home. Nevertheless, on Saturday, 30-11-1963, I picked up my one week's expenses of £7 10s 0d. and travelled by train and bus to Mount Gambier. My accommodation was in the VR Rest Hut there. On opening the door of this, I was greeted by the skeletons of deceased huntsman spiders hanging from the walls. Not exactly a home away from home. It was a bit dusty, but otherwise clean. I bought my meals locally. All locomotives operating from Victoria into Mount Gambier were oil burners.

On Sunday, 1 December, I signed on at 5 pm at the Mount Gambier loco depot. This was a small, modern, semi-roundhouse served by an electric turntable. At the far end stood a silent South Australian Railways 900 class diesel, while near to where I entered was oil-burning J class, 535, partially obscured by a pile of wood used for lighting up. It was a sunny afternoon with no wind and there was not a sound in the whole place. As I walked towards the engine, my footsteps echoed from the walls. The atmosphere was ominous. I stopped walking. It was far too quiet. What if there was someone behind that wood waiting to harm me. I wouldn't stand a chance. I could see the headlines: 'Mystery Death Beside Engine'. Of course all this was ridiculous. Or was it? Gripping my kitbag, I shuffled around the end of the wood pile and stood beside the cab of the engine. Of course there was no one there. How stupid I was. I prepared to swing up into the cab; then hesitated. Of course there was no one behind the wood, because they were waiting for me up in the cab, keeping out of sight till I stood in the gangway, then delivering a crushing blow that I couldn't possibly avoid. I paused for about 60 seconds, then dumped my kitbag noisily on the cab floor and climbed through the gangway. I was on my own, of course. But I was relieved all the same.

I set about lighting the fire. There was no wood in the cab, but with a supply so close I soon had the footplate full to overflowing. I had often watched engines being lit up at Ararat, and marvelled how easily wood seemed to burn in a firebox. Someone would throw in some burning cotton waste soaked in kerosene, lace it with pieces of wood seemingly of no particular size, then toss in a few logs. Ten minutes later this combination would be blazing merrily, ensuring steam was on its way.

Having tested the gauge glasses and carried out other pre-lighting-up checks, I threw plenty of small pieces of kindling into the centre of the firebox. This was followed by a large clump of burning cotton waste, liberally soaked in kerosene. And finally, I placed further kindling to ensure good combustion. Being satisfied that all was well, I turned my attention to oiling up. As the oil containers in the engine locker were all but empty I realized I would have to visit the oil store. Before setting out, I glanced into the firebox. Nothing! The fire was out. Not a flicker. More cotton waste, more kerosene and more wood. I placed some heavier pieces around the edges of the burnt-out remains and tossed some lighter pieces in the middle. The waste was then lit and projected, with the aid of the shovel, into the middle of this potential miniature bonfire. As soon as it landed, I delivered a flurry of the flimsiest bits of wood I could find, knowing they would burn easily. Slowly, oh so slowly, the fire began to burn. It was finally bright enough to have some heavier pieces added. Nevertheless, I was past taking anything for granted and felt compelled to wait and ensure that these fed the flames and didn't put them out. Fortunately, all went well and after making another delivery of wood into the firebox, I felt confident enough to get the oil.

I climbed down from the cab, picked up the oil bottles and walked toward the oil store. Again, silence, with every footstep echoing around the walls. Of course, the individual waiting for me had checked the oil bottles on the engine, and knowing I would have to visit the store was waiting there. No movie set was ever as cleverly designed as the scene presented by the entry to this oil store. The door was half open, with its upper glass panel obscured by a blind pulled halfway down. This blind meant that most of what was inside the store was hidden from the outside. The half-open door revealed a portion of an oil drum and a concrete pathway leading to somewhere or other. I stood outside the door clutching the oil bottles. Then, banging them together, pushed the door wide open. Finding myself still alive, I walked in. Here were drums marked Cylinder Oil and Bearing Oil. Each drum had a hand pump and making use of these I was soon on my way back to the engine.

Time was passing. The fiasco with the fire had taken an hour and the visit to the oil store a further 15 minutes and I still had not checked the spark arrestor. Leaving the oil on the footplate, I retrieved the big shifting spanner together with the hammer from the tender locker and went to the front of the engine. Climbing up to the smokebox door, I set to work on the nuts that would allow it to open. They didn't want to move, and I decided I wasn't going to make them. Returning to the cab, I was greeted with the first piece of good news for the day. The fire was burning well and devoured with ease the large quantity of heavy logs that I now delivered to it. There was no hurry to finish oiling up and I took my time. I finished at around 8 pm, just in time to greet George Twose, the VR driver stationed in Mount Gambier, who now arrived. I explained I hadn't yet checked the spark arrester. His response was not to worry, he would do it himself. We now had 100 psi of steam, and just prior to his arrival it had been my intention to rake out the wood fire and put 535 on oil. However, George cheerfully advised me to go and have my tea and leave putting her on oil to him. I was only too happy to oblige. I left the depot, had a meal, and returned 45 minutes later.

It was about this time that the South Australian crew of the 900 class diesel arrived. They were running the overnight passenger train to Adelaide. They soon had their 900 class running, and in due course moved on to the turntable and out into the yard. Their train was made up of one bogie freight wagon, three passenger cars, one of which was a sleeping car, and a brake van. With J535 now on oil firing, it was time to leave the depot. I mastered how to operate the turntable and lined it up for our engine. It easily accommodated 535, which left the shed funnel-first. The guard of our train soon appeared and effected a number of point changes that placed us at the cattle race at the Adelaide end of the Mount Gambier yard. Here we picked up a few loaded sheep wagons and took them down the other end of the yard and onto our train. This was lengthy and weighed around 600 tons. However, the first 19 miles of our journey to Dartmoor were almost flat and presented no difficulty. George checked the brakes and a long whistle brought a green light from the guard. It was now about 10 pm and we were away. Speed was restricted to 15 mph for the short distance to Rennick, just over the border into Victoria. After Rennick, 20 mph was allowed. Our trip to Dartmoor took over an hour. We jogged along at around 20 mph, with the regulator barely open and no noticeable sound from the exhaust. J535 was not long out of the workshops and in excellent condition. Everything was tight and the engine rode and steamed well.

At Dartmoor we took water from a superb water crane that delivered close to a thousand gallons a minute. Meanwhile, an assisting engine had arrived from Portland, meaning that our 600 ton load was going all the way to Heywood. After

Oil-burning J538 departs Mount Gambier for Heywood in Victoria. By the look of its load an assisting engine will come on to the train at Dartmoor. (ARHS Victorian Division Archive)

taking water, our helper, another oil-burning J, coupled on and we got under way, rolling down the short grade to the impressive trestle bridge over the Glenelg River. Over the river, the grade stiffened and both engines were opened out. With a nod from George Twose, I cut back the oil control valve and the atomizer and sent 10 shovelfuls of sand through the tubes. Smoke billowed out of the funnel blotting out the stars, then rolled away into the darkness. The steam gauge soon responded to the sanding, with the needle rising easily to the 180 mark. The train was now negotiating some reverse curves, and with both engines sending a powerful, rhythmic exhaust into the night sky our progress was purposeful and dramatic. We continued pounding away through Winnap and then on to the three mile climb up to Greenwald. The sound from both engines was magnificent. J535 proved an excellent workhorse, with only the faintest of oil fumes coming into the cab, often a clear funnel, and very easy on water. Once over the top at Greenwald it was predominately down grade through Lyons and Sinclair all the way to Heywood. On arriving there I had already been working over 10 hours and was not pleased to have to take water and oil and turn the engine. After a tiring but enjoyable 10 hours and 53 minutes, I finally signed off at 3.53 am and was pleased to get between the cool, clean sheets of a bed in the rest hut on Heywood platform.

Having had our required 11 hours off, we signed on the same day at 2.55 pm to run the 3 pm Mount Gambier goods. J535 was again the engine, and again it performed well. Leaving Heywood, we rolled in clitter clatter fashion down the short distance to Sinclair. Then, the grades gradually rose over the 10 mile section to Lyons, requiring, in a few places, heavy steaming. The next five miles to Greenwald have some heavy grades, but afterwards it is all downhill to the Glenelg River bridge, with a final uphill pinch into Dartmoor. On the Heywood–Dartmoor section we saw an abundance of wildlife, with regular sightings of emus and kangaroos, the latter often in families. On arriving at Dartmoor, George spotted the engine at the water crane and it swung accurately over the tender lid without further movement. Leaving Dartmoor, we plodded along at around 20 mph until reaching Rennick, where for the final short distance 15 was the limit. We signed off after 11 pm.

The next shift commenced with a 9.10 pm sign on, and we set out for Heywood at a little after 10. We were again in charge of J535, which performed admirably, particularly around the reverse curves and on the grades leaving Dartmoor. After resting at Heywood, we returned to Mount Gambier on J543, which, after sanding, steamed well.

I saw out my time at Mount Gambier with two days of running to Dartmoor, then changing over with something coming in the opposite direction. The first changeover saw us return to Mount Gambier with J534, and the second time with J531. After spending seven days at Mount Gambier, I returned to Ararat.

17 Warracknabeal

Back at Ararat, I was once again the junior man in the shed. I was usually rostered to fire on a Saturday, but spent most of the rest of the week either hostling or cleaning, no matter what shift I was on. And I was first in line to be sent away relieving. So it was that on one Saturday early in January 1964 I travelled by train to Warracknabeal to commence work on the following Monday. Having drawn my £7 10s. 0d. expenses, I elected to stay at O'Dea's Hotel in preference to the departmental rest huts. My expenses covered the first week at the hotel, but after that I paid out of my own pocket.

My first job was to sign on at 4.40 am, prepare the engine and run the 6 am Hopetoun and return. The driver was Hughie Shearer, driver in charge at Warracknabeal. It was a beautiful, but blistering hot day and our engine was oil-burning N class, No. 492. N class were rated at 1090 tons each way between Warracnabeal and Hopetoun, and were frequently loaded to capacity. We commenced our journey with a long string of empty GY wheat wagons, and stopping at each of the five stations on the way to Hopetoun spotted a number of these at the adjacent wheat silos, where they would soon be filled. While going over a gravel road level crossing approaching Hopetoun we noticed a cloud of dust coming up from the front of the engine. It turned out that 492's cowcatcher had worked loose and was hanging at a drunken angle below rail level. Hughie Shearer and I spent about an hour undoing the remainder of the bolts holding this now piece of scrap metal in place, and finally discarding it out of everyone's way. We could now do the shunting, take water and turn the engine, whose performance so far had been anything but outstanding.

We made up our return train, then paused for a meal. Our train of full GY wagons out of Hopetoun weighed around 400 tons. Stopping at each station on our return, we picked up the wagons we had previously left as these were now full. The train load soon reached the maximum of 1090 tons. N492 meanwhile was performing like a sick cow. Part of the problem was that engines spent a long time at Warracknabeal when allocated there, and Warracknabeal had no supply of sand to replenish cab sand boxes on oil burners. Without sand through its tubes, an oil burner soon became an indifferent steamer. If sand was still withheld it went from indifferent to dull, then to very dull. 492 obviously hadn't been sanded for ages and was at the bottom of the very dull stage.

We left Brim with a full load and Hughie Shearer remarked, 'They usually prime out of here.' And he was right. To overcome a very short stretch of 1 in 100 up grade, the engine had to be worked hard. Even though the water was barely half a glass, the thing primed for a good 30 seconds, spewing froth and foam all over the place and making the cab even more uncomfortable than the 40°C outside temperature had so far caused it to be. It was a great life firing steam engines!

In these conditions, it took a Herculean effort to get the steam gauge to register anything like 150 psi, with even greater exertion needed to keep it there. And all the while we plodded along at a near funeral pace, without the faintest breeze to provide relief from the heat. On each side of the track stretched the shimmering, harvested wheat fields, soaking up the blistering sun and seemingly enjoying it. We got no sympathy from them. Having a full load at Brim meant we went

Under a blistering sun, oil-burning N458 leans into the task of hauling its 1090 ton load up the treacherous grade out of Warracknabeal. With the regulator wide open and cutoff wound out, the exhaust shatters a tranquil sky. (ARHS Victorian Division Archive)

straight on to Warracknabeal without stopping at Lah. The speed limit for all trains between Warracknabeal and Hopetoun is 30 mph and by some miracle on this last stage of our run home we reached 25, despite steam being below 150. We were favoured with another miracle when we were sure the engine was going to prime once more, but just failed to do so. After spending 11 hours and 25 minutes on this rambling wreck, we eventually rolled into the Warracknabeal yard and signed off at 4.05 pm.

Perhaps tomorrow would be better? Not a chance. I was to sign on at 4.10 am and prepare and run the 6.30 am Hopetoun and return. At 4 the next morning there was not a breath of wind and the temperature was already rising. My driver for the day was Roy Leslie. I found him making his way to our engine, N492. During our preparation, I shared my experiences of the day before with this engine. We agreed the only way to get along with it was never to leave a station without a full glass of water and a full head of steam. This, at least, would get us part of the way to where we were going. We made up our train of empty GY wheat vehicles, tested the brakes, and were ready to depart. But first, we needed steam and water. Without making too much smoke, I turned up the oil control valve and adjusted the atomizer to suit. The needle on the steam gauge then came up to 180. With the safety valves lifting, the fireman's side injector went on until the water was bobbing out of sight in the top of the gauge glasses. In the meantime, we were treated to a spectacular sunrise that went from a soft and delicate pink to a blast-furnace red, then finally to a yellow ball of fire beating down from the sky.

A long whistle brought a green light from the guard and Roy Leslie eased us out of the yard towards Lah, our first stop. Initially, we did reasonably well. It was flat terrain and eight miles to Lah. We arrived in just over half an hour with half a glass of water and 160 lbs of steam. We spotted some GYs at the wheat silo and remarshalled our train. Once again we had a full glass of water and a full head of steam. With a slightly reduced load and only four miles to travel, Brim was reached with 170 lbs of steam and water at just over half a glass. Continuing with our full glass of water and full head of steam formula, and with the load regularly reducing, our eventual arrival at Hopetoun was less traumatic than it otherwise might have been.

We took water, turned the engine, had a meal and made up our return train. Every station had an abundance of full wheat wagons and our load out of Hopetoun was around 600 tons. Two and a half miles out was a half mile pinch of 1 in 100, followed by another one a mile further on. We departed with the water near the top of the gauge glasses and the steam on 180 and blowing off. We staggered, rather than stormed, over these two sections of 1 in 100 and fell into Goyura, the first station out with 150 lbs of steam and ¼ of a glass of water. Here we picked up a further 100 tons, recovered all our water and steam, and set sail for Rosebery, three miles away. We made it, just, and were rewarded by picking up another 150 tons. The load was now 850 tons and we had to drag it eight miles to Beulah, the next station. The only thing to do was to fill the boiler and bring the steam up to blowing off. Then depart. This we did, all the while under a sun blazing down from a cloudless sky into an atmosphere of blistering heat, and not even the faintest suggestion of any cool breeze. After eight miles of purgatory, we staggered into Beulah, hobbled around the yard, were attached to a number of full GYs weighing 240 tons, and with these in tow lurched back onto the train. We now had a full load of 1090 tons. All we needed was an engine to pull it. N492 was barely fit to be called a locomotive, and the thought of having to coax it over the next 20 miles with a full load was anything but encouraging. Nevertheless, this was our task, and we prepared for it.

The injector went on until the gauge glasses were full. With the blower on one full turn, I opened out the oil control valve until the funnel was showing much more than a trace of smoke. The atomizer was adjusted in a valiant attempt to get it to produce as fine a spray of oil as possible, thus enabling combustion to readily occur. Steam pressure rose and the safety valves lifted. A long whistle brought a green flag from the guard, the independent brake went into release, the throttle was eased open and 492 got hold of its 1090 tons and plodded out of Beulah. Speed was not an issue. Our aim was to keep the load moving and handle the engine in such a manner that it had sufficient steam to make this aim real. Eventually we were moving at 20 mph. Other things were moving too. In what seemed the blink of an eye the steam gauge needle dropped to 150. I increased the flow of oil to the burner. This slowed the fall but in no way reversed the direction. Approaching Gallaquil we were down to 140, with the water at under half a glass. The day of reckoning would come when the injector finally went on. It was approaching fast. With steam clinging to 140, the water ebbed slowly away to just over a ¼ of a glass. The day of reckoning was here. With a hiss, gurgle and whoosh the injector sent water into the boiler. These events took place against the scorching outside temperature, the smell of oil in the cab, the dull roar of the atomizer and the clanging rattle of various bits and pieces as 492 managed to move along.

With the injector on, steam dropped to 120. Then 110. Speed had long since fallen to 15 mph. Roy Leslie nudged the regulator open a fraction more to allow for the falling steam gauge. If it made any difference we didn't notice it. We had now passed Brim and were on a barely perceptible, but nevertheless real, rising grade. Water was now half a glass and I turned off the injector. Speed fell to 10 mph and the regulator was nudged further open. With the injector now off, we had hopes for the steam gauge. It fell to 100. Then to 90. We had somehow managed to get over the rises past Brim, and with steam continuing to hang around 90 we continued our forced march through Lah towards Warracknabeal. It was touch and go whether we would stall. But we didn't, and finally collapsed into Warracknabeal, signing off at 2.30 pm after 10 hours and 20 minutes on an engine that we left with 90 lbs of steam and a bob of water in the bottom of the gauge glasses.

Next day we were booked in the opposite direction. Sign on at 5.40 am for the 7 am Murtoa, changing over with the 8 am ex Murtoa. Signing on at 5.40 am meant being treated to another dramatic sunrise, and this softened the sight of the yet untried oil-burning N482. This was duly prepared and coupled on to its train, which the guard informed us weighed 1090 tons. A full load. The brake test was completed and we were ready to depart on time. The weather was warm, the sky clear and the air still.

The railway line to Murtoa was largely straight and level. Curves were few and grades, such as they were, even fewer. There was one grade, however, that commanded everyone's respect. It was two and a half miles south of Warracknabeal and comprised one mile at an average of 1 in100. In keeping with the rest of the route, this graded section bisected wheat fields that stretched as far as the eye could see in every direction. There were no buildings or any sign of human habitation.

The safety valves on 482 were lifting and the gauge glasses three-quarters full when Roy Leslie's long whistle brought a green flag from the van. With the staff for the section to Sheep Hills safely in the cab, we departed with the exhaust echoing back from the few buildings on the edge of town. The light Mikado rose to the task and we were soon bowling along at 25 mph. Steaming wasn't brilliant, but at just over 160 with a reasonably clear funnel it was a lot better than nothing. Also, there was no sign of priming. We could see the 1 in 100 coming up and the cutoff was wound out for an extra three-quarters of a turn in anticipation. On nosing up the grade, the water rose sufficiently in the gauge glasses to keep the injector at bay. It was heavy pulling, and before we were halfway up the grade speed had fallen away to 15 mph. This soon dropped to 10 mph. Steam, however, remained at over 160 and with a purposeful exhaust progress was steady. Ahead, the grade eased and tipped slightly down. As we went over the top, the engine lost its feet. The slipping at full regulator sent shudders and vibrations from one end of N482 to the other. The regulator was slammed shut and the oil control valve quickly turned back to allow for the lack of draft. As fast as it had been closed, the regulator was eased open again and for a further 10 yards we plodded on. Despite the engine being at the top of the grade, the 1090 ton load was still ascending it. Another slip, and the exhaust thundered skywards till closing the regulator checked it. Steam was quickly reapplied but to no avail. A couple of hoarse sobs left the funnel

The first main-line diesel electric locomotive arrived on the Victorian Railways in 1952. Nevertheless, 11 years later steam still reigned supreme on the VR Commissioner's consist. Looking high, wide and handsome, $D^3$639 takes the turn out at Murtoa and heads towards Warracknabeal with a VR Commissioner's special. (Ian Scutt)

and we pulled to a stand. No coaxing, cajoling, persuading or coercing, whether mechanical, emotional or verbal, would get that engine to move forward. With a sigh, the driver wound the valve gear into reverse, sounded three long whistles, received a 'back up' sign from the guard, released the brakes and let the train roll gently back towards Warracknabeal. Here, after being signalled into the yard, it was examined for any sticking brakes. When none were found, and considering we came within a hair's breath of making the grade successfully, we set off once more. Again, water and steam were well up, and the needle on the steam gauge stabilized at 160. Experience had shown 25 mph wasn't fast enough to get over the hill, and this time we approached it at just over 30. This resulted in steam dropping to 150 but the resulting momentum was worth it. We sailed over the crest at just under 15 mph with no sign of slipping.

All this had taken almost an hour. Now, however, we made good time and travelled over halfway to Murtoa, meeting our changeover at Minyip. Oil-burning N488 was at the head of the 8 am, and this soon saw us making an uneventful return to Warracknabeal. Nevertheless, our day was far from over. We hostled and turned 488, and picking up a load of empties ran tender-first to Brim, where these were exchanged for a load of GYs full of wheat. N488 performed reasonably well and brought us home without incident. We signed off at 4.25 pm after a shift of 10 hours and 45 minutes.

Steam locomotives and humans have one thing in common. They both need water. Pure water. This was not easy to find in the Warracknabeal district. The water here had a high proportion of dissolved mineral salts in it. Without treatment, this caused priming in locomotive boilers. In humans, it readily upset the digestive system, causing frequent visits to the toilet. I drank mostly tea, but even with boiled water I had to take every precaution to make sure my bowel was empty before starting work. I went through some embarrassing, and almost disastrous, situations. But still I had to drink. Working in 40°C temperatures demanded a worthwhile fluid supply to prevent dehydration. Cool water was plentiful but I dared not drink it. On arrival at a destination such as Hopetoun, you were as dry as an Afghan's armpit and parched with thirst. First, you had to turn the engine and take water. In performing this latter task, you stood on the tender tank and directed a stream of cold water into it. That water was cool to the touch, and presented the most refreshing sight as it sparkled and cascaded into the tank, and danced around inside. The temptation to gulp some down was almost irresistible, but I didn't do it. That liquid would have gone through me like an express train, as past experience had all too clearly shown. When water was taken, I walked a couple of hundred yards up the street from the station to a milk bar and purchased cold soft drinks. This self-control lessened, but didn't eliminate, a running bowel, which frequently left me drained. So it was on my first weekend at Warracknabeal I was glad not be rostered for work. I was looking forward to resting but my stomach had other ideas. It sent me to the toilet at 9 am on Saturday morning and kept me there for half an hour. And it was there that I heard my name being called around the hotel.

After washing up I made my way to the phone with the speed of a stampeding turtle. It was one of the engineman at Warracknabeal, speaking on behalf of the driver in charge. 'David, you'll have to sign on at 10.10 am and run the Patchewollock rest.' 'I haven't got a hope of being there at 10.10,' I said. 'I've got a running bowel, can't you get someone else?' I must have sounded genuine because the voice at the other end softened somewhat. It explained why they couldn't get someone else, and assured me that whatever time I could sign on would be okay. Saturday's evening meal and Sunday's lunch would be provided at the Patchewollock Hotel. Sleeping would be in the rest hut. I made my way to my room, put on my overalls, packed my kitbag, put aside some coins to buy sandwiches for lunch and walked to work. As usual, the sun beat down from a cloudless sky and there was not a breath of wind.

The engine was N488 and the driver Jack Jones. Jack had just arrived from Ararat, and like me was relieving at Warracknabeal for an indefinite period. 'Have you got a billy?' he asked. 'Yes.' 'Good, got a billy boiler?' 'No, I haven't,' I said. 'That's alright, we'll make one,' he replied.

A billy boiler comprised a length of copper tube wound into a series of curved elements, similar to the wire elements in an electric jug. The copper elements fitted comfortably into a billy of water, and when boiler steam was passed through them the water took only a few seconds to boil. I was intrigued to see how Jack was going to manufacture one of these devices. It was easy. He unscrewed one of 488's intermediate valve spindle drains. This was a suitably sized copper tube that took condensate from beneath the intermediate valve spindle, down behind the cross head slide bars to just above the ground. The copper was malleable and was quite easy to shape into heating coils. Also, the fitting that screwed into the intermediate valve spindle drain also fitted the shed line connection on the steam manifold on the fireman's side of the cab, thus enabling a supply of boiler steam to boil the billy!

Having attended to our main priorities, we got on with other tasks such as preparing the engine and making up the train. This consisted of a number of empty wheat trucks, some wagons holding general merchandise, together with a few perishable louvre vans loaded with beer and foodstuffs. As well as the driver, fireman and guard, the train also boasted a van man to assist with unloading and loading the items conveyed.

Following completion of the brake test, it was well after midday before we were ready to depart. Running funnel-first, our pace was unhurried. We stopped at each station on the way to Hopetoun. It was at these stops that the van man proved his worth, using a hand truck to unload a variety of perishable items, and sometimes delivering them to the front door of a hotel located near the station. These activities took some time. We made use of it in the cab by trying out our new billy boiler. It worked very well and we were able to drink cups of tea at will. N488 was something of an indifferent steamer. Before leaving a station, the water level would be high and the safety valves lifting. A mile down the track, steam would be down to 150 and refuse to climb any higher. Without any sand through the tubes, this was hardly surprising. However, while the steam gauge would not rise above 150, it was also reluctant to fall below this figure. Therefore, as long as we took things reasonably easy our steam supply was assured.

We arrived at Hopetoun after 4 pm. Here the train was remarshalled, water taken, and the engine turned to run tender-first to Patchewollock. Our departure for this location was just after five in the afternoon. Speed was limited to 20 mph. This meant we had plenty of time to absorb the countryside as we ventured into the hinterland of Victoria. The track was stable, but at times was no more than two ribbons of steel reaching out into a sea of yellow sand that had long since covered the ballast. This added to the sense of adventure. There were few houses in the 23 mile journey, but of those that did exist quite a number acknowledged the passing of our weekly train. People would wave anything from handkerchiefs to tea towels as we passed. They were recognized by a variety of suitable sounds from the whistle. These carried in uninterrupted fashion through the still,à late afternoon air and added a degree of festivity to our progress.

Patchewollock was reached at around 6.30 pm. In order to get our evening meal we had a quick wash up, left the train in the yard and immediately made our way to the hotel. The food was good and much appreciated, reminding us that we were still within the reach of civilization. On our way back to the train I was able to see the town. If anyone doubted that Victoria had outback regions, they should visit Patchewollock. It had two 'streets'. One ran parallel to the railway line. It came in from the south-east, was nothing but dust, and was about 150 yards long. It had a few dilapidated timber dwellings that flanked the store. This was a narrow-fronted shop that boasted a short wooden sidewalk, stretching from one side of the shop front to the other. This was covered with a skillion roof, so one could look in the windows in wet weather and not get drenched. The windows displayed a variety of bric à brac items and these extended into the shop's interior. This had a few lights. These were complimented by the globe under the skillion roof, making this emporium the highlight of town. From an unidentified source within the shop came the sound of the latest popular rock and roll music. This was in strange contrast to the overall outback setting.

The street ended in a right-angled corner, on the far side of which stood the hotel. This was a well-built red brick structure that looked smaller than it was. On the near side, and extending north, was the other 'street'. This was the width of the average road, but was merely a dusty track, disappearing over a slight rise into nowhere. From the corner were about half a dozen, melancholy, narrow-fronted wooden houses. Their ageing wooden fences separated them from the street by just a yard or two. They seemed barely habitable, their weathered and blistering exteriors crying out in vain for attention, but receiving none.

Arriving back at our train, we carried out a number of shunting moves, setting out empties and assembling loads for removal the following day. Despite the smallness of the rail yard and the relatively few vehicles in it, the shunting took a long time. When it was finally completed the engine was uncoupled and moved alongside a domestic water tap with a garden hose attached. The hose was placed in the tender water tank and the tap turned on. The engine was now taking water and the hose would remain in place overnight. It was now time to turn the fire out and stable N488. This we did, and retired to the VR rest hut for the evening. The sheets were cool and clean and we spent a comfortable night. And fortunately, my running bowel had subsided. We slept in the next morning, had a well-prepared lunch at the hotel and relaxed in the afternoon. Jack Jones signed on at 5 pm to light the engine up. We were scheduled to depart for Warracknabeal at 9 pm, which meant I signed on at 8.50 pm.

Jack had the water well up in the gauge glasses and the steam pressure healthy. Now running funnel-first, we picked up a rake of trucks, pulled them forward, and set back into No. 2 road to pick up the remainder of the train. With a load of not much more than 400 tons, the brake test was soon complete. A long whistle brought a green light from the guard and we were on our way. It was a beautiful summer night, starry and still. When the cylinder cocks were closed, the exhaust gave some purposeful sobbing beats until, with 20 mph soon reached, the regulator was eased back to make the exhaust almost inaudible. The houses that waved to us on our 'down' journey again made their presence felt. This time by switching lights on and off. And again they received a variety of appropriate whistles. Our progress south was thus a series of personalized sound and light shows. It must be mentioned that apart from the hotel staff, we saw no other human beings at Patchewollock.

Water was taken at Hopetoun and our load increased. Also, the van man spent about half an hour loading items into the guard's van and a louvre truck. We departed after midnight, and with careful handling N488's steam gauge remained on 150 for the remainder of the shift. We stopped at every station, sometimes for shunting, but always for van goods. This kept the van man occupied, who also contributed to the engine crew's alertness by uttering unnatural shrieks whenever he passed the engine. At 2 am we didn't appreciate it, but it was too dark to track him down. We pulled into Warracknabeal in the early hours of Monday morning, handed 488 over to a relief crew, and signed off at 4.50 am.

Our next turn of duty was to sign on the same day at 4.40 pm for the 6 pm Murtoa, returning with the 10.30 pm ex Murtoa. On signing on, we learned our engine was coal-burning N468. Driver in charge, Hughie Shearer, reassured us by saying, 'You'll get an oil burner at Murtoa.' Having no reason to doubt him, I thought, 'I'll put my back into this engine, and have a rest on the oil burner coming home.' We had close to a full load, and prior to departure I had the water at ¾ of a glass and had spent 15 minutes getting the fire satisfactory, resulting in the steam being right on the mark. Departing under a hot afternoon sun, 468 was soon pounding along at a little over 30 mph and approaching the notorious 1 in 100 upgrade. It steamed well, and with judicious use of the shovel in the blast-furnace atmosphere of the cab, steam remained near 180.

We were doing well until, halfway up the grade, the engine came close to priming. Froth appeared in the exhaust and it was touch and go. There was nothing we could do except keep going. Once over the grade, the engine was eased and the priming symptoms settled down and did not reappear. We made good time over the generally flat terrain to Murtoa, and after arriving safely looked around for our oil burner to replace N468. It was nowhere to be seen. N468 was the engine for the 10.30 pm to Warracknabeal. I therefore made the best of it. The night air was reasonably cool, N468 steamed reasonably well, and our load was moderate. After taking water and having a meal, we were coupled on to our train. During the brake test I got the fire in good shape, brought the water to ¾ of a glass and saw the steam rise to 180. A green light from the guard set us on our way. I opted for a short journey and made sure there was steam aplenty to enable our progress to be swift. Jack Jones took the hint and 468's speed recorder hung around 35 mph and at times right on the 40 mph Murtoa–Warracknabeal limit. This produced some pleasing exhaust sounds, sometimes amplified to please me by the cutoff being left wound out for an extended time. Jack knew I liked the sound of a brisk exhaust and on this occasion was happy to oblige. We arrived at Warracknabeal in good time and after 9 hours and 35 minutes with N468, signed off at 2.15 am.

We were booked on at 4.40 pm the next day for the same job, the 6 pm Murtoa, returning with the 10.30 pm. Our engine was oil-burning N497 with a load of 1090 tons. We departed on time with a full head of steam and plenty of water in the gauge glasses. It had been a blistering hot day. A little speed would give a draft of air through the cab and improve conditions somewhat. We tried to implement this policy, but N497 had other ideas. It didn't like being worked hard. In fact, in the early part of our trip it was reluctant to do any work at all! On approach to the climb of 1 in 100, it frothed and spewed some vile concoction from the funnel, as well as sending shuddering knocks through the big ends and axle boxes, signifying a definite carry over of water into the cylinders. The regulator was eased and the engine coaxed, petted and mollycoddled along to get us over the hill. In a sea of froth and bubble from the cylinder cocks and chimney it stalled a long way from the top. We set back about a mile and a half and tried again. The boiler was blown down, water kept at ½ a glass and steam just below 180 psi. Knowing 497's internals were very disturbed, it was treated gently. After an uneventful start, it began to cough, splutter, sob and discharge a watery substance that affected its major moving parts and for the second time that evening caused it to stall.

These stoppages had consumed well over an hour and we were in danger of blocking the 'down' rail motor as well as the 3.30 pm Warracknabeal goods from Murtoa. Once again we set back, this time all the way into Warracknabeal. While cooling our heels for the two aforementioned trains, our load was reduced from 1090 to 890 tons. Extensive use was made of the boiler blowdown, water was kept to a minimum level and steam below 180. Having thus regrouped, and well over two hours late, we left our home depot for the third time that day. The cooler night air was refreshing and the lighter load seemed to make all the difference. We made it comfortably over the 1 in 100 and continued on in the same vein to Murtoa. After turning the engine, taking water and having a well-earned meal we set out for home. Our treating N497 gently produced favourable results. Its steaming was barely satisfactory, but it showed little tendency to prime and we arrived home without incident.

A few days later I was on N497 again. It was booked on the 4.15 pm Warracknabeal–Murtoa, returning with the 8.15 pm ex Murtoa. My heart sank when I saw it, because the load in the 'up' direction was 1090 tons. I had almost finished oiling it up when Hughie Shearer arrived carrying a bag holding a number of lumps of something or other. 'The depot foreman at Ararat,' he announced, 'has sent these up here for use by crews operating out of Warracknabeal.' 'These' were water treatment tablets for use in the engine's tender. I took a few and tossed them into the tender tank. Climbing into the cab, I got busy with the steam and water. After using the injector I noticed that the water in the gauge glasses had a much healthier look and texture. With the brake test on our 1090 ton train complete, the guard responded to our long whistle with his green flag and we were moving. The funnel was almost smoke free and the steam gauge needle hovered around 180. The driver eased the regulator further open and I had my hand on the oil valve, ready to open it further when steam dropped. This took a while, but I was right on the ball, and as the funnel darkened slightly I glanced at the steam gauge. It had returned to 180. Meanwhile, speed had increased and as 497 got hold of her load the exhaust became a healthy and welcome staccato. There was no sign of priming, and with the slightest increase in the oil valve the steam gauge needle zoomed around the dial. We went blasting over the short pinch of 1 in 100 at almost 30 mph and continued on in effortless style to Murtoa. Even with a high water level, there was no sign of priming and use of the injector had little effect on steaming. The water treatment tablets had certainly made a difference! Our return trip to Warracknabeal was outstanding. The harder 497 was worked, the better it seemed to steam. I began once again to enjoy life on the footplate and look forward to the next day. Having had no major delays, we arrived home at the end of what turned out to be a shift of only 7 hours and 50 minutes.

A couple of days later, I was transferred back to Ararat.

18 Hamilton

I was still the junior man in the shed and this was reflected in the number of times I was rostered firing. This was generally once a week, on a Saturday. The remaining five or six days were either spent, cleaning, hostling or lighting up. This was the pattern for about two months. Then, on the approach to Easter, I was temporarily transferred to Hamilton. On the Thursday prior to Good Friday, I travelled on the 1.22 pm rail motor from Ararat and reported to the Hamilton loco foreman by telephone in the Hamilton signal box. I was required at the depot immediately. This was located at Coleraine Junction, a good half a mile from the station. Fortunately, an engine was heading that way and I rode on it. On making myself known, I was referred to driver Lind, for whom I was to fire on the 5.5 pm Ararat goods. He was with our engine, oil-burning J534. This was sitting on the turntable. 'Slap a bit of oil around her, will you,' he said. After oiling up, I took water and oil and we were ready to proceed to Hamilton yard. We arrived there in plenty of time for a leisurely brake test and a cup of tea, using the billy boiler made by Jack Jones two month earlier. We got away on time with a manageable load of 300 tons. J534 proved more than equal to the task and Mr Lind didn't hesitate to explore its talents. With evening closing in, we stormed over the Strathkellar Bank to the sound of a magnificent rhythmic exhaust, made all the easier to achieve after 10 shovelfuls of sand had been put through the tubes. Grades were no more than an occasion to hear a continuous, clipped exhaust, which became more strident as the cutoff was lengthened. Speed was often around 40 mph, and when worked hard uphill at 30 mph J534 produced a most beautiful sonorous staccato that was a delight to hear. And it steamed like a breeze. Use of the injector made very little difference to the steam gauge.

We were running under clear signals, and with hand staff exchanges made at around 20 mph, we ran non-stop to Willaura. While taking water there, our changeover, the 6.35 pm ex Ararat arrived. Bill Eagan was driving and Max May firing R731, with a load of only 286 tons. 731 came in blowing off, and on changing over Max May triumphantly affirmed, 'This one's going like a beauty.' They had swept the footplate clean and we entered a cab where everything was in order. Darkness had now replaced evening and 731's headlight showed us the way ahead. There was no breeze and the air was cool. Light from the full moon bathed the countryside in a soft, almost delicate illumination. Having received the appropriate staff, we whistled up the guard and got under way. At the slightest sniff of coal, R731's steam gauge needle bounded upwards. Keeping the water level where you wanted it was a picnic. For much of our journey we ran at the line speed for goods trains of 40 mph. Up grade, this resulted in classic R class exhaust sound effects echoing around the moonlit landscape. Again running under clear signals, we made good time through the superb scenery.

Travelling west, we came closer to the Grampian ranges. These were highlighted in the moonlight and etched against the skyline in a most dramatic and captivating manner, made all the more enjoyable by being viewed from the warmth of our engine cab. This was story book stuff. On arriving at Hamilton, we picked up R701, freshly prepared to run the 10.30 pm Ararat goods. Along the way we would meet, and

The loco depot at Hamilton was located at Coleraine Junction, about half a mile in the 'down' direction from Hamilton station. This panoramic view shows a portion of its eight-stall capacity. (Geoff Oliver)

change over with, the 8.30 pm ex Ararat. With the brake test and other formalities completed, R701 blasted out of the yard and away towards Ararat. It didn't steam as well as 731, but steamed well enough to send us pounding over the Strathkellar Bank and out into the moonlit countryside. The moon had risen higher and its silvery beams bathed the countryside in a delicate softness you could almost reach out and touch. When whistling for the crossings, the sound pierced the air like an audible arrow from an acoustic bow.

We met our 8.30 pm changeover at Dunkeld. It was oil-burning N470. I had been working now for almost 11 hours and was beginning to feel the pinch. Mr Lind had also been on for close to 11 hours, and the fact that we had a near full load did nothing to deter our eagerness to get to bed. N470 was soon rolling along at 40 mph on the undulating track and sounded a million dollars when urged to continue this pace uphill. It steamed quite well and we were soon rolling into the Hamilton yard. We handed the engine over to our relief and I signed off with 11 hours and 58 minutes on my time sheet.

Sleeping accommodation was in a workman's sleeping car parked in the Hamilton platform dock. It wasn't the Waldorf Astoria, but I was asleep in five minutes. I woke bleary eyed on Good Friday and barely had time to buy food from some nearby shops. Then it was back to work relieving the Hamilton yard pilot at 12.20 pm. I had been off duty for just over 11 hours. Mr Lind was again the driver and K167 the engine. As a general thing, life on a pilot was a lot easier on the fireman than on the road, particularly if the engine was hand fired.

Not today!

For a public holiday, there was an enormous build-up of freight traffic in the yard. From the time we stepped onto the footplate we worked as if we were on the main line. We pulled vast tonnages more than the length of the yard, then half-kicked and half-pushed them into a series of sidings, then repeated the process with a similar if not greater load. This required heavy steaming for extended periods, resulting in a heavy workload with the shovel. And it didn't stop. We went up and down and around that yard all afternoon. The shunters worked on both the driver and fireman's sides, so when not firing I was relaying hand signals across the cab. If there was one positive, it was the sound effects. To kick a few vehicles from the end of an 800 ton train means that for around 20 seconds the engine is worked hard, and on that afternoon it was. Many times. Moreover, getting into position to effect a kick meant blocking a main road crossing. So we would thunder down the yard over the crossing, brake hard, and on receiving the shunter's kick signal wind the reverse into forward gear and move forward following a hefty shove on the regulator, so clearing the roadway quickly. The shift lasted for seven and three-quarter hours and on signing off I was dead on my feet.

The next day I was transferred back to Ararat.

Oil-burning R class 748 and 719 stand on adjacent tracks at Hamilton loco depot. As a regular performer on the 5.30 pm Ararat–Horsham passenger, R748 was kept clean by the shed staff at Ararat. R719 was not so fortunate. (Ian Scutt)

Substituting for a rail motor, R762 waits in the Portland dock to leave Ararat with the 9.30 am to Hamilton. The fireman should have been ashamed to have that much smoke! (Geoff Oliver)

19 Portland

By 1964 Portland was becoming a busy rail centre. Export oats traffic was increasing and upgraded tracks and sidings had been put in place to improve rail facilities at the port. All freight traffic was steam-hauled and in the early 1960s the area became the exclusive province of oil burners, with oil refuelling taking place 16½ miles away at Heywood, the junction for the Mount Gambier line. Interstate traffic was also on the rise, with a daily goods train from Portland to Mount Gambier running up to six days a week, and frequently double-headed. This increase in loading was beyond the capacity of the three engine crews at Portland, and drivers and firemen from other parts of the State were drafted in to handle it. They came from Hamilton, Ararat and South Dynon. Portland North was the location of the turntable and a two-track engine shed, and all trains arrived and departed from there. Portland itself was about a mile further south and a seaside station in every sense of that term. Freight vehicles were transferred there as part of shunting moves from Portland North.

Lacking seniority, I was first in line for temporary transfers. Three of these were to Portland and I spent over nine weeks there. These comprised a few days in January 1964, a few more in May, and eight weeks in June and July of that year. I generally boarded in the railway rest huts located at Portland North, and purchased food from various local outlets. However, during the eight weeks I was fortunate to have a fortnight's accommodation in the home of a local church family.

My first job at Portland was firing for a driver from South Dynon named Henry Kakokowski. I called him Henry K, for short. We signed on at 5.30 am to run the 6.30 am goods to Hamilton, changing over with the 8.35 am ex Hamilton. Henry was only a few years my senior, spoke English with a European accent and knew what he was doing on a steam locomotive. Our engine was J547, loaded to around 300 tons. We made a vigorous start up the 1 in 52 grade out of Portland North and it soon became obvious that Henry shared my view about train running. That is, if you can run at the maximum speed, do so. And he did! We were soon rocking along at the 40 mph limit for goods trains, and with the exception of the two miles of 1 in 50 upgrade before Milltown, sat on this speed, up hill and down dale. The engine bucked and swayed and shook and rocked.

I fastened myself in the fireman's seat by placing my right elbow over the window ledge and hanging on for dear life. My left hand operated the oil control valve and atomizer, and when the injector had to go on there was a quick transfer of movements and my right hand clung to the injector steam valve.

Fortunately, J547 was equal to the task and the steam gauge needle remained between 165 and 170, not bad for the caning the engine was getting. After becoming accustomed to hanging on, I was able to pay attention to the sounds. And boy, were they any good! The exhaust blasted back over the train in a strident staccato worthy of the New York Central's 20th Century Limited.

After slowing for the staff exchange at Heywood, Henry got us moving up to 40 again in double quick time, resulting in a burst of rhythmic sound that delighted the ears. We met our changeover at Condah, 30 miles from Portland North. Here we stepped on to N497 and took the opportunity to give it a good sanding

With no one to paint their smokeboxes, both these oil-burning N class look rather forlorn as they wait for their next assignments at Portland North. (Ian Scutt)

on leaving the station. Then it was back to our 40 mph fast freight routine. 497's load was also about 300 tons. Having a trailing truck under the cab made its ride at 40 mph a little smoother than that of the J class. And it steamed well. The grades between Heathmere and Gorae required some hard working, and this in turn produced a long series of crisp sounds from the smokestack. Our arrival at Portland North was in the early afternoon, and if ever an 8 hour and 15 minutes shift seemed to end too quickly, it was this one.

Some time later, J547 and I were together again. This time it was on the 12 noon Mount Gambier. The driver was another man from South Dynon named Alan Boyd. The 12 noon was a good job. Someone else generally prepared your engine, so all you had to do was step on to the footplate 10 minutes before departure. You ran the train to Dartmoor, 42 miles 'Distant', and 19 miles from the South Australian border. At Dartmoor, you took water and changed over with the 2 pm ex Mount Gambier and ran it back to Portland North. The hours were long but convenient and the job paid well.

On this day the 12 noon was double-headed by two J class, and we were the leading engine from Portland North to Heywood. Here both engines took oil and water, and on rejoining the train first we became the second engine.

On this day, the crew on the first engine were to change over and we were to run tender-first back from Dartmoor. J547 had been sanded on the way to Heywood and was steaming well.

With a load of around 800 tons, the first portion of our journey was easy, rolling in a clitter-clatter function to Sinclair, the first station out from Heywood. The countryside began to unfold now into a series of short rolling hills, sometimes bare, sometimes wooded, and always green. The track, meanwhile, began to gradually climb, requiring the engines to be worked with increasing purpose as we progressed towards Lyons. Although speed was restricted to 25 mph, to move along at anything approaching this rate meant an increasing regulator opening

Oil-burning J541 passes under a road bridge between Portland and Portland North. (Ian Scutt)

and matching cutoff. These, in turn, produced a range of doubly pleasing sound effects because they were coming from two engines. Scenery was pleasant and wildlife plentiful. Groups of emus strutted regally through patches of bushland, sometimes looking inquisitively at the train; while kangaroos, singly, in pairs, and in families, would hop excitedly through the trees.

Soon after Lyons the grade steepened to 1 in 50 for almost two miles. J547 and its sister engine showed their mettle as they wound around curves and blasted up grade at 20 mph with throttles wide open and cutoffs lengthened. Over the grade, and there was a short downhill stretch where the engines were eased and allowed to roll on to a mile of straight and level track. They were opened up again for a final, short, uphill pinch that, once conquered, led to an eight mile roll through Greenwald and Winnap, almost into Dartmoor. This last station was reached by crossing the impressive trestle bridge over the Glenelg River and working hard up a half a mile of 1 in 50 into Dartmoor station.

After both engines had taken water, they pulled ahead from the train. J547 was uncoupled and backed into the passing loop, allowing the leading engine to back down and couple onto the load. Meanwhile, the 2 pm from Mount Gambier arrived, took water and pulled ahead to allow 547 to come onto its train. The J class on the 2 pm now backed on to 547, making it double-headed. J547 was running tender-first behind one running funnel-first, with the engines coupled together tender to tender.

It was with this combination that we rolled out of Dartmoor and over the Glenelg River towards Portland. Once over the river both engines were opened out for the mile of 1 in 50 up on the way to Winnap. The line here was quite spectacular. It featured a number of reverse curves, interspersed with two level crossings, requiring frequent whistling. Working hard up grade and winding round the curves, the tender to tender ensemble provided stirring sights and sounds as it blasted through the pleasant autumn afternoon at the head of its 600 ton plus train. Once through

Winnap, the grade again stiffened to five miles of 1 in 50 to the summit, east of Greenwald.

Running tender-first up grade meant that the water in the boiler went to the smokebox end, with the gauge glasses showing barely anything. This required the injector receiving careful attention. The impressive sights and sounds continued as the exhausts from both engines worked their way in and out of synchronization, pitting their strength against the rising grade, and winning. Kangaroos and emus were again a feature of the passing scenery. Passing through Greenwald we were soon over the top and rolling down to Lyons, with the gauge glass water levels improving dramatically. After Lyons it was mostly rolling, with the occasional minute or so of light steaming, all the way to Heywood. Here, we attached J547 to the 5.5 pm Portland–Hamilton goods, and changed over with the crew on N426 on the 4.40 pm ex Hamilton to Portland. N426 behaved itself and we were soon rolling into Portland North, where we were relieved and signed off with 10 hours and 5 minutes to our credit.

The 'down' side to Portland was the very early starts. These required one to sign on at 2.50 am, light up two engines and prepare one for the 7.20 am Hamilton. On one occasion I signed on at 2.50 am to light up J547 and J535. These were stabled in the shed at Portland North and were warm from their use the day before. In the first instance, however, this warmth was of little value. You still had to clamber over lighting-up wood piled on the footplate, check the gauge glasses, open the firebox door assembly and secure it, shine a torch through the fire hole and check the fittings in the firebox, and generally orient yourself in the darkness of a confined environment in the middle of the night. Then do it again!

While there was a water crane at Portland North, watering of engines was also by placing a shed hose in the tender when the loco was being stabled. When lighting up, you checked the tender water level and turned off and removed the hose when the tank was full. Also, before lighting up you removed the chimney cover on each engine. When the fires on both engines were well alight, one could concentrate on preparing one's allotted locomotive. On this day it was J547. I was to fire it on the 7.20 am to Hamilton, changing over along the way with the 6 am ex Hamilton. The driver was Goldwyn Patterson, known universally as Goldy. Goldy Patterson tended to take a somewhat jaundiced view of things. This was reflected in his speech, which was anything but welcoming, and in his facial expression, which was seldom smiling.

Goldy was happiest when acting as driver in charge. He did this when the usual incumbent, Jim Reid, was absent. Jim was away at this time so it was Goldy who made up the rosters and told people what to do. He had a couple of interesting characteristics. When turning a locomotive on a turntable, it was customary for the driver to get down from the cab and assist the fireman and guard. Not Goldy. He never left the driver's seat.

When running oil burners on the road, even with the best will in the world, it was not always possible to prevent the occasional fumes coming back into the cab. These were rare and soon passed. However, Goldy's dislike of them led him to fastening a handkerchief over his nose and mouth and tying it at the back of his neck, in the same manner as cowboy bandits masked their faces in the Saturday afternoon movies. He would drive like this for miles at a time, much to the amusement of anyone looking on.

In due course we moved 547 out of the shed and onto the turntable, turned it, with Goldy in the cab, and placed it on the 7.20 am to Hamilton. The load was moderate, and on completion of the brake test a long whistle heralded the guard's 'right away'. Our first stop was at the Borthwicks meatworks siding, about three-quarters of a mile from Portland North. Here, we were to set out empty refrigerated wagons and pick up those loaded. This meant leaving the train on the main line and setting back into the meatworks, picking up the loaded wagons, placing them on the train, then setting back to spot the empties. To effect these moves, the locomotive had to enter the Borthwicks building. This was equipped with a fire sprinkler system which heat from the engine's funnel would have activated. So it was, when shunting at Borthwicks, the fire was shut down and the blower turned off. You filled the boiler to near capacity and had the steam gauge right on blowing off. Shunting at the meatworks could

Although taken at Tarranginnie, between Dimboola and Serviceton, oil burners J532 and N496, coupled tender to tender, demonstrate how two J class looked at Dartmoor. (Ian Scutt)

Heading a long train of empty GYs from Portland to Hamilton, oil-burning N483 nears the end of its journey as it approaches Coleraine Junction. (Geoff Oliver)

take anything up to 20 minutes, resulting in the steam gauge showing barely 130 when you finally finished.

After the Borthwicks shunt, the additional vehicles on the train required a further brake test. Once this was completed we were on our way. After an uneventful run, we met our changeover at Heywood and climbed into the cab of J555. The shunting had been done and we were soon on our way home. There wasn't a great deal wrong with J555, but soon after leaving Heywood, Goldy brought out his handkerchief and masked up his face. This remained in place all the way to Portland North and was only removed when we were uncoupled from our train and assigned to being the yard pilot. It was now approaching midday and the last thing I wanted was to be stuck in the cab tidying up the Portland North yard. But railways do not operate to suit their employees and our pilot work lasted for one and a half hours before we were relieved. I signed off booking 10 hours and 28 minutes for the shift.

One of the drivers stationed permanently at Portland was Merv Powell. Merv was a prince among railway men. He lived at Heywood and commuted by car to work. When we ran the 12 noon Mount Gambier together we would arrive at Heywood at about 12.30 pm, take oil and water and be ready to perform any shunting around 1 o'clock; just in time for lunch. To the Victorian Railways, the luncheon menu at Heywood was shunting. To Merv, it was food. He lived close by, went home for lunch and had no qualms in delegating me to do the shunting in his absence. The guard didn't mind and I enjoyed every minute of it. Today, we had J544.

Firstly, I attended to the steam and water. The boiler would be filled to just over ¾ of a gauge glass and the injector turned off. This would knock the steam back to about 130. With the blower on at over half a turn, the oil control valve would be set to produce more smoke than usual, and the atomizer adjusted to about 40 psi. As steam pressure rose, this figure would rise. With the firing controls now at optimum settings, I settled comfortably into the driver's seat and looked out for the person organizing the makeup of our train.

'Go ahead.' The reverse went from mid gear to forward, the independent brake valve to quick release, and after a short whistle I opened the regulator. 544 moved easily down the yard until told to stop. The regulator was closed and the automatic brake valve went into a service application. On coming to a stand, the automatic brake was released and the independent brake applied.

'Back up, and kick.' The reverse went into back gear, the independent brake was released, then a short whistle and the regulator was opened firmly.

'Red light—stop.' The regulator was slammed shut and the automatic brake went into emergency for the time it took for the train to come to rest. It was then released and the independent applied. Meanwhile, the vehicles being kicked rolled away to their appointed siding. 'Set back slowly.' The independent brake was released... And so it went on, sometimes for 45 minutes; whistling, steaming, braking, up and down the yard. It was doubly enjoyable because, without making a welter of it, I had the engine sounding just the way I liked it. And it sounded superb! After the first 10 minutes, the steam gauge would show about 160 and I would ease the oil control valve back and make sure the atomizer pressure was not above 70.

In the meantime, Merv Powell would enjoy his lunch and in due course return to the engine, thank me, and take over the driver's seat. To me, it was a privilege to eat my sandwiches while being in charge of the locomotive. These interludes at Heywood were often the highlight of our trip to Dartmoor and return.

Jim Reid was the driver in charge at Portland, and while I came in contact with him on numerous occasions, I fired for him only once. This was on the 12 noon to Mount Gambier. We signed on at 11.50 am to relieve and run the banker on this train. Our engine was J553. From Portland North to Dartmoor we double-headed with J557, and from Dartmoor to Heywood we were cut in behind J559. As soon as we got going, I suggested to Jim that we sand 553. He agreed. He opened 553 out and I put 10 shovelfuls of sand through her tubes. Black smoke blanketed the countryside and steaming promptly improved. Following this, Jim eased the throttle to about three-quarters open and wound the cutoff back to what he considered an optimum setting. Having made these adjustments, he put his feet up on the firebox door, folded his hands in his lap, and when truly comfortable looked across at me and said in a half-serious, half-humorous tone, 'Great job, isn't it!' It was hard not to agree. We got on well and had a good day. He appreciated my liking steam engines, and as this one was going well he worked it hard at every opportunity. Because of the heavy load, the driver on the second engine frequently had to do the same. The resulting sound effects were exceptional and brought smiles all round, and our arrival at Dartmoor was well within the scheduled running time.

Travelling home, running tender-first behind J559 was a delight. The climb to Greenwald saw both engines working hard and close to fully extended, their staccato exhausts reverberating through the surrounding hills while beams of sunlight played hide and seek through the drifting smoke. At Heywood we detached J553 and handed it over to the crew on the 4.40 pm light engine from Hamilton. They were on J552. This became our steed for the remainder of the journey to Portland North, double-heading with J559.

A few days later my time at Portland ended and I was transferred back to Ararat.

20 Ararat Hostling

As the junior man in the shed, most of my time from Monday to Friday was spent either cleaning or hostling. The first six months of 1964 saw large amounts of wheat passing through Ararat on trains hauled almost exclusively by steam locomotives. Crews on these trains frequently worked up to 12 hours and simply dumped their locomotives at the depot before signing off. These engines needed to be serviced and prepared for further duty, and this need was met by a specific hostling crew. The depot had two drivers dedicated to hostling and they were allocated the junior fireman on their shift. Hostling shifts were 8 am, 4 pm and 12 midnight, Monday to Friday. The third hostling shift was crewed by any driver and fireman who happened to be available.

The 12 midnight shift was by far the hardest. Walking along the path to the depot, your feet crunched on the gravel in the cool night air. Passing the telephone post to notify A signal box of an engine leaving the depot, you were likely to wave to the crew of the R class on the 12.30 am Hamilton. The measured rhythm of the air compressor and the clang of the shovel as the fireman laced the firebox reinforced the fact that they were heading for the main line and you were heading for the opposite.

You signed on, repaired to the meal room for a cup of tea and met up with your mate who had the number of the first engine for the night. 'Recondition 752.'

This R class had not long come in from Geelong. Looking in the firebox you were greeted with a thick mass of glowing coals, stretching from just below the firing table all the way to the brick arch. An almost empty coal bunker revealed where this thick mass had originated. Steam was 180 and water ½ a glass. The injector was put on to raise the water level and the engine backed across the turntable and up to the water crane. The wind was just as likely to be an icy blast, so taking water could be a freezing 10 minute experience. This done, you swung down and held over the set of points leading to the coal stage. Lighting in this area wasn't exactly like Times Square, so you were careful where you walked, there being the odd fish plate, a few dog spikes and numerous pieces of coal strewn beside the track. The engine was now approaching the overhead coaling chute, so you scrambled up the wooden steps to the coal stage, called to the driver when to stop, and pulled the lever frame that sent coal into the tender. This took only a few seconds and if the wind was in the right direction you missed out on the dust. Pushing the frame shut, you trooped down the steps to the ground, walked alongside the tender on the driver's side, opened the ash pan slides, climbed into the cab and turned off the injector. The driver would have the fire doors open and the resulting glow on to the footplate made it easier to locate the grate shaker bar on the rocking levers. Left side first. You rocked the lever back and forth, pausing from time to time to peer into the firebox and check the result. It could be heavy work. If there was any clinker, your mate would deal with it using the long pricker. Now the right side. Same procedure. After shaking the grates, while most of the fire went into the ash pit, there was usually enough left around the firing table and in the back corners of the firebox to form the foundation for banking the fire. Using the shovel, and sometimes the stoker, a substantial bank of coal was placed over the remaining hot coals, then the dampers were closed and the blower

Minus its cowcatcher and headlight numbers, J548 looks a little the worse for wear as it takes oil at Ararat. (ARHS Victorian Division Archive)

shut down. If the ash pan sprinklers had been used, they were now turned off and the ash pan slides closed. The engine was then eased forward to the sanding area. You exited the cab through the door to the running plate on the fireman's side and climbed up the ladder fixed to the boiler leading to the sand box. You opened one of the two lids on this and directed sand into it from one of the suspended sand pipes, hanging on to the ladder while doing it.

Sanding complete, R752 was now driven into the shed, the hand brake put on, the air compressor turned off and the dampers closed. Steam would be around 100 and water about ⅔ of a glass. The oil containers and feeder were retrieved from the tender locker and oiling up commenced. The fireman carried out the lion's share of this. Illumination was from a kerosene-burning slush lamp, and you juggled this with the oil feeder as you undid each oil cork or attended to each trimming cup. More often than not, the oil would be cold and slow to flow, lengthening the time taken for oiling the valve motion, front and rear bogies, and tender. You thus tended to lag behind your mate, who had only to fill the hydrostatic lubricator in the cab and the mechanical lubricators, one on the driver's side running plate and one on fireman's side running plate.

He also didn't have to juggle an oil feeder and slush lamp into every nook and cranny of the unlit valve gear and whatever else you had to oil up in the middle of the night.

When the job was done, there was another engine waiting. If this was a coal-burning R class, the same process was repeated. If it was an oil burner, the procedure was a little different. After taking water, instead of taking coal and cleaning the fire, you took oil. This was done from a stand pipe, arranged so that a short hose delivered oil into the tank on the engine's tender.

The one problem was knowing just how far the oil level was from the top of the tank. In daylight, it was almost impossible to determine, and at night it was even worse. Taking oil meant you listened keenly as the oil flowed from the stand pipe into the tender tank, trying to hear when it was near the top of the tank and so turning off

Oil-burning J547 pulling loaded wagons out of the ash road at Ararat loco depot. This move was part of the tasks regularly performed by the day-shift hostling crew. (Geoff Oliver)

the oil before it overflowed. Sometimes you were successful. And sometimes, with even the keenest of attention, you were suddenly confronted with bloop, blimp, blamp blop blap blop blap blammp blomp as the oil overflowed down the outsides of the tank and into the well below as you promptly turned off the oil feed switch. Fortunately, nobody seemed to worry, so you could secure the tank lid and climb down from the tender with a clear conscience.

After taking oil, the engine was moved to the sanding area. J, K and N class had their sand boxes arranged for filling at running plate level. Oil burners, however, required additional sand. This was placed in a box in the cab, fixed in front of the oil tank. It was used for shovelling through the tubes to remove carbon deposits left by incomplete firebox combustion. Sand for tube cleaning was of a coarse grade and came from a separate sand dryer. This dryer delivered coarse sand at ground level in a 'room' attached to the sand plant beneath the coal stage. Taking the engine's bucket, you climbed down from the cab, went into this room and shovelled sand from the concrete floor into the bucket, then handed this up to your mate in the cab, who poured it into the cab sand box. This was repeated until the box was full.

With sanding complete, the engine was placed in the shed, the fire turned out, the atomizer turned off and the blower shut down. The main and intermediate oil tank valves were closed, the hand brake applied and the damper closed. Oiling up could now commence.

On occasion, you got a hostle only. This meant that oiling up was not required.

On a busy night, and the midnight shift was invariably busy, you handled six or seven engines. And this would go on from Monday to Friday.

The 4 pm hostling shift could also be severely taxing, but had the advantage of generally missing out on engines arriving late from Geelong and Hamilton.

Day shift hostling was by far the most enjoyable. You commenced at the civilized hour of 8 am and finished at the equally convenient time of 4 pm. And there was very little loco preparation. You usually only prepared the engine for the 4 pm pilot, with the shed shunt taking up most of the shift.

One would sign on at the depot at 8 am and meet up with the hostling driver. This was usually Col Stevens or Jimmy Watson. An engine from one of the overnight yard pilots would be on a turntable road and allocated as the motive power for the shed shunt. It was generally a coal-burning N or J class, or a K. An oil burner was not unheard of, but rare. We would man this engine and the day would commence. Someone from the shed would direct operations and specify each shunting movement, of which there were quite a few.

Between the ash pit roads was a downward sloping, below-ground track housing three or four open four-wheel wagons. Ash from the pits was shovelled into these, and being below ground, the shovelling effort was minimal. When full, these wagons were replaced with empties and one of the first jobs on the shed shunt was to perform this task. Next, we went to the coal stage. Empty wagons were removed from here, and trucks loaded with coal were spotted as required on the coal stage road. This occasionally took some time to enable coal unloading to take place. The loco store had its own dedicated road and we picked up the empty vehicles from this, replacing them with any wagons containing stores material, and spotting these wagons where required for unloading.

The west side of the depot housed a dedicated spur track known as the 'out' road. Any vehicles being dispatched from the Ararat loco depot were placed on here. On most days, we would transfer three or four vehicles to this road for haulage elsewhere. From here, they would be picked up by one of the afternoon pilots and included in the consist of a Melbourne-bound goods train.

The shed shunt also handled any movements required on engines or vehicles being repaired in the depot that needed to be moved to give better access for fitters effecting the repairs.

As 4 pm approached, the engine on the shed shunt would be coaled and watered, have its fire cleaned, and be oiled up in readiness for its use on the 4 pm pilot.

Each shed driver had his own set of characteristics. Col Stevens was quiet. Jim Watson had, at times, a very loud voice. If he was questioning anything, or just making fun of a situation, you could hear him halfway round the depot, saying, *'Eh, what we should arrange to be done is to ...'* He wasn't belligerent, just noisy, and generally a very good mate, particularly on day shift. His specialty was blowing short whistles. Three brief whistles would bring the turntable round to your particular road. Jim could blow for the turntable with whistles that were so precisely spaced and of such perfect pitch and volume that they were a delight to hear. Other whistles he blew while moving an engine around the depot were sounded with equal precision, economy and timing.

He also had something of a fixation with cylinder cocks. Ararat had an allocation of N class built at Newport Workshops. While these had been re-boilered, some of their fittings, such as the firebox door and cylinder cocks were of the original pattern. Thus, the firebox door was of the manual drop-down type, and the cylinder cocks were operated by a lever on the fireman's side of the cab. K class also had the same arrangement for cylinder cocks' operation. In contrast, J and N class purchased from England had air-activated cylinder cocks, operated by a short brass lever mounted adjacent to the brake pedestals in front of the driver. For much of the time, the shed shunt employed a Newport N or a K class. The cylinder cocks were thus under the control of the fireman. As soon as we got moving off the turntable, if the cylinder cocks were still open, Jim Watson would ask, 'Did you close those cocks?' 'Oh, yes Jim.' And the lever would be closed.

Sometimes, I would get in first. While standing for some time at the coal stage, the cylinder cocks would be opened. When we finally moved off, after a few turns of the wheels I would close them and there would be silence on the other side of the cab. Then there would be times after we'd been standing with the cylinder cocks open that with the first opening of the regulator would come, 'Did you close those cocks?' 'Yes Jim.' And they would be closed. These reminders didn't worry me one bit, and even though he would look rather severely in the direction of the lever on the fireman's side, the atmosphere in the cab remained uniformly cordial.

One day on the shed shunt we had N468. This coal burner was built by North British Loco and had air-operated cylinder cocks. Toward the end of the day we were engaged in moving a vehicle undergoing repairs over the drop pits inside the depot. We made a number of short moves to suit the work being undertaken and these took some time. The engine was thus standing for lengthy periods with the cylinder cocks open. In the meantime, I had to maintain steam pressure, and after placing a number of shovelfuls of coal in the firebox I placed the fire doors where they had been for some time, on the half-open notch to minimize smoke. Resuming my seat, I became conscious that all was not well on the other side of the cab. 'Can't you see you're making this too hot?' said Jim Watson, pointing to the regulator handle, which was near the half-open fire doors. 'I'm not going to work under these conditions. If you can't do better than this I'm going down to the office to get another mate!'

There was no point in explaining that I had the fire doors half open to allow secondary air to flow over the fire bed, thus providing oxygen to assist in the combustion of smoke producing volatiles and so reduce the engine's overall smoke nuisance. He should have known that, anyway. Also, the heat on the regulator handle was minimal, and no one, before or since, had ever complained about fire doors being open. Nevertheless, he was the driver.

I spoke and acted promptly. Closing the doors I said, 'I'm sorry, Jim.' And that was that. A stony silence prevailed in the cab for some minutes. Finally, we were no longer needed in the shed and were advised to depart. The reverse was wound into forward gear and the independent engine brake released. Jim blew a characteristic trademark whistle and eased open the regulator. With cylinder cocks hissing, N468 moved slowly across the turntable and out into the loco depot yard. Clear of all obstructions, he nudged the regulator open a little more and called to me, 'Did you close those cocks?' I said nothing, but gently pointed to the small brass cylinder cock lever in front of him. He glanced down. 'Oh, I'm sorry, I'm sorry,' he said with a sheepish smile and the cab atmosphere once again became most agreeable.

Both Col Stevens and Jim Watson were good mates. While Col lacked the spontaneity of Jim, for me he had one major advantage. When we were on the shed shunt, he would let me drive. And this was most enjoyable. One of the requirements was to handle the air brake in such a manner that when placing vehicles in a particular location they were placed smoothly and accurately. Judicious use of the independent brake, as well as the automatic, facilitated this. Then one could practise whistle blowing. Providing it was done advisedly, no one minded. And you could listen to the engine's sounds. You never tired of hearing the exhaust when pulling hard at 10 mph, and after coming to a stand the sound of air exhausting from the distributing valve on release of the independent engine brake was captivating. And there was nothing quite like the feel of the engine's response to the opening of the regulator. These, and a host of other locomotive nuances, contributed to the enjoyment of the occasion. And enjoyment it was. When I was enjoying myself on a locomotive it was reflected in my face and general demeanour. Col Stevens could see this and he appreciated my appreciation. Needless to say, I thanked him sincerely at the end of the day.

When firing on a pilot or out on the main line, your time accrued towards your 520 hours, this being the firing time required to be assessed as competent to fire on passenger and fast goods trains. Hostling hours, however, were not counted. So in terms of main line advancement, you were merely marking time when hostling.

Finally, another trainee engineman's class was held at Ararat, someone else became the junior man in the shed, and the likelihood of my being rostered hostling greatly diminished.

21 Pleasant Surprises

Pleasant surprises were few, but refreshing and delightful when they occurred. Two are worthy of mention.

Soon after returning from my week of relieving at Mount Gambier I was rostered for a midnight hostling shift. Arriving at the depot to sign on just before midnight, I was met by the hostling driver, a man a few years my senior named Les Swan, and Jack Costello, the night depot foreman. Jack delivered good news. 'You'll be going for a ride in a taxi to Cressy soon.'

The 6.5 pm Geelong–Ararat goods of the day that had just ended had not left Geelong until around midnight, and it had been arranged that Les Swan and I would travel by taxi and relieve it at Cressy. I climbed into that taxi with a joyful smile. Cressy was 80 miles 'Distant' and it took us two hours to arrive there. Our engine was R743 and we found it at the coal stage. Reg Boatman was the driver and Jack Thomas his fireman. They had cleaned the fire, coaled and watered their charge, and swept the footplate. They took over our taxi and went home to Ararat. We stowed our bags and I looked into the firebox. The fire was in good shape and we had just over half a glass of water.

The guard arrived and guided us through the Cressy yard and onto our train. This was mainly empty wheat trucks and weighed just over 500 tons. I had put on a good fire with the shovel and the injector had brought the water up to ¾ of a glass. Steam was close to 200. The fireman's side on this engine had its own special sound effects. The piston rod gland packing on this side was blowing badly. With every turn of the wheels the sound was huff, huff, Ssshh, huff, huff, Ssshh, huff, huff, Ssshh. Fortunately, this did not affect the engine's performance, which was otherwise satisfactory.

Also, it was not heard by the driver.

We were in possession of the staff for the Cressy–Berrybank section and a long whistle brought a green light from the guard's van and we were on our way. 743 was easy to fire. The stoker jets were well adjusted and the coal reasonable. Les Swan kept us moving at the line speed of 30 mph on the gradually rising grade, and having got used to the piston rod gland blow the exhaust sounds were excellent. The air was calm and still, accentuating the engine's acoustics. When steaming without the injector, R743 easily maintained 210 lbs of steam and a slight increase in the opening of the stoker throttle readily lifted the safety valves. With the injector on, steam pressure slowly fell to 190. By this time, however, the water level had risen sufficiently for the injector to be turned off. I considered this variation satisfactory. We were travelling on miniature electric staff and hand exchanges were made using a cane hoop. After effecting the exchange for the Berrybank–Lismore section, I resumed my seat and turned on the stoker. Coal rumbled along the stoker screw and into the firebox and smoke, but not too much, issued from the funnel. Steam sat on 210. I eased the stoker back. The engine was virtually firing itself with only minor intervention from me. This was the way they were meant to go, and this one was going well. Meanwhile, the exhaust continued to serenade the early morning air with its rhythmic staccato. And it was worth listening to, particularly when you were contributing to making it. This was railroading and the driver and I were enjoying it.

Through Lismore and on to Derrinallum. Here, we would take water and have a meal. The Derrinallum stationmaster was on hand to receive the incoming staff and Les Swan spotted the engine accurately at the water crane. The steam gauge was showing 200 and the water a shade over half a glass. I looked into the firebox. The fire was perfect. Its slope was just as it should have been. And it was as smooth as glass, with not a ripple or imperfection across the whole 42 square feet of its radiantly glowing area. I had never seen a fire like it, and I have never seen one since. I left the cab and climbed up on the tender and took water. This took about 10 minutes. Returning to the footplate, I was alarmed to find the steam gauge showing only 150. A glance into the firebox revealed why. The fire had been perfect, but it was also thin. Without fresh coal for 10 minutes its glowing surface was now 50% ash. Using plenty of blower, I put the stoker on and let it deliver coal at a fast trickle. Combustion was slow, painfully slow. A vague showing of smoke from the funnel reflected the low temperature on the grate. I turned the stoker off and carefully put coal on with the shovel. Steam had dropped to 140 and we had 20 minutes to get the engine viable for the climb away from the station. Thoughts of having a meal vanished. I had drawn Les Swan's attention to our dilemma and he now took charge. We gave the fire a slight shake and he supervised a few delicate deliveries from the stoker. After an agonizing 15 minutes, steam rose to 150. But the fire was barely three-quarters alight and in no shape to sustain steaming. While pondering our next move the stationmaster appeared alongside the cab, handed up the staff for the next section, and bade us on our way with the words, 'when you're ready'. What he really meant was, 'It's time for you to depart, now.' If we disclosed our situation we would be admitting something akin to poor engine management, if not incompetence.

Les sounded the whistle and the guard gave us a green light. There is a steady pull out of Derrinallum that does not allow for light steaming. Les opened the regulator with this in mind and with a healthy exhaust beat R743 got its train moving. After travelling about 200 yards he left the throttle, stepped into the deck and got busy with the shovel. I thought I could fire an engine until I saw him in action. He was outstanding. He had 10 shovelfuls of coal into that firebox in something like the blink of an eye. Back at the regulator, he called across to me, 'Give her one with the stoker now.' With the jets on 75 psi I opened the stoker throttle to around 70 for about 30 seconds and coal leapt from the firing table.

But it was no use. Steam dropped to 120 and three-quarters of a mile from Derrinallum station R743 pulled to a stand. We could do nothing but wait for the steam pressure to rise. Then the guard arrived. 'What's the trouble?' Les was alive to the situation. 'Air compressor,' he said, and twirled the compressor steam valve impressively. 'Looks like its okay now. So we'll only be a few minutes.' Satisfied, the guard returned to his van. Our efforts with the fire began to pay off. Within a short time, steam had risen to 160. Judging this to be sufficient, Les whistled off. The fire was now its old self. Even though the engine needed to be worked hard on the next seven miles of rising grade, using the stoker soon had the steam gauge on 210 and the safety valves lifting. We had won, and now managed to eat on the run what we had been looking forward to at Derrinallum. It was now daylight, and the steamy exhaust drifted gracefully over the trees lining the track. We went through Vite Vite, Pura Pura, and Nerrin Nerrin. Ahead now was the 12 mile climb to Tatyoon, with sections of 1 in 100. But with things back to normal these 12 miles were something of a picnic. With the steam gauge hanging around 200, 743 galloped along in fine style at close to 30 mph, with the exhaust blasting back over the train with a sound that was music to one's ears. From Derrinallum towards Ararat, the track had been upgraded and the speed limit increased to 40 mph. Following the staff exchange at Tatyoon, Les let the speed rise to 40 on the grade down into Maroona. We had been working for almost 10 hours, and after some shunting in the Maroona yard were pleased to be relieved. The morning rail motor from Portland to Ararat was now due and we used this to travel home, signing off with 10 hours and 23 minutes to our credit.

The second pleasant surprise came some months later.

I was rostered to sign on at midnight for a shift of cleaning in the shed. After signing on, I went to the meal room for a cup of tea. While drinking this, Laurie Rickard, the night depot foreman came in. 'The fireman for the banker on No. 88 hasn't turned up,' he said. 'So grab your bag, Dave, and go up to the yard and if he still doesn't turn up you run the train.' The beaming smile on my face lit up the room! Finishing my tea, I walked briskly up to the yard. No. 88 was a fast goods to Melbourne. Its booked departure time from Ararat was 10.15 pm, but frequently it did not get away until well after midnight. I found it standing near A signal box and double-headed. The leading locomotive was diesel T352, and behind this, the 'banker', R762. I climbed into the welcoming cab of the R and was greeted by Jack Jones, the driver. My first thought was that the rostered fireman would turn up and bump me off the job. Fortunately, this did not happen. No. 88 was often banked, with the banking engine coming off at Beaufort, about halfway to Ballarat, and running tender-first back to Ararat. On this pleasant autumn morning, however, we were going all the way to Ballarat. I stowed my bag and looked at the fire. It was bright, but thin. I got busy with the shovel, building up the sides and back corners, and providing some substance over the rest of the grate. With the blower adjusted, the injector went on, bringing the water up to ¾ of a glass. Steam soon rose to 180 and continued rising. I propped opened the firebox doors and checked the distribution of coal by the stoker jets. This was satisfactory. The stoker was turned off and the firebox doors closed on the hinged wedge, designed to keep them slightly apart and admit secondary air over the fire bed.

It was now well after 12.30 am. A ground disc went from red to green, then a figure descended the steps of A box with a cane hoop over his arm, walked up to T352 and handed up the hoop carrying the staff for Ararat–Buangor. We were about to depart. A long whistle from the air horn on the T class brought a green light from the van and T352 went from idle to notch 1, then notch 2. Jack Jones blew a soft whistle and eased open the regulator. With steam issuing from the cylinder cocks, 762 and 352 got their 800 ton train moving. We rolled down the grade from the yard and out onto the main line. With the water near the top of the gauge glasses and steam on 200, R762 was ready for whatever lay ahead. After running easily for a couple of miles, we came to the bottom of the six mile grade known as Mount Mistake. The T class growl became louder and Jack nudged the throttle open a little wider and lengthened the cutoff. We were doing about 35 mph and 762's exhaust hit the air with a beautifully sharp rhythm. The stoker was on, and I regulated it by watching the smoke at the funnel. Meanwhile, the steam gauge needle moved to 210, and with careful use of the stoker, sat there. As the grade steepened, the engine was worked harder and the exhaust became crisper. When the water showed ½ a glass, I put on the injector and increased the flow of the stoker. Steam dropped to a shade under 200 and remained there. R762 was a good thing. We went over the top of Mount Mistake at 20 mph and rolled rapidly down the other side. On the approach into Buangor the train was braked to 20 mph to facilitate a hand staff exchange. On 762, we simply sat back and watched them do it. This was the life! Having picked up the outgoing staff, T352 was opened up again and with our help we were soon bowling along at 45 mph towards Middle Creek. Once up to speed, the big 4-6-4 was eased to keep from going over the limit. Steam and water were easy to maintain and we were enjoying a carpet slippers ride. Middle Creek was switched out as a staff station and we rattled through at 45 mph. Soon, we were on the five mile 1 in 50 climb towards Beaufort. This was heavy pulling. The T class was soon in notch 8, and the regulator on 762 opened wide. Speed evened out at 15 mph, with the powerful exhaust beats of the R drowning out its diesel counterpart. It was an effortless performance and sounded just great.

Having steam and water to spare, I took a peek at the cutoff setting. It was a few notches off full forward gear. I ventured a suggestion. 'Could you wind her out a bit more please, Jack?' 'You want to hear her really bark?' he responded. 'Yes please.' He wound the cutoff out a couple of turns. The exhaust sharpened up magnificently and we gained a mile an hour or two in speed. For the remaining seven minutes of the climb we were treated to nothing less than a fabulous presentation of pulsating steam locomotive sounds, beautifully orchestrated in an uninterrupted symphony that was a delight to hear.

All to soon the summit was reached and we were rolling down into Beaufort. Speed was reduced to 20 mph for the staff exchange, then increased to 45 mph for the slightly undulating run to Trawalla and Burrumbeet. Trawalla was switched out and we sailed through without slowing. R762 had power in reserve, and once up to line speed had to be restrained. There was an occasional noticeable sound from the funnel as the engine was opened out to handle some minor incline. For the most part, however, we went along on a wide open regulator and six inches of cutoff, which at 45 mph was barely audible above the sound of the T class. Steam was harder to maintain when the engine was worked like this. Not that it really mattered. The steam gauge varied from 150 to 170 and this was more than adequate for the work we were doing. With 170 on the clock, I put on the injector; when the reading was down to 150 I turned it off. Steam and water were thus easily maintained. Burrumbeet was also switched out and we maintained running speed until the staff exchange at Windermere. Here, the line rose gradually over the eight miles to Linton Junction. The cutoff was accordingly wound out and once again the R class exhaust came into its own. Speed dropped to below 40 mph but the sound was still thrilling. And the steam gauge responded as well. At Linton Junction the staff was given up and we entered the double track into Ballarat. On arrival, the locomotives were detached; T352 went off to do something else and we headed to the loco depot.

Ballarat was a good depot to keep away from. If there was any work to be done, a visiting crew would be sure to do it. Arriving at the coal stage, Jack Jones used the telephone there to speak to the night depot foreman. Referring to R762, he called up to me, 'We've got to recondition it.' So at four in the morning we set about doing just that. I climbed up to take water. Ballarat was still a sizeable steam depot, but its water crane was a disgrace. To paraphrase one knowledgeable railway man's description of it, you could urinate into the tank faster than that crane could put water in it. Fortunately it wasn't raining, so I kept dry while waiting the 20 minutes for the tender tank to fill. Taking coal was next. Jack moved the engine along the coal stage and stopped it opposite one full barrow of coal, and close to another. At the back of the coal stage, and near one end, stood a small wooden building. It looked like a kind of vertical dog kennel, and gained illumination from a single electric light pole positioned close by. I had climbed up on to the coal stage and was making my way to the barrows opposite R762 when I became aware of muffled sounds coming from this building. I paused and looked around. Emerging from the gloom came a Neanderthal troglodyte figure, shuffling towards me. His nondescript clothes were solemnized by an aging felt hat, and he was equipped with the two items essential for coaling a locomotive — a notebook and pencil! He muttered something unintelligible, blinked at the coal barrows near 762, muttered something else, consulted his notebook, made a few marks in it, and shuffled back to his vertical dog kennel. It was an unforgettable three minute performance. With Jack's help, I got the coal from the two barrows into R762's bunker. Fire cleaning was next. This normally straightforward process was anything but straightforward this morning. The grates on the fireman's side were jammed. Using the fire irons, we manoeuvred the hot coals on the fireman's side over to the driver's side, and by this laborious process disposed of them. With the ash pan slides closed, and the coal stage confining our movements on one side, R762 was now oiled up. This last operation was quite miraculously achieved without anyone falling into the ash pit or tripping over whatever had been dumped beside it. We moved the engine on to the turntable in the shed and left it on a vacant stabling track. Jack delivered a Repair Card, detailing what was wrong with the grates, to the depot foreman's office and we walked briskly up to the crew meal room near the Ballarat station platform.

Following our meal, we did some shunting with a B class diesel, making up a train that no one seemed to know anything about. We were soon relieved, however, and not required to trace the train's origins or its destination. A message from Ballarat Train Control informed us that we were to run No. 9, the Melbourne–Dimboola fast goods, to Ararat, and that this would be along shortly. We were delighted. No. 9 was generally hauled by an S class diesel and ran to a strict timetable. It would get us home in no time. Soon after 7 am, No. 9 arrived with S308 on the point.

On a diesel locomotive, it was the fireman's job to check the lead seal on the air supply to the vigilance control, ensuring the air valve was always open and delivering a continuous supply of air to this safe working device. Details of this check were recorded by the fireman in the loco's log book, together with the train time and details, other locos in multiple unit if applicable, and the names of the driver and fireman. On relieving the crew on No. 9, I checked the vigilance control and made the necessary entries in the log book. We were now ready to depart. A long whistle on the air horn brought a green flag from the guard and we were away. The load was always modest on No. 9, and with lowered signal arms beckoning us on, speed was soon up to 45 mph and easy to maintain. Each staff exchange was made using the automatic apparatus and we made good time, arriving at Ararat and signing off with 8 hours and 53 minutes to our credit.

22 520 Hours

When an engine cleaner was qualified to fire, his qualification did not extend to passenger and fast goods trains. To work on these, he had first to complete 520 hours firing on everyday goods trains and yard pilots. After this, he was assessed on the road by a loco travelling foreman, and if satisfactory was passed to fire on passenger and fast goods. Much to my disappointment, hours put in firing on the Ararat shed shunt were not regarded as 'genuine' and were not included in one's overall firing tally. However, after being the junior man in the shed for over six months I finally accrued the required number of hours and was eligible to be assessed. I arrived at the shed one morning at 10 am to commence a cleaning shift. I was met by Mr Ernie Weeding, one of the depot's loco travelling foremen. 'We'll go to Buangor on the 10.55 am Ballarat goods and you can do your 520 hours', he said. I agreed immediately. Buangor was 14 miles 'Distant'. The Ballarat goods would cross No. 25, the 'down' morning passenger there, providing us with a convenient means of returning to Ararat.

We walked up to the yard. It was a sunny morning, and while a little nervous I was also optimistic. The 10.55 am Ballarat was loaded to something less than 200 tons and headed by oil-burning N class, number 498, in charge of driver Charlie Aggett. The fireman was temporarily relocated to the guard's van and I took over his duties. I brought the steam around to 180 and the water to ¾ of a glass, adjusting the oil control valve and blower to keep the engine simmering at that pressure. The footplate was then swept clean, and as departure time approached signals were pulled off, admitting us to the main line. The A box signalman arrived with the staff for Buangor, and I called the station names on it before handing it to Charlie Aggett. It was 10.55 am.

A long whistle brought a green flag from the guard which I acknowledged with the 'alright' hand signal, at the same time calling, 'right away'. Charlie blew a short whistle, released the independent engine brake and opened the regulator. Steam hissed from the cylinder cocks and N498 eased out onto the main line. As we cleared the yard, a green flag came from the van, signalling all clear from the guard. 'Green flag from the van.' Charlie nodded and sounded a short whistle, at which the green flag was withdrawn. Mr Weeding stood in the gangway on the fireman's side, observing what was going on. With a light load and easy schedule, N498 was not hard to fire. It was, however, an oil burner. And oil burners need sanding. I crossed the cab and mentioned this to the driver. He agreed. We were working slightly uphill and the time was ideal. I eased the atomizer and oil control valves back and lifted the heavy fire door. The usual procedure in sanding an oil burner was to fully open the fire door and secure it open with a metal pin provided for the purpose. There was, however, a small flanged extension piece on the right-hand side of the fire door. This accommodated the metal pin and allowed the door to be opened and secured halfway. In this position there was less chance of blow backs from the firebox entering the cab. The opening for the shovel to deliver sand was quite restricted on the halfway setting and required more skill and accuracy than that needed for a door wide open. I had tried the halfway setting a few times with varying success. So the wisest course of action would be to open the fire door wide and use the proven method.

But if I could pull it off halfway on my 520 hour exam, that would be impressive.

So in order to impress, I secured the door on the halfway flange. Charlie raised the regulator to the roof and 498 responded with a pounding exhaust. I took the shovel out of the sand box on the tender, scooped up some sand and shot it at an angle into the firebox. Black smoke from the funnel showed that the sand was doing its job. I put a second shovelful through, then a third, then a fourth, each time with excellent coordination. Smoke continued to pour from the funnel. I swung the sand for the fifth time. The shovel hit the firebox apron with a loud clang and sand coated the cab floor. Undeterred, I scooped up more sand and turning to deliver it felt a tap on my shoulder. It was the foreman. I had come unstuck. 'Don't do it that way,' he said. 'Do it like this.' And lifting the fire door, he secured it fully open and sent five or six shovelfuls of sand through the tubes with demonstrable effect. He replaced the shovel in the sand box and closed the door. 'Do it that way,' he said and resumed his position in the gangway behind me.

With her tubes now clear, the needle on 498's steam gauge zoomed round the dial in effortless fashion. It was soon close to blowing off and I had no trouble in keeping the water level satisfactory. Making good use of the Bannister brush, I swept up the spilt sand and tried to go about what I was doing as if nothing had happened. The forgoing events had occupied about three minutes, and with the evidence of my minor mishap now gone the atmosphere in the cab was, fortunately, as if nothing had happened. The one thing noticeable on the footplate was the characteristic smell of oil, common to all oil burners. Two-thirds of the way to Buangor there is a four mile grade, much of which is at 1 in 50. Charlie opened her out a little here, and with no shortage of steam we went up that grade and over the top at close to 30 mph with a near clear funnel and a resounding exhaust. The regulator was closed and we rolled easily down into Buangor. We were signalled into No. 2 road. I handed the staff down to the stationmaster who was on the ground as we passed the station platform. Charlie Aggett brought the train to a smooth stop. With both steam and water in good shape, I collected my kitbag from its place on the tender, adjusted the atomizer and oil control valves, thanked Charlie for his support and followed Mr Weeding in climbing down from the cab. On the platform, we could hear staff instruments in use, followed by the sounds of signal and point levers as preparations were made to receive the 'down' passenger train. This soon arrived and we climbed aboard. After we found ourselves a comfortable seat, I asked the burning question, 'How did I go?' 'Oh, you made it alright,' said Mr Weeding, and this left me on something of a high for the rest of the day. I could now be rostered on fast goods and passenger trains.

23 Variations to Cleaning

Being the junior man in the shed meant it was always on the cards that I would be rostered for cleaning. And so from time to time I was. Cleaning in its purist form meant one of three things; cleaning locomotives, cleaning out inspection pits or sweeping shed floors. In busy times, when engines were regularly coming and going from the depot, a cleaning shift could translate to operating the turntable for the full eight hours.

If you were cleaning, you were available for just about any task that needed an extra pair of hands. One afternoon, a GY vehicle full of bulk wheat developed a hot axle box on an 'up' train and had to be set out at Stawell. The next day, one of the shed staff experienced in these things was sent to Stawell to grease pack the hot box to enable it to be safely moved. He needed an assistant. I was on day shift and cleaning. Approaching lunchtime, Bob Cluff, the depot sub-foreman, said, 'David, you can go to Stawell with Syd Smart and help him with that hot box.'

We lugged two heavy hand-operated mechanical jacks on to the footplate of an engine that was going up to the yard. On arrival, we somehow transferred them on to the station platform. Here we had lunch and waited for the early afternoon Dimboola passenger that was to convey us. The jacks were placed in the guard's van and we accompanied them to Stawell. Another mammoth effort took them from the station platform to the GY on a vacant road in the goods yard. After making sure the hand brake was on, each jack was placed on one side of the coupler beam adjacent to the axle with the hot box. The jacks were then used to lift that end of the vehicle off its springs, enabling the journal bearing to be inspected. This had minimal damage and was replaced. The damaged wool pads and wooden wedges were now removed and the axle box interior thoroughly cleaned out. We had brought a heavy parcel of grease that resembled thick plasticine and this was now pushed and prodded into every nook and cranny of available space, up to and level with the journal bearing. This meant it surrounded the lower half of the machined journal. A wooden mallet was used to hammer the grease into the axle box casing, ensuring it was chock-a-block full. On achieving this, we closed the casing cover. The vehicle could now run. Heat from the contact of the journal with its bearing would melt the grease and provide a film of lubrication for the moving parts until new oil-soaked wool pads and wedges to hold them in place could be fitted. We lowered the GY onto its springs and removed the jacks, transporting them to the Stawell station platform to await the arrival of the guard's van on the afternoon 'up' passenger train. This returned us to Ararat at 4.20 pm. Arrangements were made for the jacks to be returned to the depot and I signed off with half an hour's overtime to my credit.

On another occasion, on arriving at the shed for a day shift of cleaning, the depot sub-foreman said, 'David, you can do the shunting today.' The crew on the shed shunt for that day were from the goods roster. How they finished up on that job I never found out but the driver, Glen Corbett, was an absolute gem and I was fortunate to have him. He was patient and forgiving to the nth degree. His engine was an oil-burning J class. Our first task was to clear the trucks full of ash from the ash road, and replace them with empties. When the empties were in place, I placed the ash trucks

In May 1964 the ARHS organized a trip to Bolangum. Their nine-car, 410 ton train was drawn by two R class, seen here approaching Ararat from Melbourne. (Ian Scutt)

With rear-end assistance, R761 heads the ARHS Bolangum special away from Ararat. (Ian Scutt)

on the out road for removal later that day by one of the afternoon pilots. Next came the coal stage. Empties from the previous day had to be removed, and five newly arrived loaded trucks, delivering some 100 tons of coal, spotted in their place. This took some time. Finally, the five loads were in place and their hand brakes were secured. The empties now had to be transferred to the out road. However, this relatively simple move had been blocked by the late arrival of a truck loaded with a number of wheel sets, to be delivered to the loco store road. Before any moves could be made, this wheel sets vehicle had to be moved from where it had been left standing, blocking the exit and entry to the loco yard. Why the pilot engine that delivered those wheel sets didn't place them directly on the stores road remains a mystery. My problem was to get them in a position where my shed shunt loco could run around them, back on, then pull and push them to their destination. And do this without disrupting other shunts and transfers. The only way to do this involved placing the wheel sets temporarily on the out road, so other things could be attended to, clearing the entrance to the stores road, and enabling the wheel sets to be correctly delivered. I no sooner had the wheel sets sitting on the out road than who should come along but Mr Jack Irons, the depot foreman. 'What are those wheels doing on the outs?' he called out to me. I had had enough of those wheels. My explanation was polite, brief, and to the point. He accepted it, and 15 minutes later had the satisfaction of seeing the items in question spotted in the correct location at the loco store. This was a load off my mind and fortunately the rest of the day was uneventful.

Two of the Ararat shed staff were permanently assigned to lighting-up duties. They would light up engines from cold and attend to the fires of locos in steam, waiting for their next turn of duty. Sometimes, with only a few engines in the shed, their task was easy. On other occasions, such as from 4 pm to midnight, they would have 12 to 14 charges to look after. When a coal burner had a heavily banked fire, smoke would ooze out of the funnel and sometimes blow around the shed, bringing with it its sharp, acrid smell, letting everyone know they were in a locomotive depot. Oil burners were a little better. They produced smoke when lit up, but when shut down, their funnel was clear. Each lighter up worked one shift. But there were only two of them, and as the depot operated on three shifts, one was always without a lighter up. This meant that someone

At Ararat, the leading engine on the ARHS Bolangum special was attached to the rear and banked the train up the 1 in 50 to the 'Stop' board on the way to Armstrong. Here it was detached, with the R on the front being easily capable of taking the train on to Lubeck, junction for the line to Bolangum. (Ian Scutt)

On arrival at Lubeck, coal-burning N428, running funnel-first, replaced the R at the front of the ARHS Bolangum special. It is seen here prior to its tender-first departure on the return journey from Bolangum. (Ian Scutt)

This is the turntable at Horsham; not quite long along enough for R720. (Ian Scutt)

else in the shed would be assigned to this task for the duration of their shift. It fell to me on more than one occasion. On arriving one morning for a day shift of cleaning, the relieving depot foreman, Mr David Robinson, said, 'David, you can be the lighter up today.' This was a step up from cleaning and, as a general thing, more agreeable. There were only two or three engines in the shed to attend to, and another two or three that would arrive later, one of which would be the engine for the Peanut.

I soon had the engines in the shed 'blown around' and, with a subsequent good conscience, joined the fitters and other shed staff in the meal room for morning tea. After this leisurely break, I once more checked on my charges in steam. Having brought each one round to almost blowing off, I decided to take a break. A GY vehicle delivering firewood, and with two doors open, was parked on a vacant track in the depot. I climbed in and found a cosy spot. I was just getting comfortable when I heard the voice of David Robinson. 'Has anyone seen Barnett, the lighter up?' I heard his footsteps fading away as he pursued his search. I slipped out of the GY and in 30 seconds crossed his path. 'You were looking for me?' 'Yes, such and such is going to run the Peanut. When it comes in, be sure and ...' So followed some advice on what had to be done with the engine for the Peanut. There was, fortunately, no question such as, 'Where have you been?' or 'Where were you?'

The depot's overhead concrete coal stage had four discharge chutes and the machinery elevating coal to service them was substantial. It was accommodated as part of the coal stage structure and housed within the upper levels, with access via an external staircase on the structure's western side.

Inside the machinery space were huge belts, pulleys, gear wheels and other mechanical paraphernalia used for conveying coal. They were accessed by a labyrinth of narrow stairways, walking platforms, doorways and handrails, all located within gloomy areas of minimal lighting and constant noise. And they needed lubrication. There were a variety of bearings on different levels in difficult locations requiring constant attention with oil or grease. They were attended to by one Vincent Smith. He was one of those characters the like of which shall never be seen again, now that elevated coal stages at railway locations are a thing of the past.

Vin Smith was of medium build and slightly below average height. His features were rather solemn and just a little severe. At times, however, they could become quite scholarly. He was single, probably in his mid-fifties, and rarely missed a day at work. His attire was an old grey pattern sports jacket, dark coloured trousers and a grey gentleman's hat. At a few minutes to nine each morning he would descend from his mechanical eyrie, and carrying his enamel mug would walk in a kind of one-man ecclesiastical procession past the turntable and inside the shed to the meal room. Here he would find himself a seat, sit down, take off his hat and place it on the table. With deliberate movements, he would then make his way to the hot water urn and having placed tea leaves in his mug would fill it with hot water. Processing back to his seat, he would place his mug on the table, make himself comfortable, and produce an orange from his jacket pocket. This he would peel with scholarly skill and consume with measured precision. He would then slowly drink his tea, at the same time participating in whatever conversation was taking place, making definitive and categorical statements that would have been at home at the United Nations. And he was well read.

I would sometimes put forward to him philosophical or biblical ideas and support them by referring to specific authors. He would reply with scholarly statements from the works of writers that he had obviously studied, usually with his features exhibiting the look of a scholar reminiscing his far away past. When morning tea was over, he would carefully collect his orange peel, rise from his seat, pick up his mug and move to the hot water urn, depositing the orange peel in the rubbish bin on the way. With the tea leaves rinsed from his mug, he would retrieve his hat, place it on his head in the manner of the learned classes, bid a refined farewell and retrace his one-man ecclesiastical procession from the shed to the coal stage, there to keep this vital depot item in smooth working order.

These events occurred three times a day; at morning tea, lunch, and afternoon tea, in rain, hail or shine! Those that knew him told me that it was only after consuming a fair amount of whisky on Saturday night that he would feel 'civilized'.

One afternoon after lunch I was sent to the coal stage to help Vin with what he was doing. We left the meal room together and he accompanied me climbing the exposed stairs to reach the top of the concrete building, and led the way through a small door that opened into an area of clanks, knocks, grinds, bangs and the slap of giant belts against huge pulleys that characterized the workings of the elevating machinery. We proceeded past various shafts supporting an array of rotating masses that creaked, groaned and vibrated and came to a small elevated store area that was home to the lubricants. Vin made a selection, some of which I carried, and we commenced work. We navigated our way over a number of levels, stopping at every nook and cranny to deliver oil or grease into shaft bearings and other items. You had to tread carefully here, watch out there, hang on somewhere else, don't bump your head on this, don't upset that, back in here then you'll be able to walk out, careful not to slip on that, and don't lose your balance here! In oiling something, you frequently looked down through bits and pieces of planking to ground level, with just a worn floorboard or two keeping you up where you were. I found locomotive cabs and footplates much more preferable. We finally came back to the small lubricant store. It was 2.55 pm and afternoon tea was at 3 o'clock. A couple of bearings that had yet to receive oil were close by. We inspected them. It would have taken no more than 60 seconds to attend to both, but Vin had a rigid system of priorities. 'We haven't got time for those now,' he said. 'I'll do those later.' So we made our way down the outside stairs, around the turntable and through the shed to the meal room for a cup of afternoon tea.

24 Working Four Shifts: Early

Early shift covered the period from 12 midnight to 8 am. On finishing an early shift, discipline was essential. It was easy to forget one's weariness and treat the daylight hours as normal. If you did, you paid for it on your next shift. You needed to sleep during the day in order to stay awake on the job in the early hours of the morning. Fortunately, I had no trouble sleeping during the day. You usually ate at breakfast and the evening meal, while 'lunch' was around 3 am to 4 am. It could be very cold in winter and played havoc with your social life, if you had one.

One summer morning I signed on in the yard at 12.25 am, to relieve and run the 12.35 am Hamilton. The engine was R762 and the driver Bob Quinlivin. Our load was 650 tons, the through load for an R from Ararat to Hamilton. All went well till we got to Maroona. Here, a simple shunting move became a major mishap. While setting back, a rail broke under the leading tender bogie, derailing it. Fortunately we were travelling very slowly and an emergency brake application stopped us almost on the spot. The derailment gang was promptly called out and they soon arrived, under the leadership of the Ararat sub-foreman Bob Cluff. In two hours they had us back on the track, with the assurance that 'that engine's all right.' So we could proceed. And we did. However, on the short climb out of Maroona the air compressor stopped, the brakes came on and the engine pulled to a stand. Picking up the hammer, I exited the cab through the narrow door leading to the running plate, proceeded along it, manoeuvred around the smoke deflector, narrowly avoided being scalded on the smokebox, and kneeling down beside the air compressor used the hammer to deliver a few wake-up calls to the compressor head. It started pumping air again and the brakes came off. Back in the cab, steam and water were plentiful and Bob Quinlivin tried to get us under way. But to no avail. R762 sat there. There was no movement and no wheel slip. So we set back into Maroona. While the steam gauge was healthy, the boiler wasn't. It had been showing signs of priming and a carry over of water was undoubtedly one of the reasons why the air compressor stopped. Before leaving Maroona for the second time, in order to reduce foaming in the boiler, I kept the steam at just on 200 and the water level as low as possible. This would enable us to make a vigorous start and minimize priming. Bob Quinlivin thought otherwise. 'Keep her blowing off, won't you', he said. I thought this most unwise but did what I was told. So with safety valves lifting, a long whistle brought a green light from the guard and we were soon pounding out of the yard. We got about half a mile. R762 frothed and bubbled, foamed and groaned and spumed and spluttered as the boiler let go all its impurities into the main steam pipe, through the super heater elements, into the cylinders and finally, out the funnel.

Once again the engine pulled to a stand. And once again we set back into Maroona. Our load was reduced to 400 tons and the boiler given a good blowdown. I was given time to get the steam and water back to acceptable levels, and when all was ready we tried again. This time, with careful management, and at least some of the impurities gone from the boiler, we made it comfortably. From then on, 762 generally behaved itself. Its performance at Maroona, however, had consumed a lot of water, making it necessary to take water at Willaura, something not normally done with an R class. With the tender replenished and steam and water levels high, we left Willaura in a positive mood. It was now after 8 am and with the countryside bathed in sunshine we covered the next 12 miles to Glenthompson without incident, sometimes reaching 40 mph. Here we were placed in No. 2 road, and on surrendering the staff were told we would be relieved by a Hamilton crew, arriving on the 8.30 am Hamilton–Ararat rail motor, and that we would travel home on this. I swept the cab clean, turned on the injector till the water showed ¾ of a glass and laced the firebox with the shovel to bring the steam round to 200. At the sound of the rail motor's air horn we left 762 and walked to the platform. After a brief exchange of information with the relieving crew, we climbed aboard. Our journey to Ararat was pleasant and we signed off at 10.25 am, 10 hours after signing on.

Not all jobs involved engines with reluctant air compressors and priming boilers. The express goods train to Adelaide was known as the Jet. It ran at 60 mph to a near passenger train schedule and was handled by senior crews from Ararat and Dimboola. It was hauled by two S class diesels and loaded to a maximum of 1300 tons. And it was popular. So popular that it sometimes required a second division to handle extra loading. A second division was handled by any crew that happened to be available. So on one early shift I was rostered to sign on at 12.50 am to relieve and run the 1 am fast goods to Dimboola. This proved to be the second division of the Jet. It comprised B84 with the moderate load of 540 tons. My driver was Eric Mason. The signalman from Ararat B box had brought the Ararat–Stawell staff over to the platform where we were standing. The staff was strapped in a pouch attached to a cane hoop, which also had a metal auto exchange ring attached to it. In keeping with the custom, I wore the cane hoop round my neck, thus making it easier to climb into the diesel's cab. It was a crisp and chilly morning. When the incoming crew stepped onto the platform, we lost no time in taking advantage of the warm cab they had just vacated. I hung the staff on the two vertical sun visors, mounted either side of the central windscreen pillar. Opening the door into the nose, I checked the seal on the vigilance control. Finding it intact, I closed the door and reached for the log book. Into this were entered, 'vigilance control checked and working okay', the train time and details, and crew names. In the background, the GM-EMD, 567C diesel engine idled away in a reassuring manner.

From time to time its sound was supplemented by the dull metallic tinkle of the three-stage Gardener Denver air compressor automatically cutting in and out. Replacing the log book, I picked up the hand lamp and awaited our departure. A long blow on the air horn brought a green light from the guard which I acknowledged in kind from the cab. The independent brake was released and the throttle advanced to 1, then 2, and so on up to notch 8. As the train cleared the platform, a further green light from the guard indicated all was well and again it was answered. I wound up the cab door window on the driver's side, from where the hand signals had been given, replaced the hand lamp and sat down. The vigilance control began to hiss. I pressed the button to cancel it and was rewarded with the characteristic SSsssPpitSShhsssas as I did so. Meanwhile B84 was accelerating up the grade away from Ararat. We were soon rolling along at a mile a minute, down the eight mile, 1 in 100 grade, through Armstrong to Great Western. Speed was reduced to 20 mph through Stawell for the hand staff exchanges. The incoming staff was surrendered at A box and that for Glenorchy picked up from B box. Back to 60 mph again and the majority of the staff exchanges now used the automatic apparatus. The brilliant headlight penetrated the darkness for about a mile ahead, and it was now merely a matter of pressing the vigilance control, attending to the automatic staff exchanger and sitting back and enjoying the ride. We made excellent time to Dimboola and our relief crew was waiting on the platform. Our next task was to proceed to the warm and snug Dimboola signal box and await the arrival of train No. 10, the Melbourne-bound Overland. We were in good company here, joining the crew who would run No. 10 to Ararat and chauffer us home. This they did, while we relaxed in a cosy and comfortable passenger car and were being paid for the privilege.

Steam engines came into their own on brisk

autumn mornings. The reassuring warmth when you climbed up into the cab was natural; on other types of motive power it was artificial. It was on a still autumn morning that I signed on at 12.25 am in the yard to relieve and run the 12.35 am Hamilton. Tom Finlay was the driver, and R706 the engine with a load of 43 vehicles for 640 tons. The crew who prepared the engine had left it standing at the head of the train, and Tom and I climbed into the cab. The atmosphere was one flavoured with hot oil, and this added to the embracing warmth that greeted our entry. The air compressor, working with a full main reservoir, sent out its intermittent rhythm, while the turbo generator serenaded us with its melodic, twangy hum. Everything seemed in order. Then I took a closer look at the gauge glasses. The water behind them had a decidedly dirty appearance. I drew this to the driver's attention and suggested we blow 706 down. He agreed. The engine was fortunately standing far enough away from buildings and other rolling stock to allow the boiler blowdown valves on each side to be partially opened. It was too dark to recognize any impurities that were blown down, but the process was continued until the water level was near the bottom of the gauge glasses. We still had a few minutes before departure, and with the steam pressure satisfactory, I put on both injectors to bring the water level up, so a second blowdown could be carried out. A fair shot from the stoker kept the steam pressure at a respectable level. Both injectors soon had the water level replenished, and on turning them off both blowdown valves were again opened.

As departure time was approaching, only a limited amount of water could be discharged.

Nevertheless, when the valves were closed and the gauge glasses tested, the water visible seemed to have improved in quality. Then another problem became evident. On looking into the firebox, I found that on using the stoker to keep the steam pressure respectable, most of the coal had gone on to the grate, but a fair amount had banked up at the back of the box, just in front of the firing table. The signalman now arrived with the Ararat–Maroona staff, signifying it was time for us to leave. The obligatory long whistle brought the obligatory green flag and we were soon rolling out of the Ararat yard. Steam was sitting on only 150, but that was enough to get us moving. I put a fire on with the shovel, then used the stoker, keeping the jet pressure at 125 psi. This proved satisfactory. Coal spread evenly over the grate and did not bank up. Steam pressure soon rose and by the time we reached Maroona, water was at ¾ of a glass. While here, the engine was blown down again. It had steamed reasonably well on the way to Maroona, but past experience dictated that we take no chances. In the event, 706 was untroubled leaving Maroona. It steamed well and handled its 640 ton load with little effort. Keeping the stoker jet pressure at 125 psi, I had no trouble with coal banking up and the engine steamed well all the way to Hamilton. Before leaving R706 in the Hamilton yard, a check in the firebox revealed the fire to be in good shape.

Here we changed over with the 4.50 am Hamilton–Ararat goods, in charge of R742 with 43 vehicles and a load of 403 tons.

Steam and water were well up on 742, and the body and slope of the fire seemed just right. With the staff on board we were soon under way and tackling the four miles of 1 in 50 grades leading out of Hamilton. The fire might have looked fine in the yard, but out on the road it didn't produce a great amount of heat. With three tons over the full load, Tom Finlay was using a long cutoff and a wide open regulator. In these circumstances, an R class steam gauge needle usually moves rapidly upward. Not this one. To get the needle to move up at all was an effort. And when it did, it was painfully slow. The stoker seemed to be spreading the coal evenly over the fire bed, but just in case it wasn't, I used the shovel to deliver coal to where I thought it might be lacking. This improved things somewhat and steam reluctantly hovered near 200. Meanwhile, R742 was blasting its way up the 1 in 50 at a constant 20 mph, the exhaust echoing around the moonlit countryside. I would have loved to have put my head out the window and listened. But I was too occupied working out how I was going to get water into the boiler without sacrificing steam pressure. When I finally did put the injector on, the steam slowly fell back to 170. We couldn't afford to lose any more and I turned the injector off. With the four miles of 1 in 50 behind us, the cutoff was wound back on a level two mile section. This respite was only temporary. Ahead was the nine miles to Dunkeld, of which rising grades occupied seven. It was the classic three-way battle. The regulator wanted steam, the steam gauge was slow in providing it, and the gauge glasses wanted water. Without any alternative, the best thing to do was to continue doing what I was doing. At least this gave us hope with the steam, but what about the water? The engine wasn't steaming well enough to leave the injector on for the time needed to replace the water being evaporated, so the water level was slowly going down. Nevertheless we pressed on. The driver was aware of my predicament and was now working 742 with kid gloves. We made Dunkeld with 170 lbs of steam and about an inch of water in each gauge glass.

The only thing I could think of doing was cleaning the spark arrestor. Tom Finlay agreed, and taking the spark arrestor cleaning tool, the heavy shifting spanner and the slush lamp I proceeded to do just that. While I was thus engaged, Tom Finlay had been looking in the firebox. On my return, he said he found the fire very thick. This was part criticism and part observation. He had, however, a most acceptable method of dealing with this situation — he was going to fire and he motioned me into the driver's seat. I was delighted and surveyed my new surroundings. The headlight switch was on 'Dim'. The cylinder cocks were open, the automatic brake valve was in release, the independent brake valve applied, and the reverse in full forward gear. Resting in the brackets provided above the driver's window sat the staff for the section to Glenthompson. Tom got busy with the fire. He used the stoker, restricting the jet pressure to 50 psi. The steam gauge needle climbed. When it approached 200, he put on the injector and brought the water up to just over ¾ of a glass. This knocked the steam back and it took five or six minutes to bring it up to 210. This achieved, he called 'right ho'. I pulled the whistle cord. A green light appeared from the guard on my side of the train. I acknowledged it with a short whistle, released the independent brake, eased open the throttle and moved the headlight switch to 'Full'. Steam hissed from the cylinder cocks and R742 moved away from Dunkeld. With cylinder cocks closed we had a brief roll down grade before beginning a five mile climb on grades varying from 1 in 60 to 1 in 120.

We were doing about 30 mph. I wound the cutoff back to between 9 and 12 inches and eased the regulator wide open. The exhaust hit the still air in a delightful staccato. A level crossing appeared in the headlight beam and I warned it of our approach with practised professional flourishes on the whistle. Speed remained just below 30 mph, with 742 really getting the bit between her teeth. At the top of the grade I closed the regulator and we rolled down grade for a mile and a half. Speed rose and I made a light service brake application to keep the speed recorder on 40 mph. Once on the level, I wound the reverse to just inside 9 inches and with the regulator wide open we sat around 40 for about four miles, with the cutoff being adjusted to suit the speed. Level crossings kept coming and each one enjoyed the challenging chime of our whistle. Tom Finlay was on top of the firing. Since leaving Dunkeld, the steam gauge had rarely fallen below 190 and was mostly around 200. And this was done without sacrificing water, with gauge glass readings being consistently above half.

In darkness, when an engine is constantly steaming, it is well nigh impossible to look into the firebox. Opening the fire doors reveals a blinding white glare from which one has to immediately look away. So Tom was relying on the steam gauge and the funnel to assess how combustion was progressing, and as the steam gauge testified it was progressing quite well. Approaching Glenthompson, I dimmed the headlight, reduced speed to 20 mph, exchanged the staff, called Glenthompson–Willaura across the cab, placed the staff in its carrying bracket, put the headlight back on full and went working steam. The next nine miles were largely level and 40 mph was again readily maintained. We were making good time. The down and up grades near Willaura were comfortably negotiated and I was soon exchanging the staff at this station. Maroona was next. By now I had thoroughly settled into the driver's seat. It was as easy as ABC to have the regulator fully open and drive using the cutoff, with the occasional independent brake application to bring speed down, or use of the automatic equipment when approaching a staff exchange station. There were a couple of noticeable grades near Maroona, and when speed fell to around 20 mph on these I wound the cutoff out and we had two two-minute episodes of lively exhaust beats. About a mile from Maroona, Tom Finlay motioned me to come to the fireman's side and he took over the driving. I had very little to do as we were rolling downhill and I was soon delivering the staff to the Maroona SM (stationmaster). As he didn't hand us an outgoing authority, it was obvious we were there for some time. It was now daylight. Tom brought the train to a stand and I examined the fire. It was flat rather than sloping, with obvious clinkering at the front. I gave it a thorough shaking and raked over the remaining coals to restore the slope. I then flushed the ash pan. The fire was now lighter and much brighter.

I put the stoker on, using only 50 psi of jet pressure. Smoke rose from the funnel and the steam gauge quickly followed suit. The injector brought the water level up to ¾ of a glass, and with the thinner fire I had no trouble in getting the steam to sit on 210. The SM now arrived with the staff for the section to Ararat. A whistle, a green flag from the van, and we were on the last leg of our journey. On these final 12 miles, R742 performed in copybook fashion. Using 50 psi of jet pressure, it was fingertip firing all the way. The steam gauge sat comfortably on 210 and water was never a problem. We stormed up the grade into Ararat yard as a fitting climax to a job well done. 742 was handed over to our relief and we signed off with 8 hours and 38 minutes on our time sheet.

25 Working Four Shifts: Day

On day shift, your morning and evening meals could usually be eaten at normal serving times. Also, if you wanted to go and see a film on Friday or Saturday night, you usually could. In the railway world, day shift brought the nearest thing to working 'normal' hours.

One pleasant summer Saturday, I signed on in the Ararat yard at 7.50 am to relieve and run the 8 am Geelong. Ron Miller was the driver and R724 the engine. The fire on 724 looked to be in good shape, with satisfactory body and slope. I built up the back corners with the shovel, then used the stoker. The steam gauge responded and the injector soon brought the water up to ¾ of a glass. I had just finished sweeping the cab floor when the A box signalman arrived with the staff to Maroona. The appropriate whistle produced the required green flag from the van, and Ron Miller eased R724 and its 800 ton load past the starting disc signal and out onto the main line. Our trip to Maroona was uneventful, with steaming requirements being minimal. We went through here under clear signals, and once the hand staff exchange was completed Ron widened the throttle and lengthened the cutoff to get us moving for the 1 in 100 grades towards Tatyoon.

With the exhaust now audible, I put the stoker on, saw smoke appear at the funnel and observed the steam gauge. It was sitting on 170 and didn't move. I increased the stoker throttle opening and coal rumbled purposefully into the firebox. This should have resulted in a definite darkening of the smoke; instead the difference was only marginal. 'Get some black smoke out of her, Dave,' came from the driver. I answered honestly, 'I'm trying, Ron.' He left his seat and motioning me to turn off the stoker, opened the firebox doors. 'Here,' he called, and I left my seat and joined him. With the throttle open, the exhaust still pounding away and the steam gauge reading 165, he pointed to the front of the grate. 'You're working with only half a fire,' he said. 'The front half is clinkered up.'

He was right. I retrieved the long pricker from the tender and got busy on the clinker. Fortunately, it broke up quite easily and use of the grate shakers dispatched it to the ash pan. I replaced the pricker, and with the steam now on 150, got busy on the stoker. The difference was remarkable. Smoke of the right colour and volume immediately appeared, and steam pressure climbed. By this time the exhaust was a rasping crackle as the cutoff was gradually wound out to handle the three miles of 1 in 100. Speed dropped from 35 mph to just over 20. The staff exchange at Tatyoon was made at this speed and this brought us to the final three-quarters of a mile of 1 in 100. The regulator went to the roof and on a long cutoff R724 blasted away from the station, the funnel almost clear, steam on 210 and water near the top of the glass.

We rolled and drifted most of the way to Derrinallum, where we found our changeover waiting. This was R763 on a long string of empty GYs. We cleaned the fire and took water on 724, then took over our new engine. The cab had been swept clean and the fire, having just been cleaned, was in good shape. Water was over half a glass and steam on 180. I gave the fire a liberal sprinkling with the shovel to keep it alive while we had lunch, and having boiled the billy, settled down to eat. We were soon suitably fortified and I brought the steam around to 210 and put on the injector. The SM arrived with the staff and we got

Even without its cowcatcher, oil-burning J549 makes a fine sight as it lifts a train of empty GY wheat vehicles up the 1 in 50 grade away from Ararat towards Murtoa. (ARHS Victorian Division Archive)

J544 performs pilot work at the 'down' end of Ararat yard. (ARHS Victorian Division Archive)

under way, facing 12 miles of 1 in 100 up grade to Tatyoon.

With a clean fire and about 400 tons behind it R763 steamed well and we made the most of it. To get anywhere on a 1 in 100 grade your engine had to be worked purposefully. Accordingly, we were soon pounding along, speed sometimes hitting 30 mph, not much smoke from the fire, and the exhaust a magnificent staccato for mile on mile. Steam never dropped below 200 and water a comfortable ⅔ to ¾ of a glass. It was fingertip firing all the way. Slowing for hand staff exchanges meant that, once completed, the engine came into its own as it was opened up and thundered away from the station.

Once past Tatyoon, we rolled almost all the way to Maroona. Here, we surrendered 763 to another crew and took over T341. This was on a goods also headed for Ararat and had priority over the train we had just brought in. I checked the vigilance control, made the necessary entries in the log book and swept the cab floor. We were not at Maroona for long. The SM soon arrived with the staff and the sound of the air horn produced a green flag from the guard. Ron Miller soon had the throttle in notch 8 and T341 proceeded to Ararat, emitting the growling splutter characteristic of its class. Compared to R763, this was nothing but a discordant jangle. Fortunately, the final leg of our journey was short, and T341 had us arriving in the Ararat yard at 4.05 in the afternoon. A relief crew was waiting and eight hours and 15 minutes were booked for the day.

On Victoria's main western line, use of automatic staff exchanging equipment was common for trains not stopping at staff stations. This applied equally to goods as well as passenger services. All R, J, K and N class engines were fitted with an automatic staff exchanger, and could thus be used to run expresses. For an automatic exchange, the staff was housed in a leather pouch attached to a small metal ring. The pouch and ring fitted into an attachment on the locomotive, which also had a specially designed pick-up device to retrieve the staff attached to the ground equipment at the station concerned. This comprised a reinforced upright post carrying fittings similar to those on the locomotive. When not in use, the items on the locomotive were stored adjacent to the cab. On steam, they were accessed by kneeling down in the gangway on the driver's side. On B and S class diesels, they were housed just below the cab and a floor panel behind the driver's seat hinged up to enable them to be used. T class diesels were not fitted with automatic staff exchangers. Ground posts were hinged at the base and swung down to lie horizontally in a specially constructed wooden enclosure.

On a locomotive, when the staff was going to be exchanged automatically it was inserted into its pouch, and the pouch and ring assembly

On 1 February 1965 R730 and R749 depart Horsham for Murtoa with their 2222 ton train. The author was the fireman on R730, the leading engine. (Ian Scutt)

Leaving the outskirts of Dimboola under an indifferent sky, oil-burning N496 and R723 accelerate their wheat train towards Horsham. (Ian Scutt)

fitted to the exchanger. This was then lowered in time to effect an exchange. On diesels, lowering and raising was done by compressed air, on steam engines it was done manually. There was an unmistakable 'clang' when the staffs were exchanged, and when heard, the equipment was raised, the pouch removed and the station names on the new staff checked and called out.

I was familiar with the procedure and had successfully used it on an S class diesel, but not yet on a steam loco. Some weeks after the recently described events with Ron Miller, and again on a Saturday, I was rostered to sign on at 10.40 am at the shed and take out and run the 11.30 am Dimboola, changing over with the 9 am ex Dimboola. The engine for the 11.30 am was oil-burning R748 and the driver Jack Jones. R748 had been prepared and all we had to do was light it up, and top up the tender water. This done, we proceeded to the yard and onto the train. After a small amount of shunting and a brake test, we were ready to depart, our train comprising a string of empty GY wheat wagons weighing 400 tons. It was a busy time. Wheat was on the move, and to keep traffic moving on this Saturday a number of stations not normally staffed on weekends were in use. Armstrong was one of them.

The signalman from B box delivered the staff. It read 'Ararat B – Armstrong', and was carried in a pouch attached to an auto exchanger ring. A long whistle, a green flag, and 748 got hold of its load up the grade and round the curve out of Ararat. With the engine pulling hard, I motioned to Jack Jones with the shovel my intention to sand the tubes. I cut back the oil control valve and atomizer, opened the fire door and sent 10 shovelfuls of sand up towards the tube plate in the firebox. Black smoke obligingly poured from the funnel, indicating that the sand was doing its job. While the gauge glass had a healthy water reading, steam had fallen to 150. Re-adjustment of the oil burner controls soon remedied this, aided by steam being shut off in preparation for the roll through Armstrong. With speed sitting on 45 mph it was time to set up the staff exchanger. On R class, there is a small box with a hinged back located beneath the driver's seat, supposedly designed to assist with automatic

R748 has the disc signal from the Ararat yard and is backing toward the weighted points that will take it down to the loco depot. The white stain on the crosshead and connecting rod show that the fireman's side piston rod gland packing has developed a slight blow. In the background, the lowered arm on the signal gantry indicates that an 'up' departure from the yard is imminent. (Geoff Oliver).

staff exchanges. A man with hands and limbs the size of a four-year-old could possibly manoeuvre something through this tiny space; but not having the physique of a midget I refrained from trying.

Kneeling down in the driver's side gangway, I reached round outside the cab and fitted the leather staff pouch into its large clip holder. The Armstrong 'Distant' signal was at 'proceed', indicating we had a clear run. On passing the 'Home', I unfastened the exchanger and casually lowered it down. I got the fright of my life. It was so heavy it nearly pulled me out of the cab with it! I was thankful that no one observed my discomfort. I slithered back from the gangway, and rose to stand up behind the driver. We passed through the station at around 45 mph. Despite the noise in the cab, the 'clang' of the staff exchangers was clearly audible. Kneeling down again, and hanging on grimly to a cab rail with one hand, I hauled up the exchange apparatus with the other. It slipped into its securing lock and I reached round outside the cab to retrieve the incoming staff. This wasn't easy. The ring attached to the pouch had to be disengaged from a rod fashioned in two reverse bends, slipped over its end, and brought into the cab. You were kneeling on a hard, swaying surface, hanging on with one hand and leaning out into a considerable slipstream. You then used your free hand to disentangle the staff assembly and bring it into the cab without falling out yourself. I achieved this, called out the names on the staff, Armstrong – Great Western, and handed it to the driver. The time for the complete operation, from the lowering of the staff exchanger to calling out the station names, took 20 to 25 seconds.

While all the 'Home' signals at Great Western were at 'proceed', the 'Distant' was at 'caution', indicating the staff would be exchanged by hand. This achieved, Jack Jones soon had the big 4-6-4 pounding up the intervening grades before Stawell.

Oil-burning N453 moves briefly from the Ararat yard to the main line to perform a shunting move. In the background, the small platform accessed by a short flight of steps is where the signalman from A box exchanges the staff with departing and arriving passenger trains. (Geoff Oliver)

After the experience with the staff exchanger at Armstrong, the rest of the day was rather dull in comparison. We ran 748 to Wal Wal where our changeover, the 9 am ex Dimboola, was waiting, headed by oil-burning N class, 426. Once sanded, 426 performed well and got us home in time for tea in fine style.

Whenever I could, I checked Monday's roster on Friday afternoon. The aim was to see what I had to look forward to over the weekend. And of course I always hoped for a firing job. It was therefore with disappointment that I walked away from the roster sheets one Friday, having been booked for 8 am cleaning in the shed on the following Monday. I wasn't working on Saturday or Sunday and resolved to make the most of a free weekend. This was improved markedly by the news I received on Saturday morning. I was no longer cleaning on Monday. Instead, I was to sign on at 8.57 am, travel per the 9 am Dimboola fast goods and relieve and run No. 86 up goods to Ararat. It was a job that came out of the blue and one that was so enjoyable in so many ways that it made one extremely thankful to be involved in running locomotives.

Signing on that Monday, I met for the first time the person who was to be my driver. It was Jack Moynihan. Jack was on the express goods roster and was working on what would normally have been a rostered day off. He was excellent company and knew how to work an engine. No. 86 was waiting for us at Murtoa. Its load was 1200 tons and it was double-headed. J545 was the leading engine with N466 cut in behind it. Both were oil burners. We were allocated 466. The cab had the familiar odour of lubricating oil mixed with fuel oil and hot steel, with each competing for nasal attention. The footplate was clean and the engine was simmering contentedly with 160 lbs of steam, ⅔ of a glass of water, and the tank heat keeping the oil at an agreeable temperature. The crew on the leading loco would handle the staff exchanges and I considered it a bonus being on the second engine. It was a beautiful day. There was hardly any wind and the sound of 466's air compressor reverberated pleasantly in the late morning air. The signalman delivered the staff to J545. Its long whistle brought a green flag from the end of the

Far removed from its tests with Laidlaw Drew oil-burning equipment, J546 backs past Ararat A signal box to pick up its goods train. The yellow spot below the boiler is flame where the oil burner enters the firebox. The items on the fireman's side pilot beam are probably a delivery from the loco depot to track gangers in the yard. The nearest of the three huts in the background behind the water tank is the sign-on location for engine crews commencing their shift in the yard. (Geoff Oliver)

train; Jack Moynihan blew a short whistle, and in harmony with 545, opened 466's regulator. With steam hissing from two sets of cylinder cocks, we were moving. I opened the oil control valve and adjusted the atomizer. Smoke appeared at 466's funnel. Speed picked up and we were soon doing 40 mph. The fireman on J545 waved his shovel out the cab window, indicating they were going to sand their engine. This they did, and a boiling cloud of black smoke trailed back over the train. While this action improved the steaming of 545, it soon became obvious from the way the leading engine was being worked that its steaming capabilities were less than ideal, and that we on N466 would be pulling more than our fair share of the load. Consequently, Jack Moynihan pushed the regulator wide open, lengthened the cutoff, and called across the cab, 'I'm giving her a bit more, to help them with the trouble they're having up front.' That was fine by me.

Meanwhile, I was observing the idiosyncrasies of the engine I was on. We had started off with 180 lbs of steam; this soon dropped to 165 and no effort of mine, except when we were rolling, would move the steam gauge needle up. On the other hand, no matter how hard the engine was worked, the needle remained on 165. In our present circumstances, N466 was blasting along at 40 mph, producing very little smoke and sounding like no N class had ever sounded.

Magnificent was a gross understatement. While steam remained constant, the gauge glass water level dropped. I increased the flow of oil to the burner and put on the injector. Still very little smoke, and as the water level slowly rose, the steam gauge needle remained rock solid. And the engine performed like this throughout the day. It was a dream to fire. No. 86 was a through goods and as we were non-stop through Lubeck, Wal Wal and Glenorchy, staff exchanges at these stations were automatic. We were making good time. And all the while N466 pounded down the high iron, producing the most fantastic and constant staccato exhaust sounds. They were a dream to hear. Shortly after passing Glenorchy, the crew on J545 managed to get something of their act together, with 545's exhaust sounding more like our own. This was timely. The three and a half miles of the 1 in 100 Bunyip Bank were up ahead and the additional power would be well used. We hit the bottom of the grade at 45 mph. Both engines were working hard and the combined exhausts delivered a sound that was out of this world. Speed gradually dropped and stabilized at 25 mph. And still the sounds continued. A little slower but just as intense and equally captivating. With the injector on, the throttle wide open and the cutoff well out, the steam gauge needle on N466 stayed glued on 165. It was an outstanding performance from an engine so easy to handle you could comfortably put your head out the cab window and listen to the most thrilling and enlivening sounds.

All too soon we reached the top of the grade and were passing through Deep Lead. Steam was shut off and we rolled for a mile and a half before three and a half miles of light steaming brought us into Stawell. Here we took water. A lengthy process, because the Stawell water crane rivalled the one at Ballarat for slow delivery, and two engines had to be serviced, not one. Thirty minutes later we were ready to depart, with the Stawell pilot attached in the rear. The staff had been delivered to J545, and with an exchange of whistle signals and a green flag from the guard we were on our way towards climbing the 1 in 62 grade facing 'up' trains. The three engines got hold of their load and soon had the 1200 tons moving uphill at a steady 20 mph. And most of the residents of Stawell heard how they were doing it, with each locomotive delivering a head-turning staccato symphony. The brakes were applied at the 'Stop' board at the top of the grade, and the pilot engine in the rear detached. It announced its departure with a long whistle. On hearing this the guard exhibited his green flag and we were moving once more. Speed rose and fell over the switchback grades to Great Western, then settled down to heavy pulling as we tackled the eight miles of mostly 1 in 100 to Armstrong and beyond. And once again the sound effects were magnificent. When heading for home and approaching the end of a shift, no locomotive crew needs encouragement to get the best out of their engine. Today was no exception. J545 and N466 stormed their 1200 tons up the 1 in 100 for mile on mile with a captivating, rhythmic and strident exhaust trailing back over the train. N466 continued its solid, 165 psi steam gauge performance, making it a dream to fire and a joy to listen to. It was an effortless accomplishment and we were soon rolling into Ararat, with the signalman from B box taking the staff from the leading engine. We rolled the length of the yard, came to a stand, and I uncoupled the engines from the train. A disc was pulled off from A box and we moved towards the loco depot. Here the fireman on J545 uncoupled his engine. Jack Moynihan and I hostled N466, stabled it in the shed, and signed off after working for a most enjoyable 7 hours and 28 minutes.

A minor footnote needs to be added to the events surrounding N466. No oil-burning steam locomotive will continue to steam as 466 did without having sand put through its boiler tubes.

The sand removes insulating carbon deposits from the tubes, enabling the combustion gases to come in direct contact with the high conductivity metal. Being well aware of this, quite early in the day described I called across the cab to Jack Moynihan, 'Shall I give her some sand, Jack?'

I was surprised at his reply. 'She's going alright, isn't she?' 'Yes, she's going fine,' I replied. 'Oh well, don't worry,' he said. So N466 went unsanded, although its performance throughout the day never faltered. However, if it had been left up to me, at least 10 shovelfuls of sand would have gone through its tubes.

26 Working Four Shifts: Night

Through a series of temporary staffing arrangements I found myself on night shift for a couple of days relieving on the goods roster. My driver was an agreeable character named Jock House. We signed on at 6 pm in the Ararat yard one pleasant autumn evening and were directed to relieve the crew on J553 on the 3.15 pm ex Murtoa. We ran 553 into the shed and proceeded back up to the yard to relieve R723 that had just arrived on a goods from Ballarat. This assignment was short-lived. We were ourselves relieved and directed to travel on the 7.30 pm Geelong goods to Maroona. This was hauled by R720, and travelling in the guard's van I watched its (rather heavy) smoke trailing back over the train. At Maroona we crossed the 10.45 am Geelong–Ararat goods, hauled by B and T class diesels. R720 was detached from the 7.30 pm Geelong and replaced by the B class. We relieved the crew on R720 and became the train engine, running tender-first, on the 10.45, cut in behind T377.

I opened the firebox doors on R720 and looked in. The fire, what there was of it, was sloping completely the wrong way. There was practically nothing in the back, while the front was so thick it was almost up to the brick arch. I tried the stoker. The jets sent coal everywhere except in the right places. I tried resetting them and this produced a minor improvement but not nearly enough to enable the stoker to be used with confidence. Steam was 190 and water just over ½ a glass. The rather easy 12 odd miles from Ararat to Maroona had allowed the crew on 720 to get by with an unfolding disaster in the firebox that was now passed on to us. I used the shovel to restore some shape and body to the fire, got the water level up and the steam round to 210. I knew, however, that as soon as we got moving I was going to be in trouble and informed the driver of the circumstances. He looked in the firebox, tried the stoker, and agreed that all was not well. He decided to bring his years of skill in handling situations like this into play and said to me, 'You sit over here,' and pointed to the driver's seat. I was relieved and delighted. He put the stoker on, and using the shovel deflected the coal being delivered in an even spread across the fire bed. Next, having got the measure of the task, he closed the firebox doors on the shovel and manoeuvred it in the required deflection arc so that a minimum of cold air went into the fire. It was then that the 'right away' came. I wound the reverse into full back gear, opened the cylinder cocks, sounded an acknowledging whistle and opened the regulator. We moved out of the Maroona yard and headed for Ararat.

With the cylinder cocks closed I wound the cutoff forward a few notches and widened the regulator. The big 4-6-4 was now well and truly pulling its share of the load. Meanwhile, from time to time out of the corner of my eye I watched Jock House manipulate the shovel to direct coal into the firebox. Steam and water levels remained well up, making the engine's performance most satisfactory. We soldiered on. Approaching Ararat I wound the cutoff well out and eased the regulator wide open. The exhaust leapt into life at 20 mph and R720 blasted up the 1 in 50 into Ararat, providing distinct relief to the discordant roar of T377. When cut off from the train, we backed down to the loco shed, hostled R720 and finished our shift by taking out S302, the loco for the 1.20 am Dimboola goods, and placing it on the train.

The next day we were booked to run the 7.30 pm Geelong. I signed on in the yard at 7.20 pm. It was another beautiful evening. I was greeted with the sight of an R class standing at the head of the train, its single-stage air compressor sounding out its reassuring rhythm, with the turbo generator running smoothly in the background. When signing on, without noticing the number of the engine, I enquired of the night depot foreman Jack Costello, 'How far do we take the R tonight, Jack?' 'All the way, David.' I had completely forgotten the difficulties we had had with an R class the night before and was euphoric at having a steam engine on the train. It was only after passing the numberplate as I climbed into the cab, R720, that I realized the gravity of our situation. I turned to the driver. 'How do I fire this thing, Jock?' 'I showed you how to do that last night,' came the reply. Yes, he might have. But I was busy with my responsibilities driving!

I checked the stoker. Once again the jets sent coal everywhere except in the right places. And once again when they had been reset, it made little difference. I wasn't going to experiment with deflecting coal from the stoker using the shovel. I considered it too risky. Instead, I used more conventional methods. In the few minutes before departure I built up the fire with the shovel. Steam was close to 200 and water well up in the glass. After acknowledging the 'right away', I experimented with the stoker on the way to Maroona. I turned off the right-side jet and cracked open those for the centre and left side. Leaving the remaining jets open, I opened the stoker throttle and observed the results. Things were still far from satisfactory. The two pronged pricker had to be used to push coal into the firebox's right-hand back corner and push it away from the left-hand back corner. Stoker jet pressure was kept to 75 psi, nevertheless I found that the right-side jet, although turned off, was still operating. The only thing for it was to supplement the stoker with extensive firing by hand.

And what an awkward nuisance this was! An R class has no shovel plate on the tender. The only access to coal is from the stoker trough at floor level. In running, some coal gravitating into the stoker trough spills out and collects on the footplate, from where it can be conveniently scooped up and delivered into the firebox with the shovel. But to extract coal constantly from the stoker trough is a different matter. It is not a shovel plate, and you often have to dig the shovel in at awkward angles to get coal on the shovel blade. This often takes time. Time you don't have when every second counts and you have the butterfly fire doors propped open. Nevertheless, on this occasion with R720, hand firing was my only alternative.

We arrived at Maroona with both steam and water at healthy levels and I had the perspiration to prove it. In keeping with good engine management, I took the opportunity to give 720 a good blowdown. We were pulling 61/1143 tons, just 17 tons short of a full load and priming was not an option. Before leaving Maroona, Jock House gave me adequate time to get the fire in good shape and have the steam on 210 and the water well up in the glass. With this achieved, a long whistle brought a green light from the guard, and with cylinder cocks hissing steam R720 got its train moving towards the rising 1 in 100 grades leading to Tatyoon and beyond. With near enough to a full load there was no playing around and Jock got straight down to business. The throttle was opened wide and the cutoff adjusted for a powerful piston thrust. Speed increased and the exhaust beat sharpened. With the stoker just trickling over, I persevered with hand firing. As well as getting coal from the stoker trough, I had to shield my eyes from the blinding glare of the firebox.

'Keep her blowing off, won't you,' Jock called across the cab. A minute or two later my efforts were rewarded and the safety valves lifted, enabling the injector to go on. We were now approaching the bottom of the 1 in 100 and speed was close to 40 mph, with the throttle still wide open and the cutoff lengthened. Coal was shooting off the shovel in a regular pattern of firing that was keeping the steam gauge needle on the mark and allowing the injector to be on for extended periods. And all the while, R720 was storming along in a rhapsody of sound that serenaded every living thing in the surrounding

The final steam locomotives produced by the Victorian Railways' Newport Workshops bed down for the night at Dimboola. (Ian Scutt)

countryside. Speed slowly dropped back, and as it did the cutoff was wound further out, until at around 25 mph it was at its maximum, reflected by an exhaust sound that blasted skywards in a strident staccato. But the best was yet to come. Following the hand staff exchange at Tatyoon, the engine was once more opened out fully to climb the final pinch of 1 in 100 on the 'up' side of that station. The sound was magnificent. Knowing we were near the top of the climb, I had things sufficiently organized on my side of the cab to take my seat and listen for what proved to be a stirring three minutes.

With a couple of minor exceptions, the next 35 miles to Derrinallum was mainly downhill. We rolled along at an agreeable pace, sometimes slowing for hand held staff exchanges and on occasion stopping at unstaffed stations to exchange the staff via a 'staff exchange box'. It was easy running and steam was easy to maintain. We took water, cleaned the fire and had a meal at Derrinallum. Our changeover failed to arrive and we were dispatched on to Lismore, the next station and seven miles 'Distant'. Here we changed over with the 6.5 pm ex Geelong, hauled by T350. After the drama with R720, T350 was quite a welcome sight. We briefed the Geelong crew on the woes of 720 and stepped onto the T class. I was invited by Jock House to occupy the driver's seat, and possibly as a reward for my efforts on the R class drove T350 for part of the way to Maroona, where a relief crew was waiting and we travelled back to Ararat by taxi, signing off with 10 hours and 48 minutes to our credit.

27 Working Four Shifts: Afternoon

Glenorchy is almost 163 miles from Melbourne, on the main line to Adelaide.

In the 1960s, the station at Glenorchy was impressive. Located at the up end of a long crossing loop, its buildings comprised a booking office and administration area. Situated towards the 'up' end of the platform, these were of generous proportions, and well-maintained. The platform itself was of sufficient length to accommodate a six-car passenger train.

Adjacent to the buildings, and positioned close to the centre of the platform, was the elevated signal box. Set well back from the platform face, this was of conventional Victorian Railways design, being of weatherboard framing with lattice windows on three sides and a low-pitched roof.

The signalman attending the 30-plus-lever frame had a good view of trains approaching from either direction, and an uninterrupted panorama of the Glenorchy yard.

Signal wires and point rodding passed from the lever frame under the platform via a platform-height, two-metre-wide tunnel. At the tunnel's exit, appropriate pulleys and levers directed each item to its point of application in the Glenorchy yard and beyond.

Trains leaving this station in the 'up' direction faced the arduous six mile long Bunyip Bank, so named because the track crossed over the Bunyip Creek. The Bunyip was not for the faint-hearted. Most trains conveyed maximum tonnage and all engine crews were well aware that their engine needed to be in apple pie order and worked hard in order to literally 'make the grade.' So it was that if they stopped for any reason at Glenorchy, the thought of the Bunyip Bank often prompted a crew to let their engine stand for as long as possible, then blowdown its boiler in an effort to remove impurities and reduce the likelihood of priming on the long climb ahead.

Travelling towards Murtoa from Glenorchy one soon reached Lubeck, the junction for the line to Marnoo and Bolangum. These locations were served by a weekly goods train, operated from Ararat. This ran out on Tuesday and back on Wednesday, with the train crew sleeping overnight in a departmental rest hut at Marnoo on Tuesday evening after a meal at the Marnoo Hotel.

'The Marnoo' was a job that ran up long hours. Typically, you would sign on in the morning of Tuesday at Ararat loco depot, take out your engine funnel-first, usually a K class, couple on to a string of empty GY wheat trucks in the Ararat yard and head off towards Bolangum.

There being no turntable or coal stage on the Bolangum line, on arrival at Stawell the engine would be coaled, watered and turned, and set off tender-first for the rest of the journey.

Once past Lubeck, speed was restricted to 20 mph. Shunting took place at a number of locations, water was taken at Rupanyup, and by the time the round trip from Marnoo to Bolangum (end of the line) and back to Marnoo was accomplished the day was far gone. Here the fire was banked in preparation for an early start on Wednesday morning.

This occurred soon after 4 am. The fire was pushed down, the engine prepared, loaded wheat trucks assembled, and one headed back towards Ararat, picking up loads of wheat at each of the three intermediate stations before Lubeck. Water would be taken at Rupanyup. At Lubeck, the

Two oil-burning N class, in the 430 number series, head south from Dimboola. (Ian Scutt)

train often exceeded 1000 tons so on arrival at Glenorchy the load would be reduced to 820, this being the maximum for a K up the Bunyip Bank.

The highlight of Wednesday was one's relief. This was usually dispatched via the 1.20 pm passenger train from Ararat, reaching the homecoming Marnoo crew at Wal Wal or Lubeck. The relief crew would take over the engine and the rest crew would travel in the guard's van to the nearest station where the afternoon passenger train to Ararat and Melbourne was scheduled to stop.

So it was that on a beautiful autumn day I was rostered to travel on the 1.20 pm passenger and relieve and run the ex Marnoo to Ararat. My driver was Bill Smith, a young, but worldly-wise fellow who had recently passed for driving.

On this day we relieved the incoming crew at Wal Wal and found ourselves in charge of K 163 at the head of some 800 tons.

The critical items in the cab and firebox were generally satisfactory, and with the cane hoop carrying the staff for Glenorchy slung over the air compressor steam valve, a long whistle produced the guard's 'right away' and we set sail.

The engine's performance was satisfactory and with the Glenorchy 'Distant' at 'caution', and the arrival 'Home' set for No. 2 road, we rolled with professional ease along the long station crossing loop, came to a smooth stand near the station buildings and surrendered our staff.

It seemed that we were going to cross something that was not yet on the horizon. In anticipation of a stop here, I had raised the boiler water level as much as possible to expedite a blowdown in preparation for the Bunyip Bank.

After about five minutes, with the water well up in the gauge glass and still no sign of any approaching train, and all signals at danger, I said to my mate,

'I'll give her a blowdown, Bill'

'Yes, alright.'

We were only one track away from the station platform, and making sure no one was around I opened the blowdown valve. On a K class this is on the fireman's side, and a torrent of condensed steam shot across the intervening track and reverberated off the platform face; or that is what appeared to be happening to any casual observer. Meanwhile, the vertical blow off discharge sent a geyser of white vapour shooting skywards, and the effect of two streams of escaping steam was visually and audibly arresting.

N453 and R705 make a fine sight as they commence their journey to Ararat from Murtoa. (Ian Scott)

I was keeping a close eye on the gauge glass to ensure its water level remained adequate when something in the corner of my eye caught my attention. Without realizing it, we had stopped with the blowdown outlet opposite the tunnel carrying the rods and wires from the signal box. While some discharged steam bounced back from the platform face, an equal amount went into the tunnel, and bouncing back from its closed end was forced upwards by the steam still coming in. The upward vapour entered the signal box through the space in the lever frame that allowed each lever to swing back and forth between 'on' and 'off'.

The results were spectacular! Fortunately, the signal box was empty and the sliding windows at each end were open. After filling the interior, surrounding the levers, and rising to the roof, the only way the trapped mist could escape was through the windows at each end. A stream of white curved away from each window, and maintaining a surprisingly compact shape ascended regally into the atmosphere like outstretched arms.

Overall, the signal box assumed the appearance of a large, marauding Viking; the windows being his teeth and the streams of ascending vapour the horns on his warrior helmet.

All this took less than five seconds to absorb. Before collapsing with laughter, I managed to call, 'Bill, look!'

With one glance he joined me rolling around the cab in laughter. You couldn't look, it wasn't funny, it was hilarious! And while that valve was open, it kept happening.

Hollywood could not have done it better.

Finally, with a shade under half a glass of water, I summoned sufficient mental resources to close the boiler blowdown.

The vapour streaming out of the end windows gradually dissipated and the interior behind them came once more dimly into view.

Our first concern was that the levers would betray our action by rusting, but as there was no one around who could fix any blame on us?

Then the hygienic aspects of the event began to be realized.

Every item in that signal box had received the most soothing, disinfecting caress, restoring it immediately to pristine condition. The next signalman would be operating a set of levers sterilized to the world's strictest surgical standards. And what about his working environment? The floor, the roof and every fitting and instrument had been sanitized to the highest levels of hygiene. Even the air he breathed had been purified!

No train arrived from either direction,

Oil-burning R719 and an unidentified R departing south from Dimboola (Ian Scutt)

and some time after our involuntary self-entertainment the SM arrived with the staff for Deep Lead, after pulling off the 'up' departure signals. His face and manner were completely normal, if not improved, and he displayed no knowledge of, or reaction to, what had recently taken place.

I had paid sufficient attention to the fire while we were standing, and with judicial use of the injector had the water at an acceptable level. Our journey up the Bunyip Bank was about to begin. It was uneventful, as was the rest of the trip home to Ararat. We arrived in good time and in good humour after a day of unexpected hilarity.

Afternoon shift was sometimes almost as good as day shift, although you frequently missed your sit-down evening meal. Commencement times often varied from around 10 am up to 5 pm, depending on traffic requirements.

One winter Saturday afternoon I signed on at the shed at 12.40 pm to take out and run the 1.30 pm Murtoa. The driver was Elso Arendshorst and our engine was R746. Elso was a clean-cut, tall Dutchman in his early to middle thirties. He spoke English with a slight accent, was good company and an excellent mate on the footplate. He was also an excellent engineman and one prepared to rise to the challenge of making up time.

Our load was 65 vehicles for 617 tons. This required banking assistance and we were pushed out of Ararat as far as the 'Stop' board on the way to Armstrong.

R746 steamed very well. We waited for some time at Stawell, crossing No. 86 'up' goods and No. 34 'up' passenger. After this, our run to Murtoa was uninterrupted. Here, we turned R746, took water, and coupled on to the 4.10 pm Dimboola–Ararat goods, cut in behind B83. This double-headed combination was charged with delivering its 700 ton load to Ararat early that evening. And it did just that. Most staff exchanges were made using the automatic apparatus, speed sat constantly around 45 mph and grades meant little. Between Great Western and Ararat, the nine mile Armstrong Bank saw speed maintained above 40 mph. On one occasion the regulator was wide open, the cutoff at 12 inches, water at ½ a glass, steam at 192 psi, the injector on and the funnel almost clear. When these observations were taken, speed was 42 mph with the engine's exhaust blasting back over the train, almost drowning out the sound of the B class. It was

An unidentified K class and R749 enjoy a pleasant winter afternoon in July 1964 as they stand waiting at Deep Lead. The disc signal below the left hand arm is pulled off, indicating they now have access to the main line. When the staff is delivered to the leading engine they will take their train on to Stawell and Ararat. (Ian Scutt)

a run like few others, with our average speed between Stawell and Ararat being almost 45 mph. We hostled R746 at Ararat and signed off after an enjoyable 8 hours and 20 minutes.

In the 1960s, weed control on the Victorian Railways was implemented using the Weedex train. This was a train of tank cars containing Weedex, an anti-weed liquid sprayed on to the track. Spraying was controlled by valves fitted in the customized guard's van and each car was connected to the other by a hose that ensured a uniform level of liquid was discharged from each vehicle as spraying progressed. Maximum speed when spraying was 20 mph, and a portable telephone line went from the spray-control guard's van to the engine cab to enable the crew to be informed when speed needed to be kept at this limit. When not spraying, speed could be increased to 30 mph.

One clear winter's day, I signed on at the shed at 12.5 pm to prepare and take out K173 for the 1.30 pm Weedex train. This was heading north-west, and for the bulk of the journey Jim Lutteral, the driver, kept speed at 20 mph to enable effective spraying to be carried out. We were to change over with the 12.10 pm ex Murtoa, and despite our slow progress travelled as far as Glenorchy before it appeared. It had not been a difficult task keeping the needle on the mark on an engine travelling at 20 mph, and the future bade well for the rest of the afternoon when we stepped onto the footplate of oil-burning N432, at the head of our changeover. Our load was a compact 19 vehicles for 503 tons. With this load we could run unassisted all the way to Ararat. The SM delivered the staff for the section to Stawell and we got under way. With the Bunyip Bank ahead I turned to the cab sand box in preparation for sanding the tubes. But I was too late. Someone had beaten me to it. There was precious little sand left; just enough for eight shovelfuls to send telltale clouds of black smoke into the cold afternoon air. We negotiated the grades to Stawell satisfactorily and N432 steamed reasonably well. After taking water, the injector went on to fill the boiler to ¾ of a gauge glass and with nearly a clear funnel I brought the steam round to right on blowing off at 180. The signalman from Stawell A box delivered the staff and we got under way. The engine made a reasonable fist of getting us to Great Western and after the hand staff exchange there Jim Lutteral eased the regulator wide open and wound the cutoff out a little. Steam was near 180 and water well up in the glass. I responded by adjusting the oil control valve and atomizer settings to handle the increased steaming.

At first things went well. Then I turned on the injector. Steam pressure fell, and no increase in the flow of oil to the burner would halt it. I tried a smoky funnel and an atomizer pressure approaching 100 psi. This effected some improvement but not enough to leave the injector on, so it was turned off. If the Newport builders of N432 had seen it now they would have quite likely disowned it. Our progress became a three-cornered life and death battle between the regulator, the steam gauge and the gauge glasses. Jim Lutteral eased back the regulator and speed dropped to 10 mph. Steam was now 130 and water at ½ a glass with the injector off. We plodded on until the water was so low that the injector had to be used. Steam plummeted to 100 and speed fell away to 5 mph. The engine was close to stalling. Steam was now at 90 psi and the only alternative to a stall was to open the regulator to a wider setting. This was done, and to compensate the injector was turned off. There was barely a sound from the exhaust, yet miraculously we kept moving. I eased back the oil control valve and atomizer, but left the blower close to hard on. Finally, the level crossing that heralded the top of the grade came into view. We staggered over the summit with 90 pounds of steam and the water out of sight in the bottom of the gauge glass. A dip in the track enabled us to pick up some momentum and both injectors went on to remedy the dire water situation. We rolled into Ararat yard with a bob of water in the bottom of each gauge glass and the steam gauge showing 110. I cut us off from the train and we were soon signalled to go over the pit. We hostled N432 and in the process found various deposits of oil clinker in the firebox, indicating poor combustion, possibly due to a misaligned burner. This was noted, and we placed the engine in the shed after a nerve-racking afternoon.

28 The Fastest 20 Minutes

After being on duty for more than four hours an engine crew were entitled to a 20 minute meal break. This would frequently occur in conjunction with having to wait in a crossing loop for a train travelling in the opposite direction. In this case, the 20 minutes would often extend to well over half an hour. There was thus plenty of time to ensure that the fire was in good shape, the gauge glass water level satisfactory, and to boil the billy and make tea. When the tea was poured into your mug, there was ample time to let it cool, enjoy your sandwiches, and drink it at your leisure. And there was always plenty of hot water for a second mug.

Boiling the billy could be done in a number of ways. On a coal burner, you would soap it all over as protection against the firebox flames, then fill it with water from a station tap and using a short fire iron hold it in the firebox for the few minutes it took to boil. You couldn't do this with an oil burner. They required a custom-made billy boiler. You screwed the billy boiler onto the shed line fitting on the oil burner manifold on the fireman's side of the cab, placed a billy of water over the copper loops, stood clear and turned on the boiler steam. You had boiling water inside 60 seconds! This was certainly the preferred method of making a cup of tea. While coal-burning locomotives were not fitted with shed line equipment, you could unscrew a gauge glass drain tube and use the billy boiler on this fitting, with the gauge glass test cock supplying ample steam. On an R class, you could unscrew one of the union nuts on the stoker jet manifold, screw on the billy boiler, turn on the stoker jets and boiling water was on its way. When the tea was made, you simply screwed the appropriate fitting, gauge glass or stoker manifold, back in place.

As mentioned, billy boilers were custom made. It was up to each individual engineman to befriend one of the shed fitters and persuade him to manufacture the required item. Fortunately, I had no trouble here. I had an excellent friendship with Jack Smyth, one of the senior fitters, and his fitter's assistant, Ray Lindell. Following a polite request, Jack and Ray produced a beautifully crafted billy boiler in copper and brass that provided boiling water for numerous cab initiated cups of tea. It replaced the one made by Jack Jones on the way to Patchewollock some months previously. And 50 years later it can still see service when I am firing on the Castlemaine to Maldon tourist railway.

There were times, however, when your meal break did not coincide with the crossing of another train. In these instances it was frequently tacked onto the end of the time allotted for cleaning the fire and taking water. If the engine was a coal burner, it would come to a stand at the water crane and after a brief glance in the firebox and at the gauge glasses you would swing down from the cab, pull the crane spout towards the train, climb up on the tender, open the tank lid, position the spout and turn on its wheel valve to let the water flow.

Meanwhile, the driver would relax in his seat, open his lunch box and begin his meal. When the tender tank was full, you turned off the wheel valve, closed the tank lid and swung down to the ground. With the water crane back in position you climbed back into the cab. If the fire was in poor shape you had to shake it, open the ash pan slides at ground level to dispose of the ash, close them up, return to the cab and place whatever coal was necessary on the fire to keep it bright. These activities could eat into your meal time. When they were finished, you found yourself scrambling around trying to boil the billy in time to let the tea cool so you could enjoy it without scalding yourself, while at the same time doing your best to avoid having to wolf down your sandwiches and instead eat them at a leisurely pace. The driver would have eaten by this time and could well be drinking his second cup of tea while you were barely sipping your first. When you finally did get settled it might be only for a few minutes. As likely as not, the stationmaster would appear with the staff, hand it up into the cab while saying 'When you're ready.' Which means, 'I've booked you as departing now. If you don't go now you'll be booked as departing late.' So you put aside the remainder of your meal and prepared to depart.

If your engine was an oil burner, things were marginally better, but only marginally. All the work fell to the fireman, while the driver could relax.

If your motive power, however, was a diesel your meal break would most likely be relaxing.

29 Fast Goods

Fast goods trains were primarily the domain of senior crews who worked on what was known as the jet roster. Annual leave, sick leave and special leave, however, created opportunities for people like me, who had passed their 520 hours exam, to fill in for a fireman who was unavailable.

My first occasion firing on a fast goods was on a winter Saturday in 1964, when I was rostered to fire on No. 38 fast goods, Ararat to Melbourne, and rest overnight. No. 38 ran from Adelaide to Melbourne seven days a week. It was usually limited to 1300 tons and comprised some four-wheel vehicles, limiting its speed to 45 mph. The 1300 tons load limit was designed to preserve time-keeping, and a second division of this train was sometimes run to accommodate extra loading. I signed on at 9.40 am in the Ararat yard. No. 38 arrived a few minutes later behind S301 and S305.

I checked the vigilance control seal and made the required entries in S301's log book. The driver was Harold Bright. Harold had a friendly face and a pleasant, rather quiet, but outgoing personality. We left Ararat at around 9.50 am, and after pressing the vigilance control and picking up the outgoing staff I settled into the fireman's seat. Speed soon rose to 45 mph.

Harold was something of a character. He seemed to have an ongoing preoccupation with women. This expressed itself in his concern for them to be satisfied. Not in a general sense, but specifically in relation to their genitalia. His conversation was never lewd or profane. Everything was referred to by innuendo and inference. A particular sexual item was always an 'it'. While never clearly stated, Harold often inferred that he was well suited to providing the satisfaction women needed. His reasoning was that women in general knew, or should know, that this area of their anatomy had to be satisfied, and were therefore responsible for seeing that this need was fulfilled. At times he developed this theme at length, often referring to the height above ground of this portion of their being and concluding emphatically with, 'You've got to give it something, Dave. And its too high up to eat grass.'

With all staff exchanges being automatic, we made good time and apart from the grades before Buangor and Beaufort, speed hovered around 45 mph. Between Trawalla and Burrumbeet, the railway line closely parallels the Western Highway. On a passenger train, you generally passed cars on the road. Today, with our 45 mph speed limit, the cars were passing us. As one late model Holden edged in front, framed in its sweeping back window was the face and waving arm of a most attractive girl. This vision of loveliness was on the fireman's side and I had a better view than the driver. As the car began to draw away, I called across the cab, 'Give her a bit more, Harold.'

'I can't,' came the reply, 'we're right on the limit now.' And so we watched our temporary dream girl fade away. After setting down the staff at Linton Junction we were soon on the double track through Ballarat. I filled the electric kettle with water and set it to boil. By the time we passed Ballarat East the kettle was boiled, the tea made, and we were having our lunch as S301 and S305 toiled up the grade to Warrenheip at the civilized speed of 20 mph.

Harold was not only a character but also something of a dandy. On our approach to Bank Box we encountered a number of signal aspects

H220, originally designed to haul the Overland unassisted between Melbourne and Ararat, visited Ararat only twice. On its first visit, it hauled a 680 ton test train up the Ingliston Bank in 49 minutes. This was 18 minutes less than its scheduled allowance of 1 hour and 7 minutes. The big 4-8-4 is seen here rolling through Ballarat East station en route to Ararat on 5 May 1949. Details of the engine's performance were recorded in the dynamometer car, attached as the first vehicle in the train. (Ararat Railway Heritage Association)

indicating we would be entering the loop there to cross something. When this became obvious, Harold checked the water remaining in the kettle for both warmth and quantity. Finding it satisfactory, he said, 'I'm going to meet the Ararat footballers at the Claire Castle Hotel in Melbourne later on. So when we stop in the loop, I'm going back to wash my hair.' I acknowledged this, and we were soon standing at the 'up' end of the loop, facing red signals. Taking the kettle, Harold went back through the engine room of S301 to the washbasin adjacent to the hostler controls and washed his hair. This took some time. Meanwhile, I kept an eye on things from the cab. In due course, a 'down' passenger train came and went. Shortly after this, one of the signals we were facing, a low speed, went from red to yellow. I went back to the washbasin. Harold was just drying his face and neck. 'We've got a low speed caution, Harold.'

'Will you take the brake off?' he said. 'She'll start to roll, and I'll be there right away.'

I went back to the cab, assumed the driver's seat and released the independent brake. Air hissed from the distributing valve and the needle on the locomotive brake cylinder gauge fell to zero. Now unrestricted, No. 38 rolled slowly out onto the main line. Harold arrived, slipped into the driver's seat, initiated the dynamic brake and we were soon rolling down grade at a controlled 45 mph. Our journey to the Melbourne yard was largely uninterrupted. On arrival, however, we were told we had to take our diesels over the pit. By the time we detached from the train, waited for signals to get us through the yard and finally found our way to South Dynon it was 5.45 pm. I was glad to get home to my parent's place in Rosanna and rest.

The next day, Sunday, we signed on at South Dynon at 3.15 pm and prepared to run the 5 pm

Melbourne–Adelaide express goods. The Jet.
Friday, 6 May 1949. After being turned on Ararat's 85 foot turntable — made specially for it — H220 waits in the Ararat yard at the head of a Melbourne-bound goods train. The Franklin air-operated power reverse, with its long reach rod from the cab, and its operating rod to the valve gear, is clearly visible on the running plate. (Ararat Railway Heritage Association)

Our locos were S308 and S300. We made our way to one of the remote loading docks at south-west Dynon and found a train examiner waiting to couple us onto our train. This done, our 1300 ton load had its brakes tested and received the thumbs up. We got away at 5 pm, and after some initial signal checks received a clear run. The Jet was an excellent example of just how efficient and fast railways are in transporting large volumes of freight. Apart from the Ingliston Bank and a couple of other grades we had those 1300 tons travelling north-west, sitting on 60 mph for mile on mile while I pressed the vigilance control and operated the automatic staff exchanger. Six hours and three minutes after signing on, we were relieved by the ongoing crew at Ararat.

There were times when the Jet had sufficient loading to warrant a second division. As there were no crews rostered to handle a second division, the roster clerk looked for whoever was available. So it was that on a fine winter's morning I signed on at 7.06 in the Ararat yard to relieve and run the 7.16 express goods to Melbourne. This rest job was the second division of the Jet from Adelaide. It was running late and the driver Jim Lutteral and I spent an hour and a half cooling our heels waiting for it to arrive. Instead of departing at 7.16 am we left at 8.45, in charge of B81 and S300. With the throttle in notch 8, and making every effort to make up time, we were halfway to Buangor when it was discovered that the continuous wheel slip indicator light on B81 was permanently illuminated. We stopped at Buangor and checked the brakes on B81 and S300 to ensure that none were sticking.

Finding everything satisfactory, we pressed on. Jim Lutteral, however, was far from satisfied with things and sent me back to S300 to check its ammeter reading. This meant opening the rear nose door on B81 and stepping across the open couplers and into the engine room door of S300 while we were running at 60 mph. An adventurous feat! The ammeter showed the loco was drawing only 50 amps. Also, S300's continuous wheel slip light was constantly illuminated.

Back in the cab of B81 I told the driver, who decided to stop at Middle Creek and test both locos for amps being drawn while they were standing. Everything seemed satisfactory and we proceeded on our way to Beaufort. Before reaching the beginning of the Beaufort Bank I assumed the driver's seat and Jim Lutteral went back to S300 and checked inside the electrical cabinet in the cab. He found the WSA solenoid contacts opening and closing intermittently. As we approached the Beaufort Bank he remedied this by placing a pencil between the WSA contacts, thus keeping them open. With the pencil in place we had little difficulty in reaching the top of the grade and on instruction I removed it as we went over the summit. Nevertheless, things were still uncertain and a note was placed with the outgoing staff at Beaufort, requesting a fitter to attend to the locomotives at Ballarat. He would have plenty to do. In addition to this difficulty, each loco had to be reversed as a separate unit because of an apparent defect in a newly replaced jumper cable. Also, the dynamic brake on each unit was defective and the train was being run without dynamic braking. So much for modern diesel electric locomotives.

We managed to reach Ballarat without further incident and stopped to enable a fitter to examine each locomotive. The faults could not be traced and he was unable to effect any repairs. Jim Lutteral decided to keep going, and making the most of our Ballarat location requested rear-end assistance to Warrenheip. This was provided by K191. I inserted the pencil in the WSA contacts on S300 and we tackled the 1 in 52 out of Ballarat East. Both units performed satisfactorily, and with K191 doing its share we soon reached the summit. K191 was detached and I removed the pencil from the switch. It apparently had some effect, and I visited S300 at other locations for pencil insertion on our run to Melbourne, chiefly before the grade from Bacchus Marsh to Parwan. By the end of the day, with due care, I had become something of dab hand crossing between the two locos at speed. We reached Spion Kop, just outside North Melbourne, unscathed, and were pleased to be relieved before 3 pm.

The next day we signed on at South Dynon at 12.10 pm for the 2 pm Jet, to Adelaide. Our load of 66/763 tons was easily handled by S class diesels 306 and 307. Our trip to Ararat was, as it should have been, uneventful. With just over half a load, 60 mph was common and we reached Ararat at 6.37 pm, pleased to hand over to the ongoing crew two units in good condition.

30 Interesting Performances

After having to cope with some locomotives whose behaviour bordered on recalcitrant, I always hoped for a footplate experience that would be more enjoyable than most and centre around an engine whose performance on the day could be regarded as outstanding. Over time it became known around the depot that I enjoyed the sound of an engine being worked hard, and was grateful to any driver who was kind enough to work his steed in a manner that produced the desired effect. This did not often happen, but when it did I made a point of recording the details of how the engine was worked in order to produce something that approached the sublime.

One fine autumn morning I signed on at 8.57 am and travelled per the 9 am Dimboola fast goods, to relieve and run the 9 am ex Dimboola to Ararat. My driver was Elso Arendshorst.

The 9 am from Dimboola was late getting away and we travelled as far as Horsham to relieve it. It was an interesting train. Its load of 43 vehicles for 1143 tons had two engines assigned to it. These were oil-burning N458 in the lead, with oil-burning R748 behind it. We were allocated to 748. The crew on N458 received the staff and we were soon on our way. 458 immediately distinguished itself by emitting a beautifully mellow sound when the whistle cord was pulled. The majority of staff exchanges used the automatic equipment, enabling line speed when reached to be maintained. As speed rose, I took the shovel out of the cab sand box and indicated to Elso my intention to use it. I cut back the oil control valve and atomizer and propped open the firebox door. Elso lengthened the cutoff and eight shovelfuls of sand went through 748's tubes, producing a satisfying boiling cloud of black smoke as carbon deposits on the boiler tubes were removed to the atmosphere. This achieved, the oil control valve and atomizer were restored to their previous settings. We repeated this once more before reaching Murtoa. The smoke was much less on the second occasion, signifying that the tubes had received a worthwhile cleansing. Like us, the boys on N458 didn't want too long a shift and on the generally level alignment to Murtoa we were soon pounding along with the speed recorder on each loco hovering around 45 mph. R748 steamed well, much of the time against the injector. On arrival at Murtoa, both engines took water. Anti-prime briquettes were made available and I placed six of these in R748's tender tank.

Once again the crew on N458 received the staff and the engine's mellow chime whistle heralded our departure, with a green flag coming promptly from the guard. And once again speed soon rose to 45 mph. Whether or not Train Control wanted a fast goods, they certainly had one! With each engine pulling less than 600 tons, their exhausts at 45 mph were rather muted. We breezed through Lubeck, Wal Wal and Glenorchy with the staff exchanger on the leading engine clanging cheerfully as it set down and picked up our safe working authority. Now we were approaching the five miles of the Bunyip Bank. Our gauge glasses showed ¾ of a glass of water and I had the steam right on 210. This was not hard as 748 was steaming like a bird. Near the foot of the grade, the muted exhausts came to life with a magnificent staccato. Elso had the regulator wide open. In an effort to maintain steam pressure, I opened the oil control valve wider and wider until it was fully open. A phenomenon I later learned was not unheard of on this engine. Speed gradually fell from 45 mph down to 30. I let the water fall to ⅔ of a glass before putting on the injector; steam fell to 200 and remained there. Meanwhile the sound from both engines was nothing short of inspirational. I crossed the cab and looked at the cutoff. It was on 12 inches. At 30 mph on a 12 inch cutoff with 200 lbs of steam entering the cylinders, R748 was putting on the most stirring performance as it climbed the 1 in 112. And on this cool and sunny autumn day it was a privilege to hear it.

The top of the bank came all too quickly and we were soon rolling down the grade from Deep Lead. We left the sound of the exhausts humming in the air as the mechanical instruments responsible for them disappeared into the distance. A short stanza of light steaming brought us into Stawell. The slow delivery of the water crane into the tenders of both engines made taking water a lengthy process. When it was finally accomplished, the Stawell pilot eased up to our van, air hoses were coupled up and preparations made for our departure. The staff was delivered to N458 and a long, short, long whistle from the rear signified that the driver of the pilot had received the bank engine key. Two long whistles came from N458—two engines coupled together move forward. Elso responded with two long whistles as did the Stawell pilot. The guard obliged with a green flag, three regulators were opened, and we were moving. Both engine crews had now been working almost eight hours and were keen to get home. The sound of the engines on the climb out of Stawell reflected this. Both throttles were wide open and cutoffs at maximum. The residents of Stawell thus received an impromptu evening serenade in steam that was an enlivening aid to the digestion of their evening meal. Our bank engine cut off at the top of the grade and we were on our own.

The switchback slopes to Great Western saw speed rise to 45 mph on more than one occasion and a hand staff exchange at that station brought us to the foot of the eight mile Armstrong Bank. Both locomotives gave it their all. Elso worked R748 hard. Once again the oil control valve was opened wide on the big 4-6-4 as it picked up its share of the load and blasted up the 1 in 100 towards Armstrong. The exhaust of each engine struck the cold evening air with an exhilarating sonorous effect, sometimes merging with that of its partner, at other times becoming individually distinct. And all the time captivating and romantic. As the grade lengthened, speed fell away. After passing through Armstrong, speed had stabilized at 21 mph. On 748 the regulator was wide open, water was at ½ a glass and the injector was on. The steam gauge registered 198 and the cutoff was at 15 inches, with the big oil burner steaming well against the injector and enjoying the heavy pulling. We went effortlessly over the summit and in a few minutes were rolling into Ararat, where our relief was waiting. It had been a magnificent day, made even better by being home in time for a well-cooked evening meal.

This outstanding performance by R748 was by no means isolated. Shortly after it occurred, I was rostered on a Dimboola job with driver Charlie Aggett, where the changeover was No. 86 'up' goods. We met this at Wal Wal in charge of R748. An R class is allowed 990 tons unassisted up the Bunyip Bank, and on this day our load was 43 vehicles for 925 tons. As we left Wal Wal, I sent 10 shovelfuls of sand through 748's tubes, and repeated this at the foot of the Bunyip Bank. The engine's steam gauge promptly registered its approval of these actions. We hit the bottom of the bank at around 40 mph with a full head of steam and a wide open regulator. A quarter of the way up, speed was 31 mph, the throttle wide open, the cutoff on 9 inches, water at ½ a glass, the injector on and steam sitting on 210. At the halfway mark, the regulator was wide open using a cutoff of 12 inches, speed was 24 mph, water at ½ a glass, the injector on and steam at 202 psi. And all the time 748 was a delight to fire as Charlie Aggett lengthened the cutoff and kept our 925 tons rolling. Needless to say, 748 matched its classic performance with thrilling sound effects, with the exhaust blasting into the air in the most magnificent manner. Three-quarters of the way up the grade, the regulator was still wide open and the cutoff had been lengthened to 15 inches. Speed had fallen to its minimum of 18 mph, water showed ½ a glass, the injector was on and steam steady on 205. And this was the way we went pounding over the summit, with R748 showing that it was more than equal to handling loads over 900 tons.

When first introduced, the R class underwent a thorough series of power tests. They were found to be able to comfortably haul 430 tons up a 1 in 50 grade. However, in the interests of operational reliability, speed, and timetabling, it was decided to limit their load on a 1 in 50 grade to 400 tons. This applied to every 1 in 50 grade throughout the State except one. This was the 1 in 50 grade in the 'down' direction, through the tunnel out of Geelong. On this half mile pinch, an R class was allowed only 325 tons.

When first constructed, the grade out of Stawell in the 'up' direction was 1 in 50. Some time later this grade was eased to 1 in 62, enabling 'up' direction loads out of Stawell to be substantially increased. Why this one section of track was chosen for load increases remains a mystery. Through loads from Stawell to Ararat remained unchanged because there was no easing of the 1 in 100 alignments that predominated after the tight pinch out of Stawell. Nevertheless, the load increases over this short section were worthwhile, as the following table shows.

And how did an R class perform with extra loading on this 1 in 62 grade? Fortunately, I was able to observe this at first hand.

One autumn afternoon I signed on at Ararat station at 1.17 pm and travelled on the 1.20 pm Dimboola pass to relieve and run the 3.15 pm ex Murtoa. My driver was Jack Green. On arrival at Murtoa we were directed to the coal stage where our engine, R703, was being coaled and watered by the Dimboola crew who had brought it in. After relieving the Dimboola men, we were signalled into the Murtoa yard and on to our waiting train. This was a bulk wheat consist of 27 vehicles weighing 500 tons. With a relatively short train, the brake test did not take long and we were on our way a little after 3.15 pm. R703 picked up those 500 tons as if they were a pocket handkerchief and was soon wheeling them along at 45 mph. Staff exchanges were on the automatic equipment as far as Deep Lead and our progress was uninterrupted over the 30 miles to this station. The engine handled its load effortlessly.

Once up to 45 mph it had to be eased back to keep within this limit. This meant that steaming was very light and the exhaust was muted. R class steam best when they are working hard and the

Locomotive	Load on 1 in 50 Grade	Load on 1 in 62 Grade in "up" direction out of Stawell	Percentage Increase %
S (diesel)	900 tons	1100 tons	22%
B (diesel)	750 tons	950 tons	26%
T (diesel)	500 tons	600 tons	20%
X	650 tons (Booster Load)	850 tons (Booster Load)	30%
C	555 tons	720 tons	29%
R	400 tons	530 tons	32.5%
J	405 tons	530 tons	30%
K or N	390 tons	510 tons	30%
A^2	385 tons	510 tons	32%
D^3	305 tons	400 tons	31%
D^1	270 tons	380 tons	40%

On a sunny winter afternoon, R748 moves through the yard at Stawell. (Ian Scutt)

lack of an exhaust beat resulted in steam falling away when the injector went on. It never fell below 150, however, and I soon found that the boiler could be filled to ¾ of a glass and that this steam pressure barely affected our speed. When the boiler feed was turned off, steam gradually rose to 210, with the water remaining still well up in the glass. Having learned from past experience, I handled the automatic staff exchanger capably and generally had a picnic. It was obvious that 703 had plenty in reserve. It would have been no trouble to increase speed to 70 mph and maintain it, so freely did the engine handle and perform.

We commenced our ascent of the Bunyip Bank at 45 mph and here the exhaust came to life as R703 stormed up the grade. When a third of the way up, speed was still at 42 mph, the regulator was wide open, water was at ⅔ of a glass, steam on 175, and the cutoff at 10 inches. The New York Central Railroad claimed to have a noteworthy train in the 20th Century Limited, but it would have been battling to sound as good as R703 on the Bunyip Bank on that sunny autumn afternoon. To this engine, 500 tons was nothing. Three-quarters of the way up the grade speed was being maintained at 34 mph, with a wide open throttle, a 12 inch cutoff, the injector off, water at ⅓ of a glass and steam on 200. The funnel showed hardly any smoke as it delivered the staccato sound of exhaust steam to the atmosphere. With all other signals at 'proceed', the 'Distant' arm at Deep Lead showed 'caution', indicating the staff was to be exchanged by hand. A service brake application reduced our speed to 20 mph, and with a swish of cane hoops the safe working authorities were delivered and picked up.

From here, it was child's play to get to Stawell. In order to expedite our passage home, we decided against having a meal here, electing only to take water. As usual, water from the Stawell water crane flowed into our tender with the speed of a stampeding turtle, leaving me ample time to get the fire in good shape. Finally, all was ready. The water was at ¾ of a glass and the safety valves sizzling on 210.We had the staff for Great Western, and a long whistle brought a green flag from the guard. Jack Green got the train moving without slipping and we were soon climbing the 1 in 62. R703 never missed a beat. Speed settled down to 17 mph and was maintained till we were over the top. Steam was readily kept on 210 and the injector used to keep the safety valves from lifting. The powerful, measured rhythm of the exhaust reflected the engine's overall performance. It never looked like slipping or stalling and could have happily continued in this manner for an hour or more. True, we only had 500 tons, not 530, but from the way the engine performed it was obvious that an additional 30 tons would have made not one scrap of difference.

We went into No. 2 road at Great Western, crossed the 'down' Horsham passenger and had a meal.

I used the shovel to build up the fire in the back corners, sides and under the firebox door, and checked that the stoker jets were still distributing coal evenly. The water was brought up to ¾ of a glass and I supplemented my hand firing by using the stoker to bring the steam round to 210. We were ready for our final climb. With the staff on board and 'right away' from the guard, Jack Green eased open the regulator. R703 responded immediately. Its 500 ton load might as well have been a perambulator for all the trouble it gave this engine. Our departure was lively and worthy of any heavy express. The exhaust shot skyward and speed rose. The regulator went to the roof. With the stoker jets at just over 75 psi, I widened the stoker throttle to set the stoker screw rapidly turning over, as it had done on the Bunyip Bank, delivering an increasing stream of coal to feed the white hot fire. We sailed through Armstrong at 30 mph with a wide open throttle, the cutoff at 9 inches, water at ¾ of a glass, the injector on and the safety valves lifting.

We continued like this to the top of the grade. I eased back on the stoker and the safety valves settled with steam still sitting on an effortless 210. In the meantime, the sound was indescribably wonderful, with the pulsating exhaust blasting back over the train. It was over all too soon. In what seemed no time at all we were rolling into

Oil-burning N489 on an 'up' goods departing Stawell. The exhaust of the bank engine is in the background. (Ian Scutt)

Ararat, surrendering our staff to B signal box and being cut off from the train and signalled over the pit. Here we hostled our engine and put it safely to rest in the depot. Six hours and 3 minutes were booked against this shift. It was so satisfying that they seemed like barely an hour or so.

N class could also perform very well. One clear winter morning I signed on at 11.25 am in the Ararat yard to relieve and run the 11.35 am Dimboola. My driver was Lance Little. Lance was tall and well built, with rather scholarly features and red hair. He was a former policeman, and carried about him a quiet dignity that was obviously a legacy of his previous role. Unlike some enginemen, he didn't mind early starts, and had confided to me on another occasion that he quite liked getting up early. Our engine on this occasion was R735, heading a light train of 18 vehicles weighing 288 tons. A most enjoyable day was ahead of us.

We left on time and R735 gave a faultless performance, steaming well and whisking us along toward our changeover. This was the 9.05 am ex Dimboola and was waiting for us at Wal Wal. We relinquished our stoker-fired Hudson and stepped on to the footplate of oil-burning N460, whose load was 720 tons. With the staff for Glenorchy on board, and steam and water readings satisfactory, we got under way. I wasted no time in thoroughly sanding 460's tubes, and was rewarded with an erupting cloud of black smoke as the sand cleared away accumulated carbon deposits. Almost immediately, and with only minor opening of the oil control valve, the needle on the steam gauge zoomed round to the working pressure of 180 psi and stayed there.

N460 steamed superbly. Lance soon had us moving at 40 mph and had to slow down for the hand staff exchange at Glenorchy. This completed, he eased the regulator wide open and adjusted the cutoff so that N460 got hold of its load with a cascade of sound from the funnel and surged steadily forward. The exhaust thundered back over the train in the most splendid staccato, and with minimum opening of the oil control valve the steam gauge needle remained glued on 180. It was all too easy. At the bottom of the Bunyip Bank the regulator was wide open and speed 35 mph. The injector was on, water ½ a glass, steam 180 and the cutoff at 9 inches. The regulator remained wide open all the way up the grade. Halfway up, speed was 25 mph, the cutoff was 12 inches, the injector on, water at ½ a glass, and steam on 180. Near the summit, speed was 17.5 mph, the cutoff 15 inches, water was just under ½ a glass, the injector was on, and the steam gauge needle had gone past 180, with the safety valves sending a geyser of steam skyward. This was in contrast to the funnel, which was clear. And all the while the sound was fantastic!

We took water at Stawell and were banked up the grade when leaving. The run from Great Western through Armstrong was a repeat performance of that on the Bunyip Bank, with 460 ready to blow off at the slightest provocation. With the injector on or off, the steam gauge needle clung on to the 180 mark like a limpet. We rounded off our time on 460 by hostling it at Ararat.

Not all interesting performances took place on the Bunyip Bank. But it was an ideal location to evaluate a locomotive over an extended distance hauling a heavy load.

31 Passenger Trains

The passenger roster comprised the most senior crews. My low ranking seniority meant that, for me, passenger trains were few and far between. Nevertheless, on rare occasions one would come my way. As happened on Christmas Day 1964. I signed on at Ararat station to relieve and run the 10.31 am passenger to Melbourne. Dave Andrew was the driver on B75 and this job enabled me to spend part of Christmas Day with my parents and sister in Rosanna. Our trip was uneventful. We arrived at Spencer Street on time at 1.46 pm, shunted the cars on our train, and took our loco over the pit at South Dynon. I slept at home that night. On Boxing Day, I signed on at 1 pm at South Dynon to take out locos S309 and S312, and run to Ararat with Dave Andrew an express goods to Adelaide.

Occasionally, there would be some unexpected disruption to the passenger rostering requiring a replacement crew member. This happened on one fine spring day when I was unexpectedly rostered to sign on at 1.10 pm and relieve and run the 1.20 pm Dimboola passenger. The driver was Leo Pritchard Kelly, a regular performer on the passenger roster. 'We'll be doing some suburban running today,' was his comment when I introduced myself. The signalman from B box delivered the staff attached to a cane hoop, which I slung around my neck for easy carrying. Our train arrived behind B83 and we relieved the incoming crew. I promptly attended to the vigilance control check and made the required entries in B83's log book. Our departure signals were all at 'clear'. Leaning out the window in the cab door on the platform side, I waited for the 'right away'.

It came at 1.20 pm and we were away on time. B83 made light work of its 250 ton load, and once over the grade out of Ararat speed was well up into the sixties. This didn't last long, however, as we stopped at Armstrong, where the staff was exchanged by hand. And this was the pattern for the rest of the run to Murtoa. We stopped at every station and hence the automatic staff exchanger was not used. Although a stopping train, 70 mph between stations was quite common. It was an enjoyable afternoon. I cancelled the audible warning from the vigilance control every 90 seconds, called the signal indications, and acknowledged the 'right away' after a station stop. These tasks provided interesting diversions from admiring the scenery while sitting in the comfortable seat on the fireman's side of the cab.

We were relieved on arrival at Murtoa, and waited a few minutes for our next assignment. This was No. 34, the afternoon passenger to Melbourne. It soon arrived behind S307. On relieving the crew, I checked the vigilance control and made the appropriate entries in the log book. The signalman delivered the staff. It was attached to a cane hoop that also carried a pouch on a metal ring for use with the automatic equipment. The 'right away' came. Leo sounded the air horn, flipped the independent brake into quick release, and gradually opened the throttle. After acknowledging the green flag from the guard as the train cleared the platform, I wound up the fireman's side cab window, pressed the vigilance control and turned my attention to the staff. We were scheduled to run non-stop for most of the way. A number of stations were timetabled as 'stop if required to pick up or set down passengers', but on a weekday afternoon a stop was seldom made. And so it proved. S307

Passengers on No. 25, on the day this photo was taken, were assured of an 'on time ' arrival as their double-headed four-car train rolls into Dimboola behind an oil-burning J class and a coal-burning N. (Ian Scutt)

had us running at 70 mph for mile on mile. As we approached Lubeck, the yellow fish-tailed arm of the 'Distant' was lowered well clear of its post to 'proceed', welcoming us on.

I opened the floor panel behind the driver, raised the auto staff exchanger, inserted the pouch with the staff attached on the metal ring, and waited. The speed recorder was showing a shade over 70 mph. With the floor panel raised, an updraft of air came into the cab bringing with it the sounds of the leading bogie in contact with the rail joints. The loco rocked slightly as we passed over some facing points and as the home signal rapidly approached there was a hiss of compressed air as I sent the staff exchanger down to its operating position. More sounds from the leading bogie, then a muffled clang as the staffs were exchanged, followed by another hiss of compressed air as the exchanger was brought up into the cab. I retrieved the staff, secured the apparatus and closed the floor panel. With the speed recorder right on 70, I called out the names on the staff, 'Lubeck – Wal Wal,' and handed it to Leo Kelly. He repeated the names and handed it back to me for hanging on the central windscreen pillar window shades. At this point, the hiss of the vigilance control made its presence felt and I pressed the button on the fireman's side to cancel it. Exchanging the staff had occupied less than a minute. We roared on with the speed recorder needle seemingly glued on 70 mph.

Staff exchanges at Wal Wal and Glenorchy followed a similar pattern to the that at Lubeck, with each station flying by and the speed rarely dropping below 70 mph. S307 rode well and the surrounding countryside looked a picture in the spring sunshine. Soon we were climbing the Bunyip Bank. At first we didn't notice it. Then speed gradually fell back to a minimum of 40 mph. We breezed through Deep Lead at 50. It was switched out as a staff station so no exchange was necessary. The speed recorder needle soon resumed its customary position on 70 and we travelled the five miles to Stawell inside even time. Stawell B box received the incoming staff before we stopped at the impressive station platform. Stawell A box delivered the outgoing staff and we sailed up the 1 in 62 at an impressive 35 mph. The locomotive's automatic apparatus was used for safe working at Great Western and Armstrong and we went over the top of the Armstrong Bank at a comfortable 40 mph. We were relieved at Ararat and had over an hour to enjoy a leisurely meal, but our day was far from over.

Our next assignment was to travel on the 5.30 pm Horsham passenger to Murtoa, and relieve

K191 looks at home on No. 25 as it rolls past the Dimboola 'Distant' with its five-car consist. (Ian Scutt)

and run No. 88 goods to Ararat. As the 5.30 pm Horsham was steam-hauled, this was fine by me. On this particular evening, the motive power was R748. I watched the big 4-6-4 back on to the four-car train. The impressive square-backed tender eased up to the first car, while the quiet rhythm of the air compressor confirmed all was well with the brakes. Declining the luxury of air-conditioning, Leo and I chose the comfort of an empty compartment in the leading vehicle, a BE second-class express car. In this you could open the window and hear the sounds; so with Leo in agreement, I did. We departed on time. R748 made a stirring start up the grade out of Ararat. Its staccato exhaust floating back over the train and in our window. 'Isn't it a beautiful sound, Leo,' I ventured. 'The side rods will fall off in minute,' came the stony faced reply. Of course they didn't, and we had the pleasure of being hauled by 748 for the next hour or so, with all its enjoyable sound effects. We detrained at Murtoa and awaited the arrival of No. 88 through goods. This arrived in due course behind B83. We relieved the crew. I checked the vigilance control and completed the entries in the log book. The signalman obliged us with the staff for Lubeck and the sound of B83's air horn brought a green light from the van. We were on our way as B83's throttle was opened and moved smoothly to notch 8. With the exception of Stawell, all staff exchanges were automatic and we ran non-stop to Ararat. Speed was maintained at 45 mph for much of the way, falling to around 20 on the two major grades. The cab heaters kept the cold night air at bay, the headlight illuminated the track ahead, and we had a pleasant journey. We rolled into Ararat around 9 pm and were relieved on arrival. Our commuting to and from Murtoa had taken 7 hours and 48 minutes.

The Christmas – New Year period always produced an upturn in passenger traffic, often requiring a second division of trains such as the Overland to handle the increased patronage. In early January 1965 I signed at 6.43 am to relieve and run the 6.53 am to Melbourne. This was

Passing through Wail on a mild spring day, oil-burning N426 heads towards Dimboola with No. 25. (Ian Scutt)

the second division of the Overland. The driver was Elso Arendshorst, who although qualified to run trains into the Melbourne yard via the Tottenham freight tracks, required a pilotman on this occasion for the suburban route from Sunshine to Spencer Street. Our train arrived 20 minutes late. It comprised 11 cars, weighing 500 tons, drawn by S300 and S301. I checked the vigilance control, made the log book entries and looked for the 'right away'. It came almost immediately and Elso got us moving. I picked up the staff from the A box signalman on the driver's side of the cab, and after calling the names and handing it to the driver returned swiftly to my side to receive the second 'right away' from the guard as the train cleared the platform. The staff was now hung on the central windscreen pillar window shades and I resumed the fireman's seat. Ballarat was our only scheduled stop, and with this exception all staff exchanges were to be automatic. Elso enjoyed a challenge, and the need to arrive on time at Spencer Street with an interstate express motivated him. S300 and S301 combined to produce 3500 horsepower and Elso soon had it wheeling us along at 70 mph for mile on mile. We barely noticed the grade between Ararat and Buangor, and with the staff exchanged automatically the station swept past in the blink of an eye. And so it was at Middle Creek. We sailed over the top of the three mile 1 in 50 grade before Beaufort at 40 mph, and skilful use of the dynamic brake kept speed at 65 mph on the curve into that station. Then back to 70, all the way to Linton Junction. We were making up time. Train Control thought so too, and gave passengers their full 20 minute refreshment stop at Ballarat.

I had put the electric kettle on at Linton Junction and it was boiling as we rolled into the Ballarat platform. We were thus able to enjoy a leisurely cup of tea and consolidate our resources for the run to Melbourne.

We made a brisk departure from Ballarat, reaching 40 mph up the grade to Warrenheip. Here the double track that had commenced at Wendouree ended, and we picked up the staff for Dunnstown. Elso kept our speed high and we recovered more time. After Millbrook it was largely down grade all the way to Bacchus Marsh. The whine of the dynamic brake rose and fell as Elso used it to keep the speed recorder needle on 70 as often as possible. We roared up the hills from Bacchus Marsh, with speed confined to 25 mph as the train snaked around the reverse curves approaching Parwan. Parwan to Sunshine was run inside even time and I gave up the staff for the last time just before we came to a stop at Sunshine platform. The waiting pilotman entered the cab. Elso sent the throttle from idle to notch 8 in a smooth and practiced sequence. Speed rose accordingly. When it reached 50 mph, the throttle was closed. Following the pilotman's advice, Elso guided the train expertly through Footscray, on to North Melbourne and passed the Franklin Street signal box. It was at this time that the measured tones of the Man in Grey came over the loudspeakers at Spencer Street station. 'Overland, second division from Adelaide, about to arrive at Platform 3; Overland, second division from Adelaide, about to arrive at Platform 3.' A few seconds later we rolled into Platform 3, just three minutes late, at 10.23 am, and were relieved on arrival.

We rested for the remainder of the day, and signed on at Spencer Street at 7 pm to relieve and run the 7.40 pm Scout Special to Adelaide. This was made up of 13 South Australian passenger cars, weighing, all up, 495 tons, and pulled by B64 and S300. Coupled behind B64, S300 was running hostler end first. All went well until just after Rockbank, when eight ground relays occurred on B64 before we reached Melton. At Melton, Train Control was informed of the situation and permission obtained to open the knife switch on B64. The knife switch was opened and we set off for Parwan. On the way, sparks issued from the trailing traction motor, No. 2 end, on B64. Control was notified of this phenomenon when we reached Parwan, and Elso was instructed to proceed with B64 'off line' and S300 only powering. This instruction was carried out and we crawled up the Ingliston Bank at a snail's pace. B64 was now included in the load, so S300 was pulling 607 tons on its own.

The defective B class was removed at Ballarat and replaced by B62. An extra vehicle was also placed on the train, bringing the load up to 540 tons. On leaving Ballarat, we hadn't gone two engine lengths when it became obvious that something was wrong. S300 was not powering. The Scout Special was brought to a stand and troubleshooting commenced. By this time Elso and I were fed up with the way things had been going and this was just about the last straw. The trouble was traced to a faulty jumper cable. This was replaced. S300 powered up and we got going at 11.48 pm, running the 57¼ miles to Ararat in one hour. We arrived at 12.48 am the next day, 1 hour and 28 minutes late, and handed our charges over to the relief crew.

The Overland was regarded by many as the pinnacle of achievement in train running at Ararat.

I achieved that pinnacle once. On a warm summer night I signed on at 11.53 pm to relieve and run train No. 69, the Overland, from Ararat to Dimboola, returning with No. 38, the fast goods from Adelaide. Jack Chandler was the driver and our locos were S304 and S301. The 14 car consist arrived on time at 11.57 pm and with the Ararat–Stawell staff in hand we climbed aboard S304.

Three minutes were allowed for the crew change, and in this time I checked the vigilance control, wrote up the log book and prepared the cab hand lamp to acknowledge the guard's 'right away'.

This came at 12 midnight. With the cab lamp on green, I acknowledged the green light from the van, called 'right away' to Jack Chandler, and felt the gentle surge of power as he opened the throttle. Our speed was soon well into the sixties and within 20 minutes we were stopping at Stawell. From here, automatic staff exchanges would allow us to run non-stop to Horsham. Setting up the automatic staff exchanger meant I was frequently on the driver's side of the cab. I would press the vigilance control for the required five seconds, retrieve the staff from where it was hanging adjacent to the centre windscreen pillar, open the floor panel and prepare the equipment for an automatic exchange. During these movements I had time to observe the speed recorder needle. It would flick up to 71.5 mph and the throttle would be dropped from notch 8 to notch 7. It would then drop to 69.5, the throttle would go back to notch 8, and in due course the needle would flick up to 70.5. With these small movements, and the occasional slowing for a 65 mph curve, our average speed from Stawell to Horsham was close to, if not right on, 70 mph.

R765 on No. 25 approaching Dimboola. (Ian Scutt)

Our stop at Horsham was something under two minutes and we were soon away, running the 21½ miles to Dimboola in well under even time. Here, we were relieved and retired to the warmth of the signal box, made a billy of tea and enjoyed a leisurely, early morning meal. We had plenty of time. The Dimboola crew that relieved us would run the Overland the 62 miles to Serviceton, where the two S class would be replaced by South Australian diesels. The Dimboola crew would then attach the two S class to No. 38, fast goods from Adelaide, and run it to Dimboola, where we would relieve them and run the train to Ararat. Our waiting time was close to three hours. No. 38 arrived behind S300 and S304 soon after 5.30 am. I carried out the necessary housekeeping tasks and we were away inside three minutes. Our train included four-wheel vehicles and was thus limited to 45 mph. All staff exchanges however, with the exception of Stawell, were automatic, and this meant we could still make good time. And we did. With the sun coming over the horizon and shining in our eyes, Jack Chandler kept our speed at 45 mph for much of our journey to Glenorchy, and the regular clang of the automatic staff exchanger announced we were one station closer to home. Progress from Stawell to Ararat was slower but still impressive, and we rolled to a stop in the Ararat yard at 9 am, handing our diesels over to our relief. The mileage we travelled that day entitled us to payment of 9½ hours.

Despite the majority of passenger trains being rostered for diesel haulage, steam performed a gallant rearguard action in the Ararat district. Train No. 25 was the morning passenger from Melbourne to Serviceton, departing Ararat at 1.20 pm. No. 25 ran as a locomotive-hauled train to Dimboola, where passengers for Serviceton changed to a rail motor for the final leg of their journey. At Horsham, the diesel on No. 25 would regularly be replaced with whatever steam loco happened to be available to haul the train the remaining 21½ miles to Dimboola. As shown in the previous illustrations, this produced a variety of motive power that included every class of main line steam locomotive then available.

32 The Jewel in the Crown

The 1.30 pm passenger train from Melbourne to Horsham was nicknamed the Peanut. It ran from Monday to Saturday. On weekdays, on arrival at Ararat, the motive power changed from diesel to steam. Ararat was reached at 5.15 pm with departure for Horsham timed for 5.30.

The B class diesel would pull ahead and reverse into No. 2 road, and the waiting R would back down. It was an impressive sight. Following a soft whistle in response to the 'calling on' signal, the long engine and tender would steal gently toward the first car. The drop of a coupling pin signified that the load was secured. With the air hoses connected, the evening air was punctuated by the tarrhn, tarrhn of the air compressor as it charged up the train line.

Then, at 5.30 pm the big 4-6-4 would whistle off and make a spirited departure around the curve and up the short grade out of Ararat. This continued well into the 1960s.

Normal train consist was one non air-conditioned car next to the tender, two air-conditioned cars and a CE van making a total of 195 tons — a walk in the park for an R class. In holiday times the load would sometimes increase.

R748 was the favoured engine. One of two oil-burning R's (719 being the other), it generally ran the 5.30 pm Peanut to Horsham and returned with No. 86 'up' goods the next day, arriving at Ararat around 2 pm. This enabled the engine to be fuelled, watered and cleaned. In the non-busy periods, there were sometimes up to four cleaners in the Ararat shed.

They would be employed cleaning 748's connection rods and valve motion, buffer beams, red lines and smoke deflectors. Then the engine would leave the shed. The next day the tender would receive attention and on the following day the boiler was cleaned. This sequence was regularly repeated so that there were times when 748 was close to spotless.

In peak times, when wheat was being moved, engine rosters would change and the first available R class would be assigned to the Peanut. Crewing arrangements, however, generally remained fixed, with the 5.30 pm Ararat–Horsham pass being run by Horsham men. And a plumb job it was. The Horsham crew would travel to Ararat on No. 34 'up' passenger, arriving at 4.25 pm. They would then swan around, have their evening meal and generally take their ease until their fully prepared engine was delivered to them at the platform just before departure. On rare occasions they would walk down to the loco depot and take out their motive power, but this was once in a blue moon.

There was, however, the odd instance when the Horsham crew was unavailable, and one fine spring day in 1964 was such an occasion. I was rostered as fireman for the 1.40 pm available crew, and for the first two hours of the shift was occupied with preparing and transferring R and N class locomotives to their various points of departure.

Then, at about four in the afternoon I was told to see the shed roster clerk.

'David,' he said, 'how would you like to run the Peanut? You could run it to Horsham, put the engine away and be in time to catch No. 88 goods back home. Officially, you'd stay the night in Horsham and travel home on 24 pass the next day, with a minimum payment of four hours!'

All this was music to my ears. My reply was enthusiastic and positive!

November 1963, and on this beautiful spring evening R735 has just stormed through Jung at 70 mph with train No. 49, the Peanut, to Horsham. This was R735's first run after spending some time in store at Ararat. Earlier that afternoon, the author had assisted in bringing 735 out of storage and preparing it to run the Peanut. (Ian Scutt)

R735 blasts up the 1 in 50 grade and around the curve away from Ararat, heading towards Horsham with the Peanut. (Ian Scutt)

R712 was the engine. It was being prepared and the driver, Ian Werner from Dimboola, was waiting for me near the coal stage where we would pick it up. Spring was definitely in the air as I walked towards that locomotive. The driver was personable and I gave divine thanks for my good fortune as I looked forward to the next few hours.

The crew who prepared the engine were at the end of their shift. They were half serious and half-humorous when, referring to the steam gauge, they said, 'We got an extra 20 pound for you.' Then they were gone.

I was quickly in the cab. The steam showed 110 and the water ⅓ of a gauge glass. I checked the fire. It was in good shape. What was needed right now was more steam. I laced the firebox with the shovel and gently applied the stoker. The smoke at the funnel showed that combustion was satisfactory.

We had moved to the telephone post that communicates with Ararat A signal box and I swung down to announce our presence. 'Driver Werner, R 712 for the 5.30 pm Horsham.' There was a pause as the signalman entered the details on his Movement of Engines sheet. Then, 'Okay, up to the disc.' I advised the driver and we proceeded away from the depot and up to the disc signal controlling the entrance to Ararat yard.

Meanwhile, the steam pressure had risen to 130.

The disc soon came off. We eased our way

On a fine summer evening in 1963, R748 accelerates the Peanut away from Murtoa. (Ian Scutt)

through the crossovers and, under the protection of signals, on to the main line clear of the 'down' end of the platform to await the Peanut. The signalman from Ararat B box gave us the staff for the section ahead. It was 5.10 pm and steam was 140. I began to have misgivings. Things were not as they should be.

Once again I laced the firebox with the shovel and put the stoker on, this time to deliver a fire that would burn fiercely and the blower was adjusted to ensure it did. Steam rose to 150 but the water was down to a ¼ of a glass. This would get us nowhere. I put the injector on. The train arrived.

B72 pulled ahead and onto No. 2 road. Our 'calling on' signal dropped and we backed on. As soon as the air hoses were connected I said to the driver, 'Ian, I'm going to clean the spark arrestor.' 'Good idea,' came the response. With that task completed I was back in the cab. I turned off the injector. The water was ½ a glass and the steam still at 150. It was 5.20. The guard appeared, noted the engine number and driver's name, announced that the load was 4 for 195 tons, and departed.

The fire was scorching and the steam gauge needle should have been zooming round the dial. Instead, it barely moved.

The dream of running the Peanut was turning into a nightmare. If 712 wouldn't steam at the platform, she certainly wouldn't steam in running. The driver thought so too. At 5.25 he said, 'David, I'm not taking this engine.'

I heaved a sigh of relief as he stepped on to the platform and disappeared towards the office of Train Control to report the circumstances. Minutes ticked by. Steam slowly rose to 160. The driver returned. 'We've got the diesel' he said.

I uncoupled 712 from the train. B72 was placed where we had been ahead of the 'calling on' arm and we moved 712 onto No. 2 road. The B class backed onto the Peanut and we relieved the crew, who then took charge of our failed R class.

At 5.47 pm B72 received the 'right away' and roared out of Ararat. Every effort was made to make up time but this was largely to no avail. Even though speed rose to 75 mph on at least one occasion and was constantly well above 60 and into the 70s, van goods at station stops meant that Horsham was reached 13 minutes late.

We stabled the passenger cars and I was in plenty of time to catch No. 88 goods back to Ararat and draw a minimum of four hours pay the next day.

After being removed from the Peanut, an examination of R712 revealed that the smokebox door had been drawing air, thus destroying the partial vacuum in the smokebox and partly preventing the hot gases in the firebox from being drawn through the boiler tubes.

Some weeks after the events with R712, I was perusing the Shed Running sheet for my next turn of duty. I had difficulty finding my name. It had obviously been a late entry. While everyone else's details were typewritten, mine, together with the driver's, were entered in pencil.

But they were worth reading. Sign on 4.15 pm, prepare, take out, and run 5.30 pm Horsham.

Signing on at the appointed time, I was pleased to discover that our engine, R762, had been prepared by the hostling crew. There was therefore plenty of time to push down the banked fire and raise steam. The needle on the gauge responded well and was soon nudging 210. I checked the stoker. Fine. The air compressor thudded into action and with both injectors tested three short whistles brought the turntable round.

The huge symmetry of steam and steel that is an R class moved out of the shed. The turntable swung us in the right direction and with squirting cylinder cocks 762 moved to the telephone post communicating with Ararat A box. I contacted the signalman. 'Driver Hilderbrandt, R762 for the 5.30 pm Horsham'.

With these details documented he replied, 'Okay, up to the disc'. We moved up to the entry point of the Ararat yard. The fire was built up using the shovel and the injector soon brought into play to prevent the safety valves lifting. The disc came off and we eased our way through the yard to the B box 'calling on' arm. The staff delivered by the signalman came in an auto pouch and I called the names on it to the driver, 'Ararat–Armstrong'.

Standing thus in readiness to back on to the train the shovel was again used to maintain the fire while the injector brought the water level up to three parts of a glass.

The Peanut arrived and the B class pulled ahead into 2 road. Our 'calling on' arm dropped.

It was just after 5.15. We eased back and coupled on. The guard advised that the load was 4 for 195 tons and while noting the engine details confirmed where we were to stop. The train line was charged and the brakes were in order. The fire was healthy with the back corners of the firebox nicely firm. Steam was a shade under 200 and water still at ¾ of a glass.

All was ready for 5.30 pm.

'Right away' came promptly. The regulator was opened, cylinder cocks hissed briefly and a strident whistle announced we were away. Having exchanged hand signals with the guard I returned to my seat and turned on the stoker. Vic Hilderbrandt had 762 accelerating up the grade and around the curve out of Ararat in masterly fashion. Smoke at the funnel indicated that all was well in the firebox and R762 began to blow off. I eased the stoker back. Armstrong soon approached. I took the staff in its auto pouch and small ring, and bending down behind the driver attached it to the engine's automatic staff exchanger. Speed was around 65 mph. All signals were at proceed and as the station approached I lowered 762's apparatus. These devices were much heavier than they looked and unless you were careful they'd take you out of the cab with them.

There was a clang indicating an exchange had taken place and I hauled up the equipment, removed the incoming staff and called the names, 'Armstrong–Great Western', then placed the metal staff rod in a cane hoop and handed it to the driver. The cane hoop was to facilitate the staff exchange at Great Western which was, on this train, invariably by hand.

The Armstrong event occupied some 60 seconds.

Meanwhile, we were drifting down a 1 in 100 grade at 65 mph. Following the hand staff exchange at Great Western, 762 sounded magnificent as it pulled away from the station with an increasingly powerful exhaust.

Stawell was passed well on time and rolling down the grade towards Glenorchy speed rose to 72 mph. The engine was performing well. It steamed effortlessly. The harder it was worked the better it went, so much so that Murtoa was reached three minutes ahead of schedule. This was railroading!

After waiting time, we made an unforgettable departure. The exhaust was sharp, crisp and clear as it met the cool summer evening. And it continued in a rising staccato as speed approached

70 mph with the steam gauge needle seemingly glued on 210 psi. Jung was next with a non-stop staff exchange. Following a familiar pattern, I set up the auto apparatus. There was the expected clang and Jung went by like a newspaper in the wind.

The final section from Dooen into Horsham produced another scintillating performance with the speed recorder needle again rising to 72.

We rolled into Horsham right on time.

R762 had given a memorable performance and was never fully extended.

We reversed the passenger cars in Horsham yard and turned and hostled our engine.

No prescribed occupational therapy could ever have had the beneficial effects of that afternoon and evening with the Peanut.

Having completed our tasks, we retired to the pleasant surroundings of the Palm Lodge guest house, ready to travel back to Ararat on No. 24 pass the next day and claim our minimum payment of four hours.

33 Nineteen Miles

From time to time I would discuss my firing assignments with the roster clerk. I was invariably told the same thing. 'David, you can't pick your jobs.' As this statement applied to everyone and not just to me, I had to abide by it. On one special occasion, however, I thought, there's no harm in asking. The occasion was an excursion organized by the Association of Railway Enthusiasts, titled Stawell Both Ways. The train was to run from Melbourne to Stawell via North Geelong, Gheringhap, Maroona, and Ararat; returning via Ballarat and Bacchus Marsh. Without asking for anything specific, I politely asked the roster clerk if, when sorting out the crews for this job, he could perhaps keep me in mind for anything on day shift. 'I'll keep you in mind for afternoon shift,' he said. This was music to my ears. I offered a brief and sincere word of thanks and made myself scarce. When the Shed Running sheet for this Saturday was displayed I was rostered to sign on at 2.36 pm, relieve and run the 2.46 pm ARE special to Stawell, recondition the engine, and run the train to a changeover point between Ararat and Ballarat. As my parents were travelling on this train, I sent them the following telegram: 'Am firing special on 24/7/65, Ararat Stawell, Stawell Ararat, then to changeover point Ararat Ballarat. David.'

On the appointed Saturday, I signed on at 2.36 pm with Herb Harnath, the driver. We were informed that the special was running an hour late, due no doubt to photo stops taking longer than scheduled. It arrived in due course behind R735 and comprised seven cars weighing 315 tons, including the parlour car, Yarra. On the footplate was a travelling foreman, Mr Eric Finlay. He explained he had recently spent some months instructing on the L class electric locos. I greeted him respectfully and having stowed my bag on the tender turned my attention to the fire. It had banked up in the back corners and around the stoker firing table and needed evening out. I retrieved the long pricker from the tender and went to work. 'No, don't do that,' said Eric Finlay. 'You don't need that pricker, use this one.' And he handed me the shorter fire iron stowed diagonally across the front of the tender. I wasn't going to argue, but I knew it would be a waste of time using it. Leaving the long pricker in the fire, I did my best with the shorter one. I might as well have used a teaspoon. It had nothing like the reach necessary to spread the fire properly. Peering into the firebox, this became obvious to Eric Finlay, who then said, 'I'll leave it to you.' The shorter implement went back in its place and the longer one evened out the back corners and under the door, finally being replaced with its end glowing red hot. It was nineteen miles to Stawell and the fire in its present condition would get us there comfortably.

The signalman from B box arrived with the staff for the section to Armstrong. The cane hoop also carried a metal ring, indicating we would make an automatic exchange. We were away from Ararat at around 3.45 pm. With ¾ of a glass of water and steam on 210, Herb Harnath had plenty to work with and he used it. R735 blasted up the grade and around the curve out of the station and was soon running at a mile a minute. Approaching Armstrong, a heavy service brake application checked the train's speed in response to the 'Distant' signal being at 'caution.' The remaining signals were at 'proceed' and I transferred the staff into the cane hoop

R735 makes a fine sight as it thunders toward a photo line between Great Western and Stawell with the Association of Railway Enthusiasts' Stawell Both Ways special, on 24 July 1965. The figure at the fireman's side cab window is the author. (Geoff Oliver).

and prepared for a hand exchange. Two R class at the head of a long freight were in No. 2 road, and with the staff for Great Western on board Herb Harnath was not content to roll down the 1 in 100 grade to that station, and once again opened 735 out so that the speed recorder was soon showing 65. The rail fans were getting their money's worth! An 'up' freight was in No. 3 road at Great Western and we were signalled into No. 2 to cross No. 34 'up' passenger. With No. 34 gone, we received the staff for Stawell, were given a green flag by the guard and under clear signals made a spirited departure. Our next stop was for a photo run by at a level crossing barely two and a half miles 'Distant'. Nevertheless, Herb Harnath eased the regulator up near the roof, and using a long cutoff had R735 pounding along in a blaring crescendo that was music to the ears. The level crossing soon arrived. We stopped, and the photographers detrained and got in position. While they were lining up, we backed up for a good half a mile, stopped, then with a powerful exhaust accelerated forward and passed the photo line with the engine delivering a reverberating staccato in the crisp air of the winter afternoon. Herb Harnath braked hard, brought the train to a stand, then backed up a little to make it easier for the passengers to reboard.

The special's seven cars held around 300 passengers. As with any large group of railway enthusiasts, a heterogeneous collection of humanity was represented. There were those who knew the driving wheel diameter, boiler pressure, cylinder dimensions and just about everything else relating to every locomotive on the Victorian Railways as well as those in New South Wales,

Oil-burning R719 at Ballarat with the 'up' Association of Railway Enthusiasts' Stawell Both Ways special, 24 July 1965. (Geoff Oliver)

South Australia, South Africa, Great Britain, India, France, Italy, Spain and a smattering of railroads in the United States. This information was available in unsolicited form every minute in an hour, every hour of a day, on any day of a month. On excursion trains, the compartments occupied by these people tended to be rather uncrowded.

Also, there were those who specialized in performance and design data. Their store of knowledge included the names and careers of numerous prominent locomotive designers, the engines they produced, their power outputs, outstanding performances, crew anecdotes, depots from which they operated and anything else that kept their wheels turning. Some of these were vehement and unpredictable. During a seemingly affable conversation on motive power, they were likely to let fly with, 'That was Gresly's idea!' 'No, it was Staniers!' And so on. They were soon on their own.

Fortunately, the majority of passengers were of more moderate and saner temperament, enjoying the opportunity to ride behind a steam locomotive at express train speeds. Most had cameras.

R735 was steaming well and once again rose to the occasion as Herb Harnath got us away smartly on the last leg of our journey to Stawell. This took us through Pinks Cutting. This is a short, sagging portion of track that commands the respect of every engineman. In the up direction, unless traversed with vigour, it can easily cause a stall. Today it was in our favour. We were doing well over 60 mph when we started rolling down it and our speed increased to 71 mph as we hit the bottom of the sag. The train had plenty of momentum and maintained this speed for half a mile. I blew a cock a doodle doo on the whistle to announce this achievement. We rolled smoothly into Stawell and the staff was delivered to the signalman at A box. Surrounded by rail fans, the guard released the engine from the train. We pulled ahead, then set back to run around the train and pick up the Yarra parlour car. This done, we were signalled to proceed to the turntable at the small Stawell loco depot. Here, we were to recondition R735 and turn both Yarra and the engine.

Pushing Yarra in front of the engine, we rolled over to the loco depot. Yarra was placed on a loop adjacent to the pit and coal stage road. R735 then reversed and using the vacant pit road proceeded on to the manually operated turntable. A number of rail fans assisted with turning the turntable, and when turned, 735 moved to the coal stage. Two barrows of coal were available and I upended these into the tender. We were opposite the water crane and I swung it over the tender tank and water was soon pouring in. The water supply at the loco depot was vastly superior to that in the Stawell yard and the tender was soon full.

It was now time to do the oiling up. This was done under the watchful eyes of an increasing number of rail fans. Their expressions varied from admiration and interest to impatience and bewilderment. The engine was now fully prepared. All that remained was to turn Yarra, run around it, and push it back to the rear end of its train. Prior to this final move we planned to clean the fire. With most of the work done, Herb Harnath moved the engine forward and I threw the points to enable us to set back on to Yarra. Herb placed 735 in reverse and backed gently down towards the passenger car.

We were about to couple up to it when the track under R735 spread, and the engine and tender wheels derailed. We were on the ground with no hope of re-railing on that day. Rail fans, however, came to the rescue of their parlour car. They pushed it onto the turntable, turned it, then pushed it past the derailed locomotive, up to the Stawell yard, and on to their train.

Meanwhile, at 6 pm R735 had its boiler filled with water, its fire knocked out and was left at the point of derailment. The 4.10 pm goods from Dimboola had arrived at Stawell. Its motive power, B81, was assigned to haul the special to Ararat where it would be replaced by oil-burning R class 719, which was being prepared to pull the train to Melbourne. I relieved the fireman on B81, but that was the last I saw of the ARE special. Train No. 145, a fast goods to Adelaide, now came to a stand in Stawell yard and I was informed that I was to change over with the fireman on it. I said goodbye to my parents and climbed into the cab of B78, the first of a trio of locos pulling No. 145, the other two being S302 and T344. I'm not sure where Herb Harnath went, but my new driver was Arthur Hupfield. We departed and I picked up the staff at Stawell B signal box. We ran the train to Murtoa, where No. 88 'up' goods was waiting. I changed over with the fireman on this and was now firing for driver Wally Ralph, our locomotives being S309 ahead of T329. No. 88 was a fast goods and S309's automatic apparatus was used for the majority of the staff exchanges. We made good time to Ararat and were looking forward to handing over to a relief crew. But no, our work was not finished; we had to shuffle some locomotives around. T329 was removed from the train and stabled. T352 was retrieved from somewhere or other and coupled and jumper cabled on to S309, with both locos then being placed on No. 88. After this we signed off, with my time sheet claiming 9 hours and 54 minutes.

34 The Psychological Factor in Locomotive Running

It was a few days before Christmas.

People were travelling in increasing numbers with additional trains being scheduled to cater for the holiday season. Also, to clear back loading, goods services were being supplemented, with a 5 pm Ararat–Ballarat set down for this day. The driver was Elso Arendshorst and I was the fireman.

Our return working from Ballarat was interesting. This was the 11.44 pm passenger, which in fact was the second division of the Overland.

The load for the 5 pm was moderate and B77 had no difficulty in arriving at its destination before 7 in the evening. On being relieved, we made the most of our time in Ballarat. The evening was warm and many of the shops and stores were still open. The major thoroughfares displayed Christmas decorations and the atmosphere was festive. Having had our evening meal, and adopting an attitude of goodwill, we walked along looking in the windows of some of the better class retail outlets and wondered if we would ever be able to afford what they were selling. We strolled agreeably around, enjoying the sights and thinking how good it was to be being paid for this activity.

As the 11.44 pm was going to be diesel-hauled we had no engine to prepare and around 9.30 pm made our way back to Ballarat station. We had a long wait. To depart at 11.44, the second division of the Overland was due to arrive at 11.24 pm and remain for a 20 minute refreshment stop. Instead, it arrived at 11.55 pm, over half an hour late. Its nine-car, 405 ton load sat comfortably in the platform. Oh for an R class! But no. Instead, we had a rather nondescript looking B76.

The 20 minute refreshment stop was sensibly reduced to 10 minutes and we were therefore 21 minutes late. We were determined to recover as much of the timetable as possible by doing our best to run the 57¼ miles to Ararat inside even time.

With the vigilance control checked and in order, I entered our names in the loco's log book, together with details of our train and its timing. The log bookings, as expected, revealed nothing about the locomotive. I readied the hand lamp and waited for the 'right away'.

This came at 12.05 am. I exchanged hand signals with the guard and we were away. There was not a moment to lose and our departure was brisk.

The double track past Wendouree soon ended and we were heading for Linton Junction. A five second press on the vigilance control produced the characteristic hiss of air and I was free to set up the automatic staff exchanger.

As the floor panel covering the apparatus was raised a rush of air entered the cab together with the muffled sound of the leading bogie striking the rail joints. As the green light of the Linton Junction 'Distant' signal flashed past the air-operated exchanger slid down its runners and into position. There was the sound of wheels going over points, then the reassuring clang as the outgoing staff was transferred to the locomotive. A flick of a small lever brought the staff exchanger back into the cab and the metal exchange ring and staff were quickly retrieved.

'Linton Junction–Windermere' I called as the driver was presented with the staff. He checked it, handed it back and I placed the metal ring on the two vertical sun visor shields on the inside of the centre windscreen pillar. Speed was increasing. 'How fast are we going, Elso? Have we reached 70 yet?'

'Too fast,' came the reply. '71, 72, 73,' and the throttle went back to notch 6, allowing the speed to ease.

It soon became obvious that B76 was a good thing and well able to recover time. On the gently falling grades to Windermere speed remained right on 70 or a shade over and with all the signals green the staff exchanger fulfilled its task and I was able to call 'Windermere–Burrumbeet' as the authority to proceed was received into the cab. And on we went. Burrumbeet passed as a blur of lights at 70 mph and the slightly undulating track to Trawalla saw the speed recorder needle sitting right on the limit, with B76 equal to the task and seeming to enjoy it.

We were doing well. A speed of 68 mph was considered slow and hence every effort was made to stay on 70. A rare exception was passing through Beaufort. Here, the right-hand curve on the 'down' side was limited to 65. A minor brake application brought the speed down and we roared around that curve and up the ensuing 1 in 50 grade in fine style. True, after two and a half miles of this we were down to a struggling 20 mph at the top, but once over, the three miles of 1 in 50 down soon had the speed back on 70, with the dynamic brake keeping it there.

Our progress so far had been swift, and there was no reason to assume that it would be anything else until we arrived at Ararat. We consulted our watches. As each station had passed, precious minutes had been recovered and our arrival time was beginning to look respectable. By this time, clear signals and no delays had become the norm. And Middle Creek was no exception. Green lights all the way. The staff exchanger was set up as the 'Distant' approached. It went smoothly into position and with the familiar and reassuring clang provided us with the permission to speed on. 'Middle Creek–Buangor' was the call, confirmed by the driver and I placed the metal ring in its appropriate place.

Once again our watches were consulted. We had departed Ballarat 21 minutes late and had recovered a quite remarkable seven minutes. At 70 mph, Buangor was less than four minutes away. After that, Ararat, 14½ miles 'Distant,' should enable more time to be recovered. This would depend on getting a good run at the couple of miles of 1 in 50 up grade on the 'down' side of Buangor.

With the clear run we had experienced so far this would not be a problem. And after this, there was five miles of down grade before Ararat. We began to relax a little. Our arrival time was improving by the minute.

Meanwhile, at about the time we were passing through Beaufort, in the orderly environment of Ballarat Train Control, miles away from our footplate action, the train controller was on the telephone. He had been contacted by the signalman at Ararat A box. No. 88, 'up' fast goods with a T class in charge, was ready to depart. Should he let it go?

The controller was far removed from the cab of B76 but he had ample evidence of what was going on. His train graph, drawn from the information received from each staff station, showed by its flat trajectory that the point to point timings of the second division of the Overland were fast. He could see also that, barring any delay, the crew on the locomotive would make up more time before reaching Ararat.

He had two options.

He could hold No. 88 at Ararat until the interstate express arrived. While this would mean 88 would incur a delay of some 25 minutes, it would enable the express train to recover important lost time. And holding 88 at Ararat would also mean it could run to Ballarat without stopping.

Or, he could let 88 go. This would mean it would take siding at Buangor to cross the express; a delay to 88 of about 15 minutes. Hopefully, it would get there in sufficient time to enable the signalman to set up the auto staff exchanger and make the road without having to delay the passenger train.

He made a few mental calculations, then gave the man in Ararat A box his answer.

'Okay, let her go.' The signalman got busy. Using the appropriate bell codes, he obtained line clear from Buangor, received authority to withdraw a staff from his instrument, inserted this staff into a cane hoop, set the road, pulled off a disc allowing access to the main line and left the box to deliver the staff to the crew on No. 88. A long whistle on the air horn brought a green light from the guard and they were away.

On arrival at Buangor the 'Distant' was yellow and they were signalled into No. 2 road. On receiving the staff the signalman called up, 'You'll cross the pass here.' The train came to a stand at the departure home signal and the fireman attended to the crossing lights on the locomotive; a red light on the danger side and a white light on the clear side. Meanwhile the signalman urgently inserted the incoming staff into his instrument, obtained line clear from Ararat A box, withdrew an outgoing staff and, having heard the air horn of the approaching passenger train, left the down 'Distant' at 'caution' and set the remaining No. 1 road signals to clear. Then, with the staff inserted into a cane hoop he hurried to the edge of the platform, where with his hand lamp indicating the point of exchange, waited for the incoming staff from the second division of the Overland.

While as yet unknown to the crew of this train, the events surrounding No. 88 fast goods were about to unfold with the most demoralizing consequences.

Approaching Buangor at well over a mile a minute, all our efforts at time-keeping seemed to count for nothing. The 'Distant' signal was at 'caution'. The throttle went into idle and a long BLAMP on the air horn let everyone know of our disappointment and disbelief. And that wasn't all. Disappointment soon turned to angry frustration and the cab roof above the driver reeled under a tirade of unprintable but understandable words. Couldn't those in authority see and appreciate the efforts we were making. Apparently not.

The signal did not change and a heavy service brake application brought the train under control. Speed dropped rapidly: 50 mph, 40, 30, 25, 20 and it became obvious what was going on. No. 88 was sitting in No. 2 road with its crossing lights well displayed. As we rolled past the 'Distant', Elso had his hand on the brake handle and was about to bring the train to a stand when the signals for No. 1 road went from red to green.

I immediately had the staff placed in a cane hoop, wound down the fireman's side cab door window and prepared to effect a hand exchange. This completed, I read out the section names: 'Buangor – Ararat A'. These were confirmed and we began to accelerate away towards our destination. It was difficult to estimate the time that this delay cost. However, being ever the optimist, I called across the cab, 'We can still achieve something.'

I could not hear the reply. Nevertheless the throttle was back in notch 8 and we were moving in the right direction. But we had lost vital momentum. It was a struggle to reach 50 mph for a short stretch before coming back to 35 at the top of the minor grade out of Buangor. From there, speed gradually dropped back over the next two and half miles until we slogged over the final summit at 15.

But now it was downhill!

Speed rose quickly.

With the aid of the dynamic brake 70 mph was maintained for the best part of five miles. Then it was well over 60 for the remainder of our journey. Smooth braking brought our train into Ararat at 12.58 am, 14 minutes late. Not on time, but a commendable effort all the same!

Despite being checked at Buangor, we had reached Ararat in 53 minutes, with our average speed for the 57¼ miles being 64.5 mph.

If train controllers underwent any special training, the psychological effects of their decisions were certainly not part of it.

35 Temporary Conclusion

As the final three months of 1965 approached, traffic levels remained high but the number of trains hauled by steam locomotives became less and less. Diesels were on the rise and whether I liked it or not, steam was definitely in decline. It was no good transferring anywhere else; Ararat was the biggest steam depot in Victoria. If steam was declining here it was undoubtedly drying up faster elsewhere. I could not see myself existing on a diesel-only railway. What to do? I had reasonable qualifications and in 1965 Victoria was in desperate need of secondary school teachers. I made inquiries, was given an interview, and told that I could be employed. An arrangement was made for me to commence in October. In September, I tended my resignation to the Victorian Railways, explaining to my associates at Ararat that I was going schoolteaching. They wished me well.

My last few jobs were firing for Elso Arendshorst on night shift. On 22 September we signed on at the shed at 4.50 pm. We took out oil-burning R719 for the 5.30 pm Horsham passenger. On arrival in the yard, we changed over with B65 that had brought the train from Melbourne. We placed B65 on the 7 pm Hamilton and ran it to Willaura, changing over there with the 5.5 pm ex Hamilton. Our new charge was oil-burning N470. This had a bad knock in at least one set of its axle boxes. The steam gauge was reading low and the driver's side injector was shut off at the stop valve. Nevertheless, 470 steamed satisfactorily. We hostled it at Ararat and Elso booked the defects.

Our evening's activities, including the return excursion to Willaura, had taken 7 hours and 5 minutes.

If a locomotive arrived at a depot with major faults, it was just as likely to be patched up and sent elsewhere. The reasoning behind this action was that, hopefully, the depot to which it was sent would effect the repairs.

The next day we signed on in the yard at 4.25 pm to relieve and run the 4.35 pm Geelong. There, at the head of the train, was N470. In the cab was the distinctive odour associated with an oil burner: fuel oil mixed with that used for lubrication, each encompassed by steel of varying grades at a wide range of temperatures. The steam gauge had been replaced but the driver's side injector was still defective. Our load was 38/840; moderate for the Geelong track. With the staff in the cab and the disc for the main line pulled off, a long whistle brought a green flag from the guard. Elso eased us out of the yard and we were soon rolling around the curve on the way to Maroona. The axle box knock was still bad, so the shed staff at Ararat were no doubt hoping that it would be fixed at Geelong. Early in our journey I sanded N470 twice. This had a marked effect on its performance and it steamed well. The single injector proved equal to the task, and despite the uncomfortable knock in the axle boxes the engine handled the load well and our progress was satisfactory. We were to change over with the 2.15 pm ex Geelong, and this was waiting for us at Derrinallum.

N470 was handed over to the Geelong crew, with advice concerning the driver's side injector and the knocking axle boxes. Our changeover locomotive was T337, hauling 57 vehicles weighing some 550 tons. Our trip home was uneventful until we reached Ararat. Powering up the 1 in 50 grade into the yard, we discovered that all the signals were against us. Elso returned the throttle to idle and brought the train to a stop. A departing 'up' goods came into view. Its passage blocked the crossovers into the yard and we were delayed until it had cleared. A disc signal went from to red to green. Elso released the brakes and opened the throttle, moving it gently from notch 1 to notch 8. T337 spluttered, shuddered, vibrated and refused to move. The throttle was closed and I was dispatched to A box to report our stall and ask for assistance. Soon after rejoining T337, J523, the A box pilot backed down on to our loco and coupled on. Elso cut in the isolating cock on his brake pedestal and advised J523's driver that he had control of the brakes. Two long whistles from 523 were answered in kind from our air horn and Elso once again opened T337's throttle. This time, with J 523's help, the train moved smoothly into the yard. Here our relief was waiting and we signed off after working 8 hours and 13 minutes.

The next day was my last. We signed on at 6.25 pm for the 6.35 pm Geelong. T381 was in charge, with a load of 52/1055. This was increased at Minnera where we picked up a further three vehicles, bringing the total to 55/1093. We changed over at Derrinallum with the 4.15 pm ex Geelong. This was headed by T353 with a load of 50/450. Our run back to Ararat was uneventful and we were relieved there in the yard after being on duty for 9 hours and 3 minutes. I shook hands with Elso and thanked him for having me with him. He responded graciously and thanked me for firing for him.

I made my way through the light and shadow of the Ararat yard at 3.30 am and found my way for the last time to Leslie House. I had settled the account for my last week's board and was thus free to leave. There was no point in going to bed. The Overland would be along and depart Ararat at 5.25 am and I decided to catch it. Most of my things were packed and it took only a few minutes to find space for the few items remaining. I changed out of my overalls and put on clothes suitable for travelling. I switched off the light in my room and took my suitcases and bag outside. Leaving them there, I returned silently inside and went to the kitchen. I wrote a note to my landlady, thanking her for having me and explaining I had caught the Overland home. This was placed on the kitchen table. I left quietly, picked up my things from outside, walked over to the station booking window and purchased a second class single ticket to Melbourne. I didn't have long to wait. The whine of the dynamic brakes on the S class hauling the Overland heralded the train's arrival. Three minutes were allowed for a change of crew. Making my way to the rear, I found a BJ, second-class sitting car with plenty of spare seats. Climbing aboard, I found a comfortable seat, stowed my luggage in the rack above, and settled down. We were soon on our way. The long train glided smoothly out of Ararat and in a few miles was running at line speed. Arrival at Spencer Street was on time and I bought a ticket to my suburban station at Rosanna. My school teaching lasted little more than the blink of an eye. After a few false starts, I settled into a career of industrial advertising, public relations and technical documentation. This allowed me to pursue my railway interests in an ongoing manner. Thus my resignation from the footplate was merely a temporary conclusion.

Glossary

Ash pan slides: The horizontally placed sliding openings which form the bottom panels of the ash pan on a coal-burning locomotive. These panels are fitted with an air cylinder which enables the enginemen to open and close them as required. The ash pan is fitted with sprinklers which can deliver water to assist in quenching hot coals and ash, either in the ash pan or discharged into an ash pit.

Atomizer: On oil-burning locomotives, the burner delivering oil to the firebox has two machined passages through it, one above the other. The upper passage carries oil, gravity fed from the oil tank on the locomotive's tender. The lower passage carries atomizing steam. This steam combines with the oil and delivers it into the firebox in a stream of atomized particles ensuring the oil is highly combustible and causing it to burn in a solid, high-temperature flame. Atomizing steam is controlled by a valve on the fireman's side of the locomotive cab, known as the atomizer. The atomizer is equipped with a pressure gauge to enable the fireman to provide atomizing steam at a pressure in line with the steaming requirements of the locomotive.

Blower: A device similar to a gas ring on a cooking stove, fitted in the smokebox of a locomotive and through which steam is passed up the funnel to the atmosphere, creating a partial vacuum in the smokebox. In response to this vacuum, atmospheric pressure forces air up through the grate in the firebox, thus promoting combustion.

Booster: A small auxiliary steam engine attached to the rear pair of the locomotive's carrying wheels. It is cut in to give extra power when the train is climbing a steep grade, or when starting.

Consolidation: The name given to a steam locomotive having a 2-8-0 wheel arrangement.

Cutoff: The distance live steam is admitted into the cylinder before being cut off and allowed to use its expansive force to push the piston for the remainder of its stroke. Thus: a cutoff of 12 inches means that for the first 12 inches of the piston's stroke it is being pushed by live steam. At 12 inches the live steam is cut off and for the remainder of its stroke the piston is pushed along by the expansive properties of the steam in the cylinder.

Distant signal: A yellow fish-tailed arm with a black bar. Its normal position is *caution* with the arm being horizontal, displaying a *yellow* light. At *proceed*, the arm is lowered 45 degrees, displaying a *green* light. Distant signals are the first to be seen when approaching a main line station and provide the train crew with a clear indication of the aspects of other signals at that location. Thus if the Distant is at 'proceed', the crew can expect other signals to also be at 'proceed'. If the Distant is at 'caution', the crew reduces the speed of the train and prepares to find other signals at stop.

Double-heading: The use of two locomotives coupled together at the front of one train.

'Down': Any train travelling away from Melbourne is classified as a 'down' train.

Ease up: The instruction given to the driver of a locomotive about to couple on to a train. It can be given verbally or by hand signal.

Gauge glass: A transparent oblong glass, approximately nine inches long, housed within bolted together front and rear metal frames, and mounted at eye level in the engine cab. It indicates the level of water in the locomotive's boiler. It is one of the most important cab fittings. It is watched constantly and checked, via valves and test cocks, frequently.

Home signal: A red square-ended arm with a white bar. Its normal position is *stop* with the arm being horizontal, displaying a *red* light. At *proceed*, the arm is lowered 45 degrees, displaying a *green* light. Home signals are used to control the movement of trains into, and within, major sections of railway.

Hostling: Term used to describe the main activities involved when a locomotive has finished a turn of duty. These are fire cleaning, taking coal and water and filling sand boxes — sand being dropped on the rail to improve adhesion. Oil-burning locomotives have their fuel oil tank filled, tender water replenished, rail sand box topped up, and cab sand box filled — the cab sand is passed through the boiler tubes to keep them clean by shovelling it into the firebox where the combustion draft takes it through the tubes and out to the atmosphere.

Hudson: The name given to a locomotive having a 4-6-4 wheel arrangement.

Injector: The steam-operated device used to transfer water from the locomotive's tender into its boiler.

Kick: A shunting move where the locomotive makes a vigorous start pushing a rake of wagons, then brakes hard and the shunter coordinating the move uncouples some wagons from the rake and they roll to their allotted destination using the momentum received from their first push.

Mikado: The name given to a locomotive having a 2-8-2 wheel arrangement.

Over the pit: The general railway term referring to a locomotive proceeding to a depot to have its fire cleaned and be otherwise serviced — the pit being the ash pit into which the remains of the engine's fire are deposited.

Pacific: The name given to a locomotive with a 4-6-2 wheel arrangement.

Pricker: A long steel fire iron with a short, right-angle extension on one end. Used for making up and disposing of a locomotive's fire. Stowed along the length of the tender, on the fireman's side.

SM: The accepted railway abbreviation for stationmaster.

Staff: A safe working device used to ensure that only one train is present on a single line section of railway. The staff was a metal rod stored in an interlocking instrument at the station the train was approaching and released only when the signalman at the station in advance gave his authority. From Mangalore to Albury the safe working system was miniature electric staff, enabling the staff to be picked up and set down at speed, using apparatus mounted on the ground and an exchanger fitted to the locomotive.

TR point or Telephone post: A location on the departure track from a locomotive depot equipped with a telephone connected to the nearest signal box controlling the movement of locomotives from the depot on to train running tracks.

Train examiner: A railway employee who inspects the brakes and other below-frame items on each vehicle of a passenger or goods train prior to its departure from its station of origin.

'Up': Any train travelling towards Melbourne is classified as an 'up' train.

Unit Conversion Tables

Imperial to Metric and Metric to Imperial

Unit	Imperial to Metric	Metric to Imperial
Length	1inch = 25.4mm 1inch = 2.54cm 1foot = 30.5cm 1yard = 914cm 1 mile =1.61 km	1 mm = 0.0394 inches 1 cm = 0.394 inches 1m = 3.28 feet 1 km = 0.62 miles
Mass (Weight)	1 pound = 454 gm 1ton = 1.02 tons	1 kg = 2.2 pounds 1tonne = 0.98 tons
Area	1 inch^2 = 6.54 cm^2 1foot^2 = 929 cm^2 1 yard^2 = 0.836 m^2 1mile^2 = 2.59 km^2	1 cm^2 = 0.155inches^2 1 m^2 = 10.8 feet^2 1 m^2 = 1.2 yards^2 1 km^2 = 0.386 mile^2
Volume	1 pint = 0.568 litres 1 gallon = 4.55 litres	1 litre = 1.76 pints
Speed	1 mph = 1.61 km/h	1 km/h = 0.621 mph
Pressure	1 psi = 6.89 kPa	1 kPa = 0.145 psi
Power	1 hp = 0.746 kW	1 kW = 1.34 hp

About the Author

From an early age David Barnett became familiar with railways. His father Frank was a founding member of the Victorian Model Railway Society, which came into being in the early 1930s. His mother, Iris, was sympathetic to her husband's railway interests and together they took David on railway excursions.

Frank was able to express his railway interests through a unique gift. He could imitate a steam locomotive chime whistle with complete accuracy. He complimented this with equally realistic sounds of locomotive exhausts, air compressors, cylinder cocks, safety valves and a range of other audio effects that gave the listener a complete locomotive experience. These sounds were captured on a 12 inch, 78 rpm recording produced by W&G.

So it was that David Barnett was able to enjoy steam locomotives seven days a week without leaving home.

In his teen years he developed a number of contacts with engine crews at North Melbourne and Ballarat. He was a frequent guest on their footplates on locomotives performing a variety of duties, including yard pilots, fast and pick-up goods, and stopping and express passenger trains. His steam locomotive experience included Y, E, D2, D3, D4, A2, C, K, N, J, X, R and S.

He studied mechanical engineering to diploma level at the Footscray Senior Technical School and joined the Rolling Stock branch of the Victorian Railways in 1957. He served in the Investigating Engineer's Office, the Locomotive Design section of the Rolling Stock Drawing Office and as an assistant engineer at Newport Workshops. These positions were interesting but not fulfilling and after two years he resigned.

He studied Theology for three years at Ridley College, a resident college of the University of Melbourne. He was a private student and the course took a toll on his finances.

To boost these, he rejoined the Victorian Railways in 1963 as an engine cleaner/trainee engineman and was posted to Ararat, then the largest steam depot in the State, having an allocation of 60 engines.

After qualifying as a fireman he relieved at a number of outstations and sub-depots, including Mount Gambier, Portland, Hamilton and Warracknabeal. It was at these locations, and also at Ararat, that he experienced all the vicissitudes of railway life and learned to handle the idiosyncrasies of a variety of locomotives.

With the decline of steam, he resigned toward the end of 1965 and pursued a career in industrial public relations and advertising, and later in technical documentation. Throughout his life, however, he has maintained an active interest in railways and locomotive running.

Index

STATIONS, PLACES AND TOWNS